"IT'S ALL MENTAL"

James Ketchell

"IT'S ALL MENTAL"

James Ketchell

First printing, 2021
ISBN: 978-0-9934722-1-3 (paperback)
ISBN: 978-0-9934722-2-0 (eBook)
Ketchell Publishing

ABOUT THE AUTHOR

James Ketchell is a record-breaking aviator, adventurer and motivational speaker.

On 1st February 2014, James became the first and only person to have rowed across the Atlantic Ocean, successfully summited Mount Everest and cycled 18,000 miles around the world, in what the media dubbed 'The Ultimate Triathlon'.

In 2019, he flew his open cockpit gyroplane over 24,000 nautical miles, around the world in 175 days to set the first ratified circumnavigation for an aircraft of its type.

However, it was an inauspicious start for James. In 2008, he broke his legs and dislocated his ankle in a serious motorbike accident. The prognosis was that he would likely suffer a permanent walking impairment and would not be able to continue the active, physical lifestyle he had so enjoyed…but he defied the odds.

No stranger to overcoming adversity, James is also a motivational speaker and talks with candour and enthusiasm about his approach to taking on challenges. "Without doing anything special", he tackles physical adventures that most of us have only imagined experiencing.

James struggled through his teenage years, with no ambition and very little confidence, leaving school with no qualifications. He has spent the last ten years passionately working to inspire young people, as well as sharing his lessons learnt with companies around the world. James' key message is that we can all set ourselves inspirational goals and achieve them: the capability to succeed lies within.

James' first book, *The Ultimate Triathlon*, was launched in April 2016 and is endorsed by Bear Grylls.

DEDICATION

This book is dedicated to my Uncle Dave who passed away in October 2020, celebrating the most wonderful uncle I could have asked for. My earliest memories were from Christmas when he would visit and tell me stories about how he knew Father Christmas and how he had been in contact with him prior to visiting us. Of course, as a child, I thought this was absolutely wonderful. I remember running downstairs on Christmas morning to open my presents, then playing with them all day. Dave was just as enthusiastic as me, which was great!

We had some fabulous times as a family with Uncle Dave at the annual Royal Tournament (the world's largest military tattoo and pageant) in London. He was particularly knowledgeable when it came to the different regiments.

My fondest memories are the swashbuckling stories of fun and adventure that he would tell me, sometimes made up, but other times based on my great grandfather. Other memories include exploring the streets of London as tourists together. He had a story for almost every street we would walk down, from an old pub in the city, to Chinatown in the West End. He would have made a fantastic tour guide.

My first trip to America was to attend Dave's wedding in Sacramento, California. I was ten years old and couldn't sleep for weeks, I was so excited. It was the biggest trip by far that I'd ever embarked on: going to America at that young age seemed to me like going to another world.

Dave was a fantastic speaker and could easily hold a crowd, with his audience often hanging off his every word! He was also a natural leader and his non-confrontational demeanour enabled him to take control of most situations.

He was well-liked and knew a lot of people. I always looked up to my Uncle Dave and there is no doubt that my ability to speak and tell stories is something that he helped influence from a young age. I hope I can continue to do him proud and will never forget the wonderful memories of a special man.

ACKNOWLEDGEMENTS

There are simply so many people who have supported and helped me over the years that it's difficult to put in writing without inevitably forgetting something or someone.

I will start the acknowledgments in order of events as they unfold in this book. Firstly, I would like to thank Ash for being such an amazing rowing partner and all round great guy; it was an absolute pleasure to spend the time together that we did. Huge thanks to all of the sponsors and charities involved with the Indian Ocean row, along with Euan, for all his generous support.

Phil, for our time together in the Amazon, which was an absolutely fantastic experience – I still remember it like it was yesterday.

Anthony, for giving me the opportunity to cross the Atlantic Ocean in a pedalo and manage the project. Your kindness and generosity has not been forgotten. You wanted an adventure and boy, did you get one!

Ian, for all the filming you have kindly undertaken for me and for our continued friendship.

There are a lot of people who were involved in my flight around the world, but I need to say a huge thank you to the *Magni* family for believing in me from the very start. Andy and Steve from Magni UK, you were both there from the beginning and supported me the whole way: I will never forget that. *General Aviation Services Egypt*, for their fantastic flight support. Peter, for all the help with my flight training and for ongoing advice and support.

All of my sponsors played a pivotal role in getting me around the world but I'd like to say thank you to Jonathan from *Cain International*, David from *Barratt Homes* and John from *DHL*, along with everyone involved from the charities. All of the team at *Newgate Media*, especially Guy and Louise – thank you.

I need to give a special acknowledgment to Pru from *PAC Copywriting* – you are firstly my friend and secondly my editor. This was not easy but we did it! You gave me space when I needed it and chased me when I needed a kick up the backside! Without your support I would have really struggled. This is the second book we have worked on together and I'm sure there will be a third in time… thank you!

My family have always supported me, no matter how stressful it may have been at times. Thank you to mum, dad and my brother Jeremy and his family, Max and Yaz. I think about you all every day when I'm away.

I'd also like to thank all of my friends, who have always supported and encouraged me.

There are so many people who have had a great impact on me and ultimately, if our paths have crossed and you are reading this, it's probably because you have helped me in some way. Thank you so much.

PROLOGUE

I'd like to thank you for purchasing a copy of my book, *It's All Mental*. I sincerely hope you enjoy reading it.

My aim when writing was for this to appeal to anyone who is interested in building resilience, pushing themselves towards a goal, open to new ideas and is perhaps looking for their own purpose in life, whatever that may be.

I have experienced more emotions than I thought possible in the past decade as an adventurer and have learnt to accept things that are outside of my control. I never thought I would have been able to achieve half the things I have managed to, but somehow I have. I want to take you on a journey of fun and adventure, sharing the emotional highs and crippling lows along the way, and describing how I went about doing things that most people would only dream about. In reality, they are far more achievable than you might think!

Whether you want to have your own adventure, set up a business, or simply try something new, I set out to make you realise that we are all far more capable than our own minds would have us believe. Complex challenges can be overcome with the right attitude, strong work ethic and determination to never give up. Do not underestimate the compounding effect of breaking a task down and doing one small thing every day. I can tell you from experience, it can take you a long way.

I also want to acknowledge that I have been very fortunate to have experienced the things I have. However, this has come off the back of taking advantage of opportunities and often pushing myself into situations outside of my comfort zone. I also made a habit of always doing more than I was asked to do, which I knew would improve my chances of new, bigger and better opportunities coming my way.

I didn't wake up one day and decide that I was going to be a professional adventurer! There was no master plan as such: it just happened slowly over time. I had found something that I enjoyed doing and decided to do more of it, with one thing leading to another. I was able to find purpose and perspective with my adventures and it afforded me opportunities to connect with so many wonderful people around the world. If you put yourself out there and treat people in a way that you would like to be treated, you'll be amazed at the things that come your way.

In 2013, at the age of 31, I was eagerly preparing for another adventure. No sooner had I announced that I was going to cycle around the world, the next opportunity presented itself to me. I hadn't given a great deal of thought to what I was going to do after the cycle as I had 18,000 miles ahead of me to focus on. However, on meeting Ash, I was drawn to his enthusiasm and willingness to help others. A volunteer Scout leader, he wanted to row a boat across the Indian Ocean, from Western Australia to Mauritius. I thought it was a great idea and, as I got to know Ash, it soon became something that felt right to be involved with, for reasons you will find out as you read on.

I am keen to hear your thoughts once you've read the book, and am open to all forms of feedback. Perhaps there will be something that resonates with you, or you would simply like some advice and help for your own adventure. Either way, I can be contacted at james@jamesketchell.net.

INDEX

1

The Indian Ocean

With Euan and Ash in tow, I set off from Heathrow Airport on a crisp March morning. There was quite a gathering at the airport to see us off including family, friends, sponsors and even the charity representatives. I was excited; we were flying with Emirates and Euan had managed to work his PR magic to gain us access to the Business Class lounge. It wasn't just me who was excited – Ash and Euan were buzzing too. We had worked extremely hard to get to the start line and this massive project was now happening. We were determined to enjoy this five-star experience so we toasted the start of our journey with champagne and lobster!

Euan, one hell of a PR guy, was in full-on promotion mode, telling anyone who was passing and prepared to listen what we were doing. As we were about to board the plane, Euan wouldn't let us on without first telling the air stewardesses at the door who we were. They smiled and said well done; it was all a little embarrassing but by this point, it was certainly the champagne talking!

We took our seats, and it didn't take long for the six hours to pass before we reached Abu Dhabi, our first stopover. By this time, the alcohol had started to wear off and we were feeling a little jaded. Luckily, we only had a two hour layover and were soon back on board another aircraft, bound for Perth. Ash and I looked down at the Indian Ocean below us, chatting about our impending row. Euan was a couple of seats in front and, unbeknown to us, had taken sleeping pills to get him through the 11-hour flight to Perth and was happily in the Land of Nod.

Outside the airport, we jumped into a taxi. Prior to heading out to Australia, Euan had managed to line us up with some free accommodation with a luxury hotel brand called *The Mantra Group*. We had an amazing three-bedroom apartment in a high-rise building in the central business district of Perth.

We were all running on adrenaline on arrival but, with the time difference and the long journey, we soon came down from our high and just slept on and off for almost two days solid. It wasn't the best use of time but I just looked at it as a bit of a reset before things got busy.

Once our body clocks had adjusted, we were all keen to start exploring what Perth had to offer. I had passed through Perth when I cycled around the world in 2013 but didn't see the city at all, as I was in and out in about two days. I was amazed at the number of people who were out running and cycling; it was refreshing to see so many fit-looking individuals and there was something about the place that I immediately liked. It just had a good vibe.

Our plan was to stay in Perth for around four or five days, then head up to Geraldton, but we ended up staying in Perth for about a week. One evening, the three of us went out for dinner. Ash and I realised that we wouldn't be able to indulge quite so much for the coming few months, so we were probably overdoing it a bit with the food and drink. We also knew that we would lose a lot of weight out in the ocean. We had found a steakhouse that was laying on a 'Steak Challenge'. If you managed to eat all of the food, your photo would go up on the wall. It was a typical male testosterone thing to do, to be honest!

I think the steak was about 1.5kg and was called a Tomahawk but the strict rules decreed that it wasn't just the steak that had to be consumed, it was absolutely everything, including multiple plates of fries, vegetables, corn on the cob and salad. The real issue was eating absolutely everything inside the 30-minute limit. There was a judge who started the clock and who would also decide if we'd eaten enough, not just pushed food around the plate, claiming it was all just fat. I guess they needed to be pretty strict: these steak challenges were not cheap so they couldn't afford to be giving too many away!

Ash said that there was no way he would even attempt it, so it was Euan and I who decided to take on the dare. The waitress brought the food over with sparklers and announced out loud that we were taking on the challenge.

She counted down – "3,2,1 Go!" – and the clock started. We both tucked into our meals, whilst laughing and joking. By the halfway point, we had both consumed over half the food. I, however, made a tactical error: my mistake was drinking Coke. Euan was drinking water and I didn't realise that the gas from the Coke was making me extremely bloated and every gulp I took was filling me up even more. I was by now sweating profusely and my body temperature had risen considerably. I was just forcing food down and gagging after every mouthful.

Euan completed the challenge but I missed the deadline with about five mouthfuls left; I was literally on the verge of passing out. The waitress took the plates away and I quickly went to the bathroom and was promptly sick. I felt seriously unwell and, looking back, it was fun at the time but not something I would try again!

The following morning, now feeling much better, I was chilling in bed when I noticed Ash shaking violently: he was having an epileptic fit. It was the first time I had seen Ash actually having one, even though we had spoken about it many times.

I had first met Ash back in 2013, before I was due to cycle around the world. I was speaking at a Scout group where Ash was one of the adult volunteers. He expressed a keen interest in rowing across the Indian Ocean; he had already started researching the trip as he certainly knew what he was talking about. Quite quickly, he asked if I would consider teaming up with him. I joked that I was a little busy as I was literally only a few months away from cycling around the world, but it sounded like an interesting proposition.

It wasn't uncommon for people to approach me with various expedition ideas, however this was different: Ash had an incredible story to tell. He had survived Hodgkin lymphoma, a type of cancer of the immune system, after three gruelling rounds of chemotherapy. He had also lived with epilepsy his entire life, something I knew very little about. Ash wanted to raise awareness and funds for *Young Epilepsy*, a UK charity working on behalf of young people with epilepsy.

At the time I was pretty busy with my cycle preparations but was impressed with Ash's commitment and motivation to undertake this challenge. He wasn't talking about it, he was *doing* it. Every time I spoke with him, he'd update me on sponsorship opportunities to turn his dream into reality. I found it very inspiring and had a gut feeling that this was certainly going to go somewhere.

When I undertook the specialist epilepsy training, I was always told not to panic when I witnessed a fit. It's not a pleasant experience for someone who doesn't know what's going on or has no understanding of seizures. It goes against your instinct to just watch because most people naturally want to help. Ash had told me that I didn't need to do anything and it would always pass in a few minutes. I quickly got Euan's attention so that he could see what was happening as well.

Just as Ash had said, he started to regain consciousness after a few minutes. Whilst he seemed totally fine, the after effects of the epileptic fit meant that he pretty much slept for the entire day. I've been told that the aftermath leaves you with a feeling similar to being awake for a very long time and feeling hugely sleep-deprived. It was a real eye-opener for me, to realise that this could happen anywhere and at any time, without warning. We had thought long and hard about how we managed the risk of seizures on the boat, which he would inevitably have at some point. At night when I wasn't on deck and asleep in the cabin, Ash was going to wear a bicycle helmet to protect his head if he collapsed, as well as a safety line attaching him to the boat. It's not usually the seizure that's the problem, it's what your body hits when you pass out that often causes greater harm. As long as Ash wasn't injured in any way, he could always sleep off the effects in the cabin.

Before we departed for Geraldton, we had a lot of media interviews lined up by Euan. He had thrown himself into the project and was working hard to secure as much PR as possible, which helped raise the awareness of our chosen charities too. I wasn't looking for self-promotion but I quite enjoyed the interviews and knew it was good publicity for our sponsors as well.

Our time in Perth had been great but it was now time to head up to Geraldton. We had an apartment booked there, part of the same hotel group with which Euan had agreed a sponsorship deal. We hired a car and literally stuffed it full of our kit. It was about a four-hour drive (260 miles), mostly along the coastal road. Once out of Perth, the road reminded me of cycling across Australia and we even saw a few cyclists loaded down with equipment. We stopped off about halfway for a toilet break and to get some drinks and ice-creams, in a small town called Jurien Bay. We were soon on the road again, with Euan at the wheel.

I remember seeing a white car coming towards us, on the opposite side of the road, but didn't think much of it. The next thing we knew, it had turned around and was chasing us down. It was an undercover police traffic patrol car and apparently we were speeding! The police car had equipment on board that could calculate the closing speed of both cars and work out our speed, which I thought was quite clever. The guy was actually fairly friendly but told us to slow down and gave us a ticket, before he let us carry on. I was in the back of the car and, whilst the patrol man was doing his job, I had been secretly filming in the back. I thought it would make good content for our documentary!

A couple of hours later, we arrived in Geraldton. The apartment was absolutely great and close to the marina where our boat was going to be kept. The following day, we headed down to Geraldton Yacht Club, who had kindly let us use their facilities to store our boat and use the space to do any preparation work that was required. It was a great sight to see our boat, the *James Lewis*, sitting there looking as clean and shiny as the day it left the UK! The boat was named after the son of one of our sponsors, who tragically passed away with complications due to epilepsy. Both Ash and I thought this was a fitting tribute.

We first met with Edrick, who Ash and I had been in email contact with prior to our arrival. The boat was shipped from the UK to Perth in a container and then transported by road to its destination at the yacht club. Edrick gave us a tour around the building and showed us where our boat was going to be based, outside in a secure compound. He gave us a set of keys to the place and basically told us to make ourselves at home and to let him know if we needed anything.

After some lunch, we started unpacking the boat and going through our list of jobs, of which there were many. When we shipped our food, it was all packed in boxes; literally hundreds of dried ration packs for our Indian Ocean crossing, with various flavours like Spaghetti Bolognese, chicken pasta and chocolate pudding. I had eaten many of these types of meals before and I used the same company, *Be-Well Nutrition*, who had supplied my food for the Atlantic row some years earlier. All of the food was laid out on the grass inside the compound and it all needed to be placed into waterproof ziplock bags, which we then put in our day bags: one bag of food per person per day. We had decided that 100 days of food would be enough as we were aiming for around a 75-day crossing, possibly quicker if the weather was favourable.

We decided back in the UK that we would purchase any chocolate for the crossing in Australia. Euan sent an email to the marketing team at Coles, a large Australian supermarket chain and, a few hours later, we were in the local store speaking to the manager, who told us we could literally have as much of anything as we wanted. We ended up with two trolley-loads of chocolate and anything else we thought we would need. Although we did already have some, we also took the opportunity to stock up on more tinned fruit, especially peaches. To be honest, it was probably a bit excessive but it was all very exciting and it was easy to get carried away.

All of the chocolate was stored separately from the day bags, right in the bottom of the boat in the hull; these little compartments stayed a lot cooler in the hot weather. We had a lot of equipment – cameras, laptops, sat phones, tracing devices, fishing kit and even a harpoon! In hindsight, we probably had too much stuff. We had to find space for all of it but our little boat had a lot of usable space so it wasn't a problem.

A few days later, we had completed the first stage of packing and were ready to launch the boat off the slipway into the water and row it around to the harbour. The yacht club had given us a berth to use, which was in a perfect location on a corner. The boat was sitting on a custom-made cradle that had been fabricated back in the UK as the trailer was not shipped with the boat. It was a very short walk over to the slipway and one of the yacht club members came over with a pick-up truck to help lower the boat down the slipway. We pushed it out from the compound and over the flat ground relatively easily, but needed to secure it before it got near the slope of the ramp. If we hadn't have done this, it would have hurtled off down the ramp and we wouldn't have had the strength to hold it back.

We secured some lines to the boat and a line to the pick-up truck and the cradle. The rope connected to the cradle tightened up and we gradually let gravity pull the boat into the water, with a few of us holding on to the lines. Before it got too far into the water, Ash jumped in and assumed the rowing position. The boat slowly floated away from its base – it was a fantastic sight to watch. The local media were there, watching and filming the launch and Euan had doubled up again as our cameraman to capture the moment. There was no pontoon to tie the boat to so I waded out and jumped on. Everything had gone perfectly: the truck slowly pulled the cradle out of the water and the *James Lewis* was just floating effortlessly in the blue water, with the sun sparkling off its white carbon composite sides. There was no wind and it was lovely and warm. The conditions could not have been better.

We turned the boat around and started to make the short row around to the marina. The boat was gliding through the water like it was floating on air and it felt brilliant to actually be on the water. On the short row to the marina, we tried out the *Raymarine Auto* tiller which was our auto pilot: it was working perfectly. I even turned the water maker on and straightaway it jumped into life, with fresh water coming out of the little tube onto the deck. The GPS was also working perfectly and Ash was rowing the boat at 3.5 knots with ease. If we were to average that speed for the crossing, we would be doing very well. However, I was aware that the water was as flat as a pancake so it wasn't really an accurate representation of the conditions that we would face out at sea.

Ash rowed the boat into the marina where we saw Euan standing by the pontoon, signalling for us to come over. A local news crew was actually still hanging around, waiting for us to come in so that they could interview us. We were getting a lot of attention, a lot more than I was expecting!

We secured the boat and went back to the yacht club to tidy up the mess that we had left, including empty boxes and bits of rubbish. It didn't take long and we went straight to Skeetas restaurant and sat out on the patio overlooking the marina. The sun was setting and the water was glowing from the low angle of the sun. It really was magical, sitting there with a cold beer and relaxing, just enjoying the moment. Euan raised a glass and said, "Well done lads, you've made it. You said getting to the start line would be the hardest part and you have achieved it." The three of us made a good team: we all brought different things to the table and it worked really well.

We were scheduled to leave in about five days and were now closely watching the weather. We were looking for a wind blowing out of the east to get us away from the shore, off the continental shelf and out into the deep ocean. Over the past few days, we had got quite friendly with the locals who all came out to look at the boat, most of whom were sailors or had little fishing boats. Apart from the normal comments like, "You guys are bloody crazy!", everyone was extremely friendly and supportive.

Edrick asked if we would like to give a talk to the members at the yacht club, which both Ash and I were happy to do. They had been very kind to us so this was a good opportunity to say thank you.

It was a sit-down dinner and we would be given as much time as we wanted to tell our story and convey our objectives.

During my time in Perth, I had met a woman called Kat. She was a bubbly, happy person and was interested in our row. Both Ash and Euan agreed that she was a nice person to have around. Kat was staying with us in the apartment and her mum was renting a small place around the corner, so we made sure that they also had an invitation to come to the dinner. We headed down to the yacht club early to get the laptop set up. Ash was going to meet us later as he was working on the laptop and sat phone connection. About an hour before the guests arrived, I had a message from Ash to say that he had just woken up from an epileptic fit and really wasn't feeling well enough to come down. I said it wasn't a problem and that he should just rest. I gave the talk, which was well-received. I lost count of how many times I heard Ash and I referred to as "crazy pommies!"

With only a few more days until we were due to leave, the weather was not looking good. We made the decision to delay the start until it looked more favourable. By now, we were pretty much ready. We were probably carrying far too much stuff but everything we wanted to complete had been taken care of and the 'To Do' list was almost ticked off.

It was now the night before we were due to depart. Earlier in the day, we had visited the Immigration department to sign us out of the country. They laughed and joked, "You know, tonight you'll officially be illegal immigrants so you must leave tomorrow!"

That evening, we went back to Skeetas restaurant and had a huge blowout meal but didn't go overboard on the drinks! Back at the flat, it hit me that I actually wasn't quite as organised as I'd thought. Whilst Ash was very well squared away with his personal items, I still had my clothes, laptop, sat phones, cables, spare batteries and tools everywhere. By this stage, I was pretty tired and needed to get to bed so I decided to sort it out in the morning. With hindsight, that wasn't really the right thing to do, as I've learnt over the years. So the following morning I was up early and quickly packed everything away.

We had some breakfast and headed down to the boat. Ash and I had a few bags between us and we were wondering where all of this was going to go: the boat was well packed and neatly organised but now we were filling it with our personal stuff and loads of fresh fruit. I had learnt whilst rowing the Atlantic Ocean in 2010 that food – at least for me – played a big part in my mental wellbeing. It really does make a massive difference to how you feel, so I suggested we take a lot of fresh fruit to make the first week or so easier; it wouldn't keep for that long so it would need to be consumed fairly quickly.

Again, Euan had worked his magic and managed to create something special with the media; even media crews from Perth made the journey up to Geraldton. It was starting to get quite busy, with lots of locals arriving to see us off and news crews asking for interviews. We still hadn't finished organising our things but I told Ash that everything was in the boat and we could tidy it up a bit later after we had departed.

We both *FaceTimed* our families back home, Kat then hugged me and gave me a book which she said I was to open one page at a time when I was struggling. I'd really enjoyed my time in Western Australia and had created some fantastic memories. Ash had said his goodbyes to everyone and was waiting for me in the boat. I shook Euan's hand one last time and stepped on board. I was now running on adrenaline and felt very fired up, having felt slightly nervous all morning, with butterflies in my stomach.

When you're about to embark on an ocean row or something on a large scale that you've spent a long time preparing for and which you know is going to be difficult, it's inevitable that you will feel anxious.

As soon as you leave your comfort zone, you will naturally not want to be there: it's human nature. A comfort zone is a psychological state in which you feel at ease with your environment, everything is relatively familiar and straightforward, and you are not particularly stressed. However, you only ever really grow when you step out of your comfort zone.

The subconscious brain will work in a way to talk you out of things, to get you back to a place which feels safe and familiar. The purpose of this is to protect you, so when you're facing a situation that doesn't feel normal, the brain is programmed to make you question your choices!

If your preparation has been thorough, you will at least be in a semi-confident state but the truth is, you will be wondering whether this is really a good idea or not: that's the brain talking and not usually the heart. In your heart, you know you want to be there, you know you have worked hard to secure the funding and to make it happen. It's usually been a hell of a journey just to get to the start line. Now, there is nowhere to hide. You don't have another day to get ready or the opportunity to put that task off – that's it – time's up!

At this point, the mind gets very clever, coming up with lots of good reasons why you need to either back out or take some more time to get ready. You suddenly start to justify your decisions, thinking it's time to back out and that you're doing the right thing. If you get to this point mentally, you're going to struggle to get back on track. When it comes to rowing across an ocean, or any other monumental task, you have to want it badly – and I mean 100%, not 99%. You need to want it as if your life depends on it!

It's very easy to talk about something but it's a completely different story doing it. I have a mantra that I tell many young people I meet: "Your actions are a measure of who you are." I am personally still working on this! There are times when I said to myself that I want to do X, Y and Z, yet my actions still didn't show it. Thankfully, Ash and I were in a good place mentally and were both looking forward to what lay ahead.

2

False Start

Euan slipped the lines and, as the boat moved away from the dock, I could hear loud cheering and clicking cameras. I was in a heightened state of awareness and small things became very noticeable: the markings on peoples' clothing, their hair colour, their voices. My brain was working hard to process everything that was going on around me. Ash rowed out whilst I was filming.

It didn't take too long to get out of the harbour and eventually the cheers from well-wishers quietened down. Sea conditions were calm with no swell to make things difficult and Ash rowed for a good few hours. We still had full phone coverage so I was streaming to *Facebook* and putting pictures on social media. I was sending pictures to Euan to give to the press, who were apparently loving them. Our apartment and the other buildings in Geraldton were getting smaller. It was pretty hot so we were both drinking a lot to stay hydrated. In the rush that morning, I'd forgotten to take a sea sickness tablet; I didn't usually suffer but it's always a good idea to take precautions for the first few days. Thankfully, both of us were feeling fine.

It was soon time for my two-hour rowing shift. There is no right or wrong way to row across an ocean in terms of shift patterns. Obviously, you cannot row all the time! When I rowed across the Atlantic, I slept at night for around six to seven hours and would just let the boat drift; for the most part, it would drift the right way in the currents. With two of us rowing, the plan was to have someone on the oars 24/7 to keep the boat moving. We knew it would be tiring to begin with, but this was the way that most crews row across an ocean.

As Ash was rowing out and I was filming him, I hadn't taken too much notice of our GPS repeaters out on deck, which displayed our speed, heading and a course to steer. It can be set up to display more but that's all we really wanted and needed. It was a little demoralising to see that I was only just averaging two knots, even with a light following wind. We were fully loaded and whilst the boat felt incredibly stable, the downside was the impact on our rowing speed. It's hard to judge what's really needed and what's not; we knew we would quite quickly eat through a lot of the extra fresh food but we also had a lot of emergency drinking water packed in the hull. We were not competing in a race so we had no restrictions on what to pack. However, we were still very optimistic and knew that when the winds picked up, we would also see the boat speed increase.

We decided to run the autopilot whilst I rowed. Ash turned it on, we set it up to hold the desired course, the foot steering was disengaged and the tiller itself was doing the steering. It was working perfectly and, although we weren't moving particularly quickly, we were looking good. The sun was starting to set and the lights of Geraldton were shining, creating an orange glow in the sky over the town. The temperature had started to drop and it cooled down quickly, to the point where we were both starting to get quite chilly. I pulled out my *Nothing's Impossible* hoodie that was branded with our charities' logos and carried on rowing. Ash boiled some water and made up a ration pack meal. He already knew which meals he liked the best as he'd been sampling them back in the UK!

Both of us were not in the least bit tired as we were still fuelled by the excitement of our departure. I swapped over with Ash after my two-hour shift had finished and made myself a Spaghetti Bolognese meal. Thankfully, neither of us were having problems with sea sickness which can be extremely debilitating. One of the first symptoms is usually loss of appetite but I was ravenously hungry so that was a good sign. It was now dark and our eyes had adjusted to the low light. The moon was out and shining brightly so we didn't actually need any head torches or lights on. We did have our navigational lights on despite the AIS (Automatic Identification System) telling us that there were no other ships around.

Our boat was now running on the two 12-volt gel batteries that powered the electrical system as there was no sunlight for the solar panels to utilise. We could see a slow discharge which was to be expected when the power goes out and nothing comes in. We decided to run our fuel cell, a device that uses methanol fuel to create electricity. It's not burned but instead produces electricity through a chemical reaction; the only by-product is water and a small amount of carbon dioxide. As we turned the device on, we could see the flow of electricity come in through our controller unit which displays the battery levels, and the charge flow in and out. It was working perfectly.

The only thing that Ash and I were struggling with was the temperature. It really had plummeted and we had virtually every layer of clothing on. We each rowed our two-hour shifts throughout the night with little bits of rest here and there. Eventually, we could start to see the sky to the east brighten up and it wouldn't be long before the sun made an appearance over the horizon. Almost immediately, the temperature started to rise as the sun climbed into the sky.

I was starting to feel quite tired now but as the sun came up, it gave me another boost of energy. The wind and sea state had settled and it was now very calm. We had lost the lights of the Australian coast overnight but we were not in international waters yet. We hadn't seen any commercial vessels but were treated to an amazing spectacle from a pod of whales. Neither Ash nor I are wildlife experts but we think they may have been humpback whales. They moved gracefully with absolute ease through the water, which really was a magical sight.

We decided to stop rowing for 20 minutes whilst we both had some breakfast. We had run the autopilot all through the night and our batteries had more charge going in than going out now that the sun was blasting down on us. Overall, the first night had gone very well. As we had stopped rowing, we turned the auto pilot off; it was now very quiet with just the sound of water gently lapping up against the side of the boat. After breakfast, Ash took over the oars and I lay down for a while which was the first proper sleep that I'd managed to get. We had plenty of power and it was working well, so we decided to continue to use the autopilot; it just made things easier and all we needed to do was pull the oars.

The morning passed by and the wind started to gently pick up, coming directly from behind, which was useful. We still couldn't get the boat moving that fast unless we really pulled hard, which was not possible to sustain, but we were moving at around 2.5 knots which was OK. By mid-afternoon, we had both pulled a couple more shifts each.

Whilst Ash was rowing, we noticed that the autopilot had stopped. We turned it back on again and it stopped working almost immediately. We disconnected the tiller from the rudder and I used the foot steering to continue. Ash looked at what was going on but there was nothing obvious to see. The piston that pushed the tiller up and down was not hot and there was nothing blocking it so we couldn't understand what the issue was. We pulled out the instruction manual and started looking through the troubleshooting section. We went through everything and tried all the factory resets but we were unable to get it working and found ourselves in a bit of a conundrum. We called the manufacturer via the sat phone and they were very helpful but we were still unable to identify why the autopilot had stopped working.

We now had to make a decision to either try and somehow get back to Geraldton to fix it, or carry on and make the whole journey without it. This would have been perfectly feasible as there was always one of us on the oars who could steer and I had rowed the Atlantic Ocean on my own without an autopilot, so it wasn't critical. I think it was just frustrating because we had it working so well and wanted to use it. I called Euan to ask his advice, who said we should go back to Geraldton. He also said he could organise a boat to come and get us. I said we would call him back.

Ash and I spent some time deliberating whether or not to turn round. We had been out just over 24 hours and hadn't travelled a massive distance, almost 50 miles from where we started. But we hadn't rowed directly 50 miles away from the coast, we had actually been rowing north west; our current position was about 30 miles from the coast. We didn't want to declare an emergency as this wasn't one, it was a technical recovery. We spoke with Euan and he was liaising with Geraldton Yacht Club. Apparently there was a fishing charter boat not too far from our position which was happy to tow us back in. We passed on our current position (latitude and longitude) to Euan to convey to the fishing vessel.

About 30 minutes later, the sat phone rang and it was the captain of the boat coming to tow us back in. The first thing he said to me was, "Do you have insurance?" I confirmed that we did so he asked if I could provide our updated position and tell him our direction of travel. As I gave him the coordinates, he must have input them straight into the GPS as he said they were about three hours away. They would be approaching from the south so we turned the boat around and tried to make progress towards them but the wind made it virtually impossible. We deployed the para anchor which held us in position because there was really no point wasting energy by trying to row towards them and not even making one knot.

Both Ash and I made some calls home to let everyone know what we were doing, as the tracker would show us heading back to the coast. Euan called again to inform us that the local news crew were asking what was going on. Euan hadn't mentioned anything to the media so we suspected that it was perhaps the yacht club who had mentioned it. Euan pointed out that our return had to be managed correctly, from a PR perspective. "You guys are only coming back in for a technical stop, then you'll be back out again and we can probably use this as a second chance to gain some positive PR and support," Euan said. He always had a great angle in his head for a story, so we trusted him and knew it would be well handled.

We had our navigation lights on and after a few hours, we eventually saw a light on the horizon, from the direction that our recovery boat would be travelling. I looked on our chart plotter: if they had AIS, we would have been able to confirm it was the vessel. Slowly but surely, it was getting closer and we could make out the outline of the boat, which wasn't particularly big. The sat phone rang and it was the captain again, confirming that he could see us and would be with us shortly. We pulled in the para anchor as we didn't want the line or the para anchor itself to get tangled up in their propeller or rudder. It was fairly easy to deploy and retrieve: it's basically like a parachute that sits in the water, with a line attached to the boat. As the wind pushes the boat backwards, the para anchor will fill with water and slow the boat's movement through the water. This is what we would use if the wind changed direction and started pushing us back. It had been an essential item of kit when I rowed across the Atlantic.

Once we pulled the para anchor in and stowed it away, we started to get ready for the arrival. We wanted to use the bridle, which was a rope permanently fixed to the bow (front) of the boat; we attached a long line to it and this would be used as the tow line. By now, the recovery vessel was a lot closer and in VHF radio range. They wanted to circle around us a few times before coming in close. We could hear the chugging of the diesel engine and when we were downwind of it, we could smell the diesel fumes. There was a young-looking deckhand on the boat with long dreadlocks, who was moving around and organising ropes. The captain was at the helm and the rest of the crew were paying passengers who had chartered the boat to go fishing.

They came in close and I threw the bow line which the deckhand missed the first time. I quickly pulled it in, launched it back and he caught it no problem the second time. Thankfully, the sea state was fairly calm so there was not a massive amount of movement. Before we disembarked the boat, we locked the rudder in position so it would track straight under tow. The deckhand put some fenders out as we pulled the *James Lewis* up alongside to make the transition. Ash packed some of the electrical kit, sat phone and laptops into a bag, then boarded the boat. Just before I left, I shut the hatch door and locked it into position.

Once we had both boarded, the captain came over and shook our hands. "Well done guys," he said, then offered us a drink. The sun was now starting to set and the rest of the folk on board looked pretty tired. Ash and I were still running on adrenaline so we were buzzing. The captain did say to us that it would take around 12 hours to motor back to Geraldton with our boat in tow. We set off and the *James Lewis* was tracking nicely as we moved along at around five knots.

After about an hour, we noticed that the winds were picking up and the sea state was starting to become quite choppy and confused. This was starting to roll the boat a bit more but the *James Lewis* was still looking good under tow.

However, some of the guys on our boat were not looking so good as debilitating sea sickness took hold. The deckhand made some dinner for everyone. I was impressed with this guy who was moving all over the place making everything happen but I guess that was his job. The captain would shout for him to do something and he'd jump up and do it. Even when the boat started to roll around a bit more, he was moving about like a mountain goat. He cooked up some pasta and chicken, which Ash and I quickly polished off as we were hungry!

It was now dark, although the moon was out and reflecting beautifully off the water. Some fold-out beds were made up and put on deck and most of the guys tried to get some sleep. Mobile phone signals were intermittently coming in and cutting out, so I used the sat phone to call Euan to let him know our estimated ETA. The adrenaline had now worn off and both Ash and I were starting to feel pretty tired. The deckhand found some more fold-out beds and we lay down.

I was tired but found it hard to sleep as my head was spinning. "Have we done the right thing?" I thought to myself. I managed to drift in and out of sleep but it was also pretty cold, which was keeping me awake. It was a good job I *was* awake as I heard a loud crack and instantly bolted upright to see that the tow line to the *James Lewis* had snapped. Ash and the deckhand heard it too and were now awake and on their feet. The deckhand was lightning fast and shouted to the captain that the boat had just become separated.

Everyone was now awake and ready to help. The captain spun the boat around and circled up on the *James Lewis*, which I noticed was not sitting in the water straight and was badly listing over to one side.

The entire deck was covered in water and my heart sank. Getting the boat attached again was not really a problem: the rope had simply snapped so we used a long hook to pick up the broken tow line. The deckhand used another rope to reattach it to the bow line but the captain came over with a tyre and told him to tie the broken bow line to that and the new tow rope to the other side. The tyre would act as a spring and take up some of the tension. The captain said that we should have used this to begin with but the sea had been calm.

As the sea was now a bit rougher, it was causing the tow line to slacken off and then tighten up which no one had noticed since we were trying to get some sleep. This action had also caused the boat to list over slightly when the tow line was snapping tight. Water had started to fill the boat which made it heavier and caused it to list over even more to one side. It took a good hour or so to get the rope secured and the boat under tow again. We could now only motor along at about 3.5 knots due to the way our boat was sitting in the water. The captain apologised and acknowledged that this was less than ideal but we just needed to get both boats back to shore. We also noticed a lot of water in the cabin when we shone our flash light on it which had possibly come in through the vents. It was pretty obvious to both me and Ash that this could have quite a bad outcome as the electrics could be damaged.

We continued to motor on, watching the *James Lewis* under tow, sadly no longer looking like the sleek, fast, modern rowing boat it was when we climbed off it. It was in rather a sorry state as it was dragged through the sea, taking on even more water as the deck was now almost at the water line. We knew we would be back in around five hours and could quite clearly see the glowing lights of Geraldton.

Knowing that we had a fair bit of work ahead of us to dry out the boat and assess any damage, the hours passed very slowly. We had full signal on our mobiles which were vibrating every few seconds with messages coming through. I heard a 'clunk' and thought, "Not again!" This time, the tow line hadn't snapped but the metal rail it was tied to on the fishing boat had bent. As our boat was now filled with water, the weight had probably doubled, especially as it was listing and creating a huge amount of drag in the water. The captain wasn't happy but he realised he should have secured the tow line on a stronger anchor point on his boat. He turned the engine to idle and disengaged the drive to the propeller. This allowed the *James Lewis* to move closer to us so that the line would slacken enough for him to tie it to a more solid point.

It was dark and cold and to be honest, I think everyone on board just wanted to be back in port and on dry land. We got chatting to the rest of the crew who had chartered the boat to take them fishing for a few days but apparently they had caught virtually nothing. Their trip was coming to an end and they joked that they hadn't expected to catch two crazy pommies who were out rowing. Whilst some of them were quiet, most of them were very supportive of what we were doing.

By now, we only had a few hours left and could clearly make out Geraldton and some recognisable buildings, such as our apartment and the harbour walls. As we got closer to shore, the water became shallower and the sea started to flatten out. This allowed the captain to increase speed a little. It wasn't long before we were back in the harbour but not the harbour we had departed from almost 48 hours earlier, but this time, the commercial harbour.

There were film crews everywhere with big lights set up and I could see Euan standing there. Ash and I looked at each other in surprise as we hadn't expected this scale of media presence. As we docked, the media flash lights started going off as the photographers snapped away. It was a shame that the *James Lewis* was filled with water and clearly its deck should not have been half submerged in the water.

It was still dark but the lights from the crews really lit the whole area up. I wasn't fazed by the media but it was incredibly frustrating to see our boat in this state. The rest of the guys on the boat joked that we were celebrities.

As Ash and I stepped off the boat, we made sure to thank the crew profusely who had towed us back in. Euan said that the media just wanted to know what happened and why we had come back. Very quickly, there was a reporter standing in front of us, asking questions, with a cameraman at her side, pointing a light and camera at us. We explained that the boat had performed well and that everything was fine, and that we only returned because we were still close enough to shore. We would have carried on had we been another few days out. We repeated the same thing to a few different news crews and they were all really understanding, with not one of them asking any awkward or probing questions. As quickly as they were there in front of us, they had their story and were gone.

3

Preparing Again

It was now just the captain, Ash, me and Euan who were hanging around. To be fair, the captain wasn't a ruthless guy but he pointed out that we did need to talk about the cost of the recovery because he would have to refund the guys who chartered the boat for their fishing trip, bearing in mind they came in early. I asked how much we were talking and he confirmed that it was $15,000 Australian dollars. I asked for his bank details and we exchanged email addresses. We were all pretty tired by now and it wasn't as if we could run off with our boat without paying the guy so we agreed to communicate further on email.

It was now fully light and people were starting to make their way to work. We had secured an apartment from the hotel at a good rate, bearing in mind that our sponsored accommodation had now run out. I had a hot shower and crashed out on the bed. I remember waking up at about two o'clock in the afternoon. Euan had moved his stuff into the new apartment and was moving around. He said that there had been a lot of media interest so he had lined up a radio interview in a few hours' time.

It was the first time I didn't really feel like doing any PR but made sure that I sounded enthusiastic. Ash was now up and about too so we all headed down to Skeetas for a late lunch (I certainly wasn't expecting to walk back in there quite so soon!). The staff asked what had happened and how come we were back; we explained the situation and realised that this would not be the last time that we would have to explain it. I guess they felt pretty sorry for us because when we came to pay the bill, they said, "Don't worry guys, this one's on us."

We needed to get back to the boat to get it lifted out of the water but first had to collect the cradle so we had something to put the boat on. As luck would have it, the yacht club told us that the cradle was now in the commercial port and we found it sitting outside a boat repair yard. When we arrived back at the boat, we saw that the rowing seat was missing and not attached to the rails anymore. How this had happened, I had no idea, as it was a very secure fit. Either way, it was not there so we also needed to get a new one sent to us. This was a real nuisance as it was a custom-padded seat that attached to the base of the rowing seat.

The crane driver slid two heavy-duty lifting straps under the boat and attached them to the forks of his mobile hoist. He started to lift and the *James Lewis* slowly rose out of the water. We noticed that the dagger board had snapped and was still hanging on by the line it was attached to – another thing that would need to be repaired! Once it was up in the air, the boat was slowly driven over to the cradle. As the mobile crane moved, water was still coming out of the gunnels on the side of the boat (these let the water flow out when a large wave engulfs the boat). This was good as it would have had to be pumped out anyway. The driver gently sat the boat down on the cradle, took the straps away and then drove back to the dock.

This was the first time that Ash and I were able to get on board and assess the damage. There was literally water everywhere in the cabin, with oranges and tinned fruit floating about. We took a bilge pump out from another compartment and started to pump the remaining water out. It didn't take long for it to clear out, then we used a sponge and bucket to get the last of the water out.

We decided that the best course of action was to strip the boat of its entire contents, to at least begin to dry everything out. The mattress was soaked so we pulled it out and placed it over the back of the boat to dry. Ash jumped inside the cabin and checked the electrics; everything was working apart from the water maker, the device we used to turn salt water into drinking water. Without this essential item of kit, there would be no crossing at all. Ash checked the fuse, which showed no sign of being broken. We decided to come back to the water maker and just carried on getting everything out of the boat. We took all the food out of the hatches which was all fine as it was wrapped in waterproof bags. We made a list of everything that needed attention: the auto pilot, broken dagger board, water maker, the fuel cell which was also not working and the lost rowing seat. What we had envisaged being a simple tow back into port for a few days turned out to be an absolute nightmare, not to mention the bill we still had to pay for the recovery.

I had now received an email from the captain of the recovery boat with his bank details, which he followed up with a phone call. This debt needed to be dealt with fairly urgently but our project funds were dwindling rapidly. We were going to have to use the funds that had been put aside to ship the boat back to the UK from Mauritius and I'd possibly need to use some of my personal savings too. I needed to get back to the apartment to look at the finances properly so I could get this bill paid; I had a feeling that the captain would not want to wait for long.

Back at the apartment, I pulled out the laptop and made the bank transfer. Boy, it hurt! I think with hindsight, despite the broken autopilot, if we had known how costly this was going to be in terms of money and time, plus damaged equipment, we would have undoubtedly carried on without the autopilot. However, hindsight is a great thing so it was now up to us to get back on track. Life is 99% about how you respond to situations and we were both highly motivated and determined to get back out there.

I said to Euan, "Let's get back down to the boat!" I wanted to see the captain to let him know that I'd made the transfer. Euan needed five minutes so I sat back down again. I don't really like asking for things but I decided to send one of our sponsors, Gordon, an email update. He was an extremely successful and very generous businessman who had personally put some funding into our project. He was a big supporter of *Over The Wall*, one of the charities we were raising money for. I didn't expressly ask for help, I just updated him on what had happened and explained that we might struggle to ship the boat back from Mauritius as we had no choice but to spend the funds that had been allocated for that on the recovery.

When we arrived at the boat, Ash was inside the cabin, still attempting to get the water maker working. He said that he was going to have to take it out to look at it more closely. If I'm honest, the whole situation wasn't really sinking in. I was looking around at our kit strewn all over the floor, mixed in with bags of expedition food. Later on, the owner of the boat builder's, whose space we were using, came over and said, "Hey guys, I've just had a call from the Port Immigration. You need to drop whatever you're doing and head over there now as an absolute priority."

One thing that we had overlooked was the fact that we were technically now illegal immigrants in Australia as we had not been officially cleared back in through Customs. I remember joking with the Immigration agent when she cleared us out on the dock and now we were back…a situation I had not expected to be in.

We rushed straight back to the apartment and picked up our passports. Obviously Euan was OK as he hadn't left the country but I wasn't really sure what to expect and didn't know if Ash and I were in serious trouble or not. We parked up outside the small building. I walked in first and was ready to start apologising for not coming sooner. It was the same woman as before, working behind the counter. She looked at me and said, "Ah, our rowers are back!" Luckily, she said it with a smile on her face which I took to be a good sign. We handed our passports over, laughing and joking for a few minutes, before she asked us how long we intended to stay before leaving again. We were not entirely sure, so she said, "No worries, I'll just give you a standard tourist visa; you have six months so just let us know when you want to leave." We thanked her and left. As we were walking back to the car, I said to Ash, "I bloody hope we're not here in six months!" He agreed, with a smile on his face.

We headed back to the boat and continued to tidy up. Whilst I was picking things up and generally organising our kit, I looked up and noticed the captain of the recovery boat walking over. He said, "Lads, I've received the money, thank you. Good luck with everything." I still felt a sense of frustration at the scale of work that was ahead of us and how much time we'd lost. Yet, for the first time since returning to Geraldton, I was starting to realise that perhaps we could use this extra time to better prepare ourselves.

Ash, Euan and I sat down that evening and looked closely at the timescales. We needed to gain an understanding of just how long it was going to take to get everything fixed and back on track. We also needed a new seat to be shipped from the UK. During the day, I'd received an email from the seat manufacturer who said it was going to be at least a month to get the new one shipped out to Australia.

I had hoped to be able to turn things around in two weeks but it was becoming quite obvious that we were going to be around for a lot longer. We also needed to consider the cost of extra accommodation. As if someone was looking down on us, as we were talking about finances and how we were going to manage this, I happened to check my phone and noticed that Gordon had sent a reply in response to my earlier email that morning. He had kindly offered to pay the fee for the tow, which was a massive help and really took the pressure off the budget, in the short term anyway. We were extremely grateful for his generosity.

That evening, we spoke about all sorts of options, in terms of what we were going to do for the next month. It certainly wouldn't take that long to get the boat ready. Ash was understandably missing his family and the reality was that another month in Australia before we had even departed was another month that he would not be able to see them at the other end. I'd made the decision that I didn't want to go back to the UK. Euan only had another two weeks left in the country and had planned to see some friends before heading back to the UK. That night, when Ash had gone to bed, Euan and I spoke about how we could arrange a flight to get Ash back to the UK. It didn't make sense for Ash to spend the whole month kicking about in Australia. We agreed that Euan would speak to Paul and James from *Balmain* and I would speak to Richard from *Ofsure*, and we might be able to arrange Ash a flight home. Richard, Paul and James were all really great supporters and sponsors of the project.

In less than 24 hours, they had agreed to split the cost of a flight home for Ash. The following day, we decided to have a barbecue outside our apartment in the communal area. It was glorious sunshine and the three of us were chilling and generally enjoying the outdoors, with Euan cooking the steak and burgers. After we'd finished our food, Ash went to the toilet, so Euan and I quickly decided that we should tell him now about the flight home to see his family. Ash came back out and cracked open another beer and sat himself down in a chair. I said to Ash, "Overall, we've had a fairly good day today, completing various jobs, but we have some more good news." Ash replied, "Oh yeah?" I told him that Euan and I had spoken to the guys from *Balmain* and Richard from *Ofsure* and that they'd agreed to pay for his flight home. Ash didn't seem an overly sensitive person; he was a fairly quiet, extremely hard-working individual who just got on with things. His eyes welled up at the news that he would soon be seeing his family again! He hugged Euan and me and thanked us both.

We decided that the best thing to do was to use the next week to finish all the jobs on the boat before Ash went home. Once Ash had flown back, I planned to stay with Kat in Perth, whilst Euan would spend some time with his friends. Over the next few days, we cracked on with various tasks on the boat. Now that we had a plan, it was as if we all had a massive injection of enthusiasm and motivation. Ash set to work on the water maker which he stripped out and took back to the flat. We had also managed to identify the problem with the auto pilot. Both Ash and I spent quite a lot of time on the phone with the company's technical support team who provided excellent customer service and dispatched the new part that we needed. Our 'To Do' list had halved and, despite it being in many pieces on the apartment floor at one point, Ash had managed to get the water maker working again.

One job that we would need some help with was repairing the dagger board. Luckily, the owner of the boat builder's yard offered to do it for us, in between other jobs. The dagger board is a small, retractable board that, when deployed, can help keep the boat tracking straight when a crosswind is coming from the side. We removed the damaged one and showed it to the boss, who said it was apparently an easy fix.

He was a nice guy, with a calm, easy-going persona, who had been working in the boat industry his whole life.

Even though we had taken the mattress out of the boat to dry out in the sun, it was still wet. We didn't want to leave it out whilst we were away so we found a local laundrette that we thought may be able to help dry it out for us. Ash and I walked in later that day with it. Before we could even speak to the woman behind the counter, she said, "Ah, so you guys are the rowers, we've heard all about you!" She kindly offered to put it in her drying room and advised us to come back in a few days.

We needed to purchase a few things from the local chandlery, *Max Marine*, owned by John and his wife, Carole. They were very friendly and we chatted for quite a while as they were interested in what we were doing. Over the course of the day, we returned a few times to pick up various bits and bobs. The people of Geraldton extended a huge amount of generosity to me and Ash, for which we will be forever grateful.

A few days had passed since we made our plans to head back to Perth. Euan was leaving Geraldton that night on a flight to Sydney, so we drove him to the airport. We would see Euan in a few weeks when he was back but the apartment wasn't quite the same without his energy, positivity and easy nature. The next day, Ash and I went back to the laundrette to collect the mattress, which was still slightly damp inside but dry enough for us to take away. We put it back in the boat, without the cover on; it got pretty hot in the cabin in the daytime so we relied on the heat to dry it out further.

We decided to drive back to Perth that afternoon: the quicker we got back, the more time Ash could spend with his family. There were plenty of flights back to London from Perth so securing a flight would not be a problem. Before leaving Geraldton, we gave the boat a final check and made sure that we'd locked the cabin hatches. We also made sure that we thanked everyone who had helped us over the past week and let them know that we would be back soon.

It was a beautiful afternoon, not too hot, just a stunning, cloudless, deep-blue sky: perfect conditions for the coastal drive, dotted with several national parks. Although I'd already cycled across the country, Australia really is a vast place; thousands of miles of absolutely nothing but truly stunning. When we arrived in Perth, we drove straight to Kat's apartment; it was a lovely, little place just outside the city with a pool in the garden. Ash managed to book his flight to leave the following day and we waved him off. Kat and I joked that he must promise to come back and he laughed. The disappointment of what had recently happened was long behind me: I felt I was in a good place and I really liked Perth.

The next day, Ash called me to say he had arrived home safely after a good flight. I could understand how he must have missed his wife and kids a great deal. I speak to my parents a fair bit as they are my best friends, however I had been away many times before and we were all used to me being absent for long periods. Technology has evolved dramatically, even since I completed my Atlantic row, so I was now able to *FaceTime* my parents any time I wanted.

Over the next couple of days, I hung out with Kat's brother. We went cycling along a disused railway line that had been turned into a recreational path. I was now eating cleaner and doing some form of training most days, which was certainly beneficial and I was starting to feel more energised. I was enjoying my time in Perth but it was important that I didn't lose sight of the mission. I made sure to touch base with Ash regularly when I had something of value to tell him. I had received an email from the company that was making a new seat for the boat, informing me that it had been shipped and would probably be with us in about a week. I was surprised it was going to take so long but I was just pleased that it was on its way.

I could now see some light at the end of the tunnel, in terms of a new departure date.

Ten days had now passed and it wasn't long before Ash would be heading back out to Perth. I had been in Australia for over a month; the summer heat in the day was starting to subside and the evenings were getting colder.

Ash called me from the airport as he was about to board the plane for Abu Dhabi where he was due to stop over for a few hours then carry on direct to Perth. It was quite a journey which had really knocked us for six when we first arrived in Perth. I knew we needed to take this into account when Ash arrived so made sure that we had at least 24 hours doing nothing before we headed back up to Geraldton.

Kat and I both drove to the airport that evening to collect Ash. We waited in the Arrival's Hall; we knew that his flight had landed but it must have taken a while to get through Immigration as it took some time for him to come through. With Ash now back in the country, this was quite an occasion, so Kat was filming as we wanted to capture the moment that he came through the doors. The doors slid open and there he was, with a big smile on his face. We hugged each other warmly and went straight out for something to eat. Ash was hungry and had plenty of enthusiasm. You wouldn't have known that he'd been travelling for almost 24 hours!

The next morning, I was pleasantly surprised to see that Ash was fine. Kat had managed to take some time off work and had borrowed her mum's 4 x 4 *Jeep* to drive us back to Geraldton and would stay with us for a day, before heading back. Euan was due to arrive in Geraldton a few days later on a flight from Sydney.

We drove straight to the apartments that we had initially rented. The following day, we all went down to the boat. Nothing had been moved and everything was in its place; the mattress had dried out nicely and the boatyard owner had repaired our dagger board whilst we were away. There was not a massive amount to do now, it was just a case of waiting for our seat to arrive.

The following day, Euan flew back into Geraldton so I used the truck to pick him up: he was impressed. The truck had character and looked cool (at least we thought so, anyway!). We headed down to the boat and hung out for a few hours with the boss of the boat builder's. He passed around some beers as it was coming to the end of their working day. Having spent almost six weeks out there, I could see why so many people from the UK emigrate to Australia. I think Sydney may be different but certainly on the west coast, the pace of life is much slower. No one appeared to be rushing around like mad men. People in general are so much friendlier, all saying hello to one another, regardless of whether they actually know that person or not. I think the weather made a big difference as well; most people finished work at around 4pm and would spend time with their families, having barbecues, running, cycling or just generally enjoying various sports and activities outdoors. Both Ash and I also noticed that people appeared to be far more active than back home in the UK.

It was now Friday evening and Euan had to leave Geraldton on Monday to head back to Perth, then ultimately the UK. He asked, "So, when are you leaving, guys?" We would never have guessed that we'd still be in Australia by the time Euan had to fly home. I had been checking the weather with Ash and there was no favourable weather window in the forecast at all. There was no rain or extreme weather, it was literally just a case of the wind blowing the wrong way and at a speed that we would not be able to row against. This would inevitably happen whilst we were at sea but we wanted to see two or three days of favourable winds to help us get clear of the coast and out into the deeper water, at the very least. We didn't want to get pushed south; if anything, we needed to head north where the winds are more established and coming from the east to push us west. It was obvious that we would not be leaving before Euan.

We'd waited this long now so another week or so wouldn't really matter. It was far from ideal though: we had haemorrhaged virtually all of our project funds and really needed to get going. Sponsors were understandably asking how we were getting on and wanted to know when we were going to be leaving. This time round, we had ourselves and the boat squared away properly. It wasn't that we were unprepared before, it was just that now we'd had more time to set things up exactly as we wanted them. The key to this was in the detail; a lot of small elements often come together to make something of epic proportions possible.

We mulled over our options, considering what we were going to do for the next week or so until we had favourable weather. We hadn't long returned from Perth but the thought of just hanging around in Geraldton wasn't something that appealed to us. Making decisions with Ash was easy; he was very laid back and always looked at things in a logical way. He too could see that there was nothing we could do as the weather was out of our control.

That evening, Euan left. It felt quite emotional saying goodbye to him as the three of us were a good team, with every one of us bringing something different to the table. That night when Euan left, Ash and I spent the evening relaxing and looking at the weather again in more detail. The forecast only showed ten days out, but there was some good news. We could see a change in the wind direction, which was just what we needed. It was however nine days away.

4

Second Try

The favourable weather window was looking more established and we absolutely had to take advantage of this opportunity. The days passed quickly and it was soon time to set off again. The boat was packed and ready, it just needed to be lifted back into the water. This time, it wasn't lowered in on the cradle using a slip way, it was simply lifted up and lowered in using the crane. It was soon time to get in the boat. Before I could step in, one of the reporters on her mobile shouted at me, "James, Euan's on the phone. He wants to speak to you before you leave and he sounds steaming drunk!" That made me chuckle. I spoke to Euan briefly, who was clearly very excited. It was odd not having him there but we needed to get moving.

We slowly floated out of the berth on the morning of 3rd July 2015. Ash would row the boat out and I was juggling the filming and live streaming from my phone. It didn't take long to get clear of the harbour but this time round, there was no media boat following us out: it was just the two of us.

We had a following wind that was providing some assistance and Ash was easily moving the boat along at close to three knots, which was fantastic. We were finally back out where we wanted to be, in perfect weather conditions and with the boat in prime condition. The first two-hour shift literally flew by; I was eager to jump on the oars and see how it felt. We both rowed as hard as we realistically could, considering this was a marathon not a sprint. Again, neither of us had any problems with sea sickness, which made things easier.

We were both running on adrenaline for the first night and I wasn't able to sleep for even one minute. I was expecting it to be cooler at night as it was almost two months later and the summer was coming to an end. Thankfully, it wasn't much colder, although we were prepared for the weather this time round. We had purchased some extra jackets to keep us warm at night; just a few degrees can make all the difference, taking you from slightly chilly to positively cosy.

As the sun rose the following morning, the first night was now behind us and we had lost sight of land. We had made good progress during the night and the boat was working well. I felt pretty tired but Ash still looked strong. Both of us had been up for over 24 hours now with no sleep. When the sun broke out over the horizon and started to rise, it almost instantly warmed up, as if someone had just turned the heating on. This made me feel sleepy but I knew it would only take a few days to get into a rhythm. The morning sun shining down on our faces was a great feeling.

I made us some breakfast then was ready for my shift, having quickly polished off my muesli. The boat was moving through the water nicely, feeling smooth and efficient. In the daytime, the sun would shine down on the water, creating a dazzling array of reflections and making it look very inviting. We were hopeful of seeing some large sharks; we knew these waters were inhabited by great whites although they had probably migrated to warmer waters by now. Every now and then, I'd see a fin or some splashing in the water but as quickly as I noticed some kind of wildlife, it was gone. Over the course of the day, Ash and I took regular, retrospective looks at the GPS repeater on deck and we had calculated every conceivable crossing time, depending on our speed. I knew that the novelty of doing this would wear off soon enough! The day shifts would always go quite quickly: for the most part, we would either be eating, rowing or just chatting.

It wasn't long before the sun was beginning to set and another day had almost passed. I was starting to feel really tired now and I knew I'd struggle on the night shifts. When it gets dark, your body naturally wants to sleep. Ash had the first real night shift on the oars where the sun had completely passed over the horizon. It wasn't particularly dark as the moon was shining bright and I was able to get some sleep. Before I knew it, I heard a voice calling my name; it was Ash telling me that it was time for my shift. I felt like I was drifting in and out of consciousness but after the third or fourth time I heard my name, I knew I had to get up. Everyone is different but as soon as I know I have to get up, I start moving quickly.

For a lot of people, tiredness is very much a mental thing. You feel slightly tired and your brain is telling you to rest and sleep. If you are able to overcome that mental barrier, you realise that you might not be as tired as you thought you were and actually feel pretty good. I thought I knew what extreme tiredness was, having already rowed one ocean, but in 2011, I came very close to finding out what my limits were as I was descending from the summit of Mount Everest with pneumonia. There is a famous saying that Navy Seals use: "When you think you are tired, you are only at 40% of your maximum capacity." I do believe this: when I had no choice but to keep going or I would simply die, I managed to find that extra strength from somewhere and easily surpassed my expectations.

Two hours on and two hours off would be a brutal regime for most people. It's not that you don't get enough rest, it's the fact that you are only sleeping for a maximum of two hours at a time. It just takes some getting used to! That night was a really tough night for me. I was falling asleep on the oars, trying to row, but my head kept nodding up and down. At one point, I fell back off the seat and woke up leaning on the hatch! I have no idea how long I was asleep for but I only had thirty minutes of my shift left, so I jumped back up on the seat and finished the last thirty minutes as intensely as I could. I felt guilty because every time I fell asleep, I was letting Ash down but I knew that after a few days, I'd be fine.

I managed to get through the night. Both Ash and I were very tired as the adrenaline had long worn off and we were about to start our third day at sea. "If you can survive three days at sea, you can survive three months at sea," I joked with Ash. Another day passed and the evening was rolling in. Both of us had managed to get some sleep during the course of the day and were feeling a little bit fresher, giving us confidence that slowly but surely, we were starting to get used to the pattern. No matter how good we were feeling, the time always passed more slowly at night.

I'm often asked about the mental side of rowing an ocean and to be honest, I believe that ocean rowing is 90% in the head and 10% actual rowing. It's more about surviving the environment and staying on what I call an 'even keel'. You can't let yourself get too down when things aren't going well as the next day usually brings new feelings and new weather. When things are going well, I consciously take a few moments to enjoy them and realise how lucky I am to be in this amazing place doing something great, which most people will never have the opportunity to experience.

I knew how important it was to stay in a mentally positive state. I maintained it by constantly trying to stimulate my mind, thinking about all the things I wanted to do when I was back home, the people

I wanted to see, the places I wanted to travel to and the new skills I wanted to learn. Whilst I was not rowing, I was constantly making notes in my little, black book, jotting them down every time something popped into my head. You have a lot of time on your hands to think when rowing an ocean and it's critical that you keep your mind in a positive place. As soon as your mind wanders to a negative place, it can be quite difficult to get it back. Everyone has their own ways of dealing with this but for me, it's visualising the end goal, whilst also trying to enjoy the moment and embracing the ups and downs.

I mentioned to Ash that we had not checked our sat phone messages or emails. I turned it on, waited a few minutes to gain reception, then heard a flurry of "beep, beep, beep" as messages of support were coming through. The messages really help with morale but sometimes they can have the opposite effect. You are not interacting with people in the normal way so you can find yourself reading into things in far greater detail than you would do at home. You might read a message and think, "What do they mean by that?" or "Are they being funny with me?" This is another example of how your mind can quickly run away with itself if you're not mindful of the mental challenge you're undertaking. The dynamics are different on your own and this time round, I was with Ash, which I actually preferred as we connected well and I really enjoyed his company.

The next few days passed and we were both starting to get into a rhythm. Our bodies had now got used to the dehydrated ration packs and everything abnormal was becoming normal! Everything had its place and going to the toilet, aka "bucket and chuck it," was a formality that we would mostly do at night on deck when the other person was asleep. I did accidentally step in the bucket once, straight after using it but quickly cleaned it up and only told Ash the following day!

We had been on the water for five days and were making very good progress, now around 300 nautical miles from our starting point.

However, we noticed that the wind had started to shift round, now blowing from north to south, which made rowing extremely difficult. Rowing with a following wind and sea is very easy: for the most part, the boat will just glide through the water with the momentum of the following sea to keep it moving. But rowing at a 90° angle to the following sea and wind can be very challenging. The boat will roll from side to side and waves will often break over the boat, inevitably slowing up the speed. The wind speed was progressively picking up and rowing was now difficult. Our boat speed had dropped to just over one knot, nevertheless we continued on.

Despite having a very slim build – a side effect from chemotherapy treatment when he was younger – I was impressed that Ash always rowed hard and put huge effort into whatever he was doing. We weren't sure at what point that Ash would have an epileptic fit but apparently they were most likely to happen when he was tired. We had both been extremely tired but so far, he hadn't had a seizure.

Rowing was becoming really difficult so I decided to call our weather router on the sat phone, just to get an idea of what was coming. We both wondered if an area of low pressure was coming our way as the cloud cover had started to build and we no longer had the sun shining down on us. Our weather router was based in Canada and he would send us text messages with a forecast every day. However, we had not received one that day or, if he'd sent one, it hadn't reached us. I managed to get through and he gave us an update but it certainly wasn't the update we were hoping for. We did indeed have a large, low pressure system coming right at us.

There was nothing we could do: we couldn't outrun it or row around it, we just had to go directly through it. The wind speeds were forecast to be around 50 knots, which was a lot of wind that would dramatically change the sea state. It was going to be at least a few days before we could row again. With this news in mind, we decided to get a head start on the weather and deployed the para anchor. We were barely able to make much progress anyway. The boat itself was relatively tidy but we decided to remove the seat and stow it in the stern cabin. We also locked the rudder in position and generally tied down anything that could move.

It almost felt like a weight off our shoulders as we knew that we'd be staying put for a few days whilst this weather system passed. We grabbed some extra ration packs out of the lockers and stowed them away in the cabin. It's not ideal going out on deck in very high winds as we could quite easily have been knocked overboard by a rogue wave or a sudden roll in the boat. We would obviously have to go on deck to use the toilet bucket when needs must but apart from that, we wanted to avoid being on deck.

It was the end of day five and we were now sitting on the para anchor. The wind speed hadn't started to pick up yet as it was only blowing at around 20 knots; it was now more comfortable as the para anchor was holding us into the sea so we no longer had the side to side rolling motion. That evening, we lay chatting in the cabin. We both knew that we would at some point have to spend some time stationary on the para anchor as it's very rare to not spend at least a few days at anchor in bad weather during an ocean row. We were just hoping that this would happen a little further along on our journey. Nevertheless, we both remained upbeat and positive.

We did notice that our battery level had fallen to below 50% which was a lot lower than we had seen before, especially as we had not been using the autopilot. We only had the GPS and AIS on in the daytime so this was a bit of a worry. We figured that if we turned almost everything off that didn't need to be on, it would help. We needed to leave the GPS and AIS on as this was effectively our radar and would make us visible to other large, commercial vessels. We could also see the position of other vessels around us in relation to our position. We turned down the brightness on the screen, which would also save some power. Unfortunately, we were never able to get our fuel cell working again in Geraldton due to water damage, so we couldn't use that to top the batteries up.

The wind had certainly picked up during the night. Every now and then, we would hear the waves which would get louder and louder and then, "Smash!" They would hit the boat with such a force: I'll never forget what that feels like, which at times can be quite scary. The boat was built to withstand virtually anything but every time a large wave hit the boat, it literally felt like it was going to break into pieces. Of course it never would have done as it's made from layers of carbon fibre, which are incredibly strong. Despite the pounding of the waves, we did manage to get some sleep.

When I woke up the next morning, I could see out of the hatch that the sea state had worsened. Intimidating waves were breaking on the boat and our British Ensign flag was blowing fiercely in the wind. I was unsure of the wind speed but I knew it was a lot! The direction was straight out of the north, so over time, it would push us slowly south. We wanted to avoid this because if we ended up too far south, it would be difficult to get back on course again. I noticed that our drift was very minimal but we were being taken southeast, the direction we had come from, which was certainly demoralising this early on into the row. The battery level was now even lower at around 40%, however there was some sun around in patches that was occasionally breaking through the clouds, so we hoped to see this put some charge back into the batteries.

It was hot and humid in the cabin: the air was pretty stale as the hatch had to be locked overnight so no fresh air had managed to get in. I opened the hatch and breathed in some fresh, oxygen-rich air. Just as I did, a wave came crashing over the top and soaked me and the inside of the cabin, which was a sober reminder of why the hatch had to be closed!

It doesn't take long to get fed up lying in a small cabin. It can be quite claustrophobic but thankfully, Ash's slim build made things a little bit easier as we lay next to one another. As the morning passed, it began to warm up even more. Both our bodies were now sweating and it was beginning to feel pretty uncomfortable. We could only open the hatch for a few seconds at a time to let the fresh air in and the stale, carbon dioxide-rich air out. I had learnt from my time in the Atlantic that it's important to have something to focus on and take your mind off things when facing a mental challenge. Sometimes listening to music that evokes great memories helps and can change your mood instantly. I listened to audio books to pass the time. We also put some social media messages out via our comms team, communicating that we were safe and well and waiting for this storm to pass before we could carry on. We explained the reason for the tracker showing us as hardly moving and actually slowly drifting back.

The sea state was getting worse by the hour as the *James Lewis* would rise and fall over the crest of the waves, which were engulfing the boat. Occasionally, a freak wave would pick the boat up and smash us down again but the para anchor was doing a great job of holding us steady into the oncoming sea. If we had been 'beam on', meaning that the waves were hitting us from the side, we would almost certainly have been rolled over.

I had just closed and locked the cabin hatch after letting some fresh air into the cabin and suddenly noticed that the boat was starting to turn away from the oncoming sea. The para anchor line had obviously slackened off and, just as that happened, the boat was hit by a monstrous wave that lifted the boat up and threw it over with such a force, I had no idea what was going on. There was a moment of darkness for a split second and the next thing I knew, there was a violent tug from the para anchor where the line had abruptly tightened, pulling the boat round again. I felt very disorientated but quickly became aware that we had taken a massive hit. Initially I wondered if the boat was still intact; the impact was so brutal, it felt like a car crash. My senses quickly sharpened to a heightened state of awareness and I shouted, "Ash, are you OK?" Initially there was no reply and I realised with dread that something was wrong. Within a second or two, I could see that the boat was OK and there were no visible cracks, although I noticed Ash lying face down on the soaked mattress.

After what felt like a lifetime, but in reality was perhaps not even a minute, Ash was responsive and lucid but had clearly taken quite a hit to his head from what I could work out, and judging by the headache he said he had. Safety was our absolute priority and, whilst being out in the ocean in a rowing boat is for the most part quite safe, things can escalate very quickly. It only takes one small thing to go wrong, then another and another, and before you know it, you're in a whole world of trouble. Another large wave hit the boat hard, listing it over to the point where I thought it might completely roll over again. It was a stark reminder that we were still in a very vulnerable position, being tossed and turned as wave after wave pummelled the boat, enduring the relentless Indian Ocean. We still had months at sea ahead of us and we were only 300 nautical miles off the Australian Coast.

I was breathing hard and was running on adrenaline. It was like a second sense had taken over my body: my thinking was slow but I still had clarity of mind, enough to notice that the batteries for the boat's electrical system had now fallen to an incredibly low 25% and were showing no charge coming in. It was like our problems were compounding. This added to my concern as I could not see a reason for this, although it would not have stopped us continuing.

Occasionally in life you will find yourself in very difficult situations.

I have learnt over time that you just have to go with your gut feeling and make the best decision you can at the time, based on the situation you are in and the information you have. Sometimes you'll make the right choice and sometimes you'll make the wrong choice: either way, you often have to analyse the situation fast, as I had to. We were not even in the worst of the forecasted winds yet and had already taken a serious battering. If we continued on and the conditions worsened, it would have made a rescue almost impossible from any passing vessel.

The risks were mounting up and I was uncomfortable with the bang to the head that Ash had sustained as he drifted in and out of consciousness. In my head, I knew that I didn't have much choice about what needed to be done. After some deliberation and a slightly jaded conversation with Ash, I made the difficult decision to activate the EPIRB (Emergency Positioning Indicating Radio Beacon). I had to put safety above our quest to cross the Indian Ocean. Ash had a family waiting for him at home and we didn't know if there would be any repercussions from his head injury.

I pulled out the sat phone and called the UK coastguards. Although we were in the Indian Ocean, it would be the UK authorities who would organise a rescue and coordinate with Australia's coastguards. I confirmed that we had intentionally activated our EPIRB and explained our situation. The operator on the other end of the phone was very calm and reassuring. She said she would call us back and 15 minutes later, the sat phone rang. They advised us that the closest vessel was now en route to us but it was still six hours away and heading to a port in Melbourne, Australia. The vessel was called the *Dubai Charm*, a 250-metre long, 100,000-tonne crude oil tanker! The operator told me that they had passed on our vessel's details and sat phone number.

With our AIS, the *Dubai Charm* would have no problem finding us as they got closer. I felt a sense of relief to know that help was coming but I was wondering how on earth we were going to get on board this thing! I was aware of the sea state and the fact that they would have to bring this massive vessel alongside us. We had no way of manoeuvring the boat and I was very concerned by the para anchor that was trailing out from the boat. I didn't want to retrieve it as it would mean that the boat would be very vulnerable to being rolled over if one of us wasn't on the oars, and that wasn't possible. I decided to just leave it out and would tell them on the radio when they got closer. We still had hours to wait until they arrived and it was like time had slowed down: one hour felt like three. Ash was resting and we both knew that this was going to take all of our strength to somehow get up on board.

I packed all of our personal and electrical items into a dry bag, including laptops and cameras. I was concerned that it would be nearly dark by the time the *Dubai Charm* arrived and we certainly didn't want to be doing this at night, even if they did have lights. A few hours later, I could see a vessel displaying on our chart plotter. I clicked on it to open up an information box that displayed all of the vessel's details. There she was – *the Dubai Charm* – still just over 40 nautical miles away.

Another hour passed as I was looking for her out over the horizon. Eventually I glimpsed something; as our boat would rise and fall with the swell, I could just make out the bridge on the vessel. It would appear then disappear behind a wave but it was gradually getting closer. As I feared, we were running out of daylight. I heard the VHF radio come to life, "*James Lewis*, this is *Dubai Charm*, over" in an Indian accent. Before I could answer, they repeated the same thing and I answered back to establish communication. They asked how our injured crew member was, referring to Ash. "He is stable at the moment," I replied. "OK, we are going to hold back and pick you up in the morning at first light, it's too dangerous in the dark.

We see you on our AIS, so we will come alongside you tomorrow and pick you up." He was very calm and made it all sound relatively easy, which was actually quite reassuring.

I found it hard to sleep that night. I made a few sat phone calls and spoke to Euan, who was disappointed for us but knew that safety was the absolute priority. I asked him not to divulge this news to anyone until we were safely on board the tanker. The night eventually passed and I think I slept for about an hour as my mind was racing. This project had been something that Ash and I had worked extremely hard to make happen and it was effectively over. I couldn't stop thinking about our sponsors and our charities – so many things. The hardest part is getting to the start line; securing the finances was ever so difficult and many people declined to help us, but for the few that did, we felt a massive responsibility on our shoulders to not let them down. What made it harder was the fact that we would have to abandon the boat and hope that it could possibly be recovered at a later date.

5

Dubai Charm Rescue

As the sun came up, we knew that we were only a few hours away from making this dangerous transition on to the tanker. As if someone was looking down on us, the sea had calmed just a little, though the wind was still blowing around 40 knots. This was going to be very risky as we were right on the weather limit for this rescue, in my opinion.

"*James Lewis*, this is *Dubai Charm*" came over the radio and I quickly acknowledged the call. "You will be on our starboard side, we will come alongside you and throw ropes down to you to tie on to your boat; we will then lower a rope ladder." I confirmed that I had copied the message and explained that Ash would need to be winched up. He was unable to climb a rope ladder, as his epileptic seizures come with no warning and can strike at any time, so it was a risk we couldn't take. We were ready for it on our boat and had planned for it, but we couldn't plan for it climbing up a rope ladder on the side of a tanker.

It would take them at least an hour to position themselves. Both Ash and I were now out on deck, with our life jackets on, ready to go. We could clearly see just how big this tanker really was, as we were now looking up at this truly gargantuan vessel, whose sheer size made us feel tiny and insignificant. We figured that it was probably 60 feet or more just to climb up to the deck. I looked up to the sky and muttered under my breath, "Please help us." Who I was speaking to, I had no real idea, I just knew that this was a potentially very dangerous thing to be doing and we needed all the 'help' we could get!

If it had been a calm day with not a ripple in the water, it would have been no problem at all. I checked the cabin door was locked for the last time and looked up, just as the bow of the boat was coming level with us. I could see the safety hats of the workers on deck: they were a long way up, that's for sure! They started to throw ropes down and it didn't take long before we attached one to our boat. This pulled us in to the side of the vessel, which caused us to be smashed against the side every time a wave picked up our small boat. The size and weight of the *Dubai Charm* meant that she was not rolling or really moving in the water; it was the fact that our boat was being bashed around that made things difficult. Workers on deck were still throwing ropes down to us, some of which were very heavy. With the momentum of a 60-foot drop, they picked up a lot of speed by the time they hit the boat. If any one of these ropes had hit us on the head as they came hurtling down, it would have undoubtedly knocked us out. We both shouted for them to stop throwing ropes down as we were already tied up and moving along with the vessel now. We noticed that the deckhand workers were walking our boat back towards the middle of theirs as we had established a line close to the front. We were now positioned almost exactly in the middle of the ship. The captain called on the radio and said, "OK, you guys are doing great, stay where you are for a few minutes, I'm going to turn the vessel to port and put you on the lee side out of the wind." I acknowledged the message.

I looked up and saw some netting being lowered down; I wasn't sure why as the plan was to use a rope ladder. As the netting was lowered, it immediately caused a problem. It was catching on the gates that hold the oars in place and causing the boat to list over to one side when it was rising and falling with the waves. I started to try and cut it away as it could potentially tip our boat over, which would have been catastrophic. Thankfully, the deckhands who were assisting could see this happening too and quickly pulled the netting up. By this point, there were ropes everywhere and I was worried that they were going to get caught up and make it very difficult for us to get off without getting tangled up.

All of this was happening very fast. I looked over to Ash and saw him getting into a harness that had been lowered down, then he put his life jacket on over the top of it. I took our bag and tied it to a rope: up it went. Another rope was lowered down for Ash so he tied the knot and was now connected to the rope. We both looked up at the mess of ropes that were dangling down. It was possible that Ash might get caught in a rope that was already tied to our boat if they just lifted him off the boat then and there. The crew shouted down for Ash to climb to the back of our boat and jump into the water, clearing himself and his connected rope away from the tangled mess.

As I watched Ash manoeuvre himself round to the back of the boat, I felt a whack to the side of my face, which took me by surprise and really hurt for a few seconds. I had been hit in the face by a swinging rope and it knocked the *GoPro* off my head strap and into the water. "No!" I thought. Up until that point, I had the whole rescue mission captured on camera but it was now on its way to the bottom of the Indian Ocean.

No sooner had that happened, I looked at Ash who had now inflated his life jacket and jumped into the water. He was only in the water for a few seconds before he literally flew up like a rag doll. There must have been ten guys on the end of the rope, he was moving so quickly. I watched him get to the top where a barrage of arms and hands took hold of him and pulled him over to safety. It was a massive feeling of relief.

I turned and looked for the rope ladder and, as if it had been purposely placed in front of me by a higher power, something just took over and my body started moving. Without thinking, I leapt off the boat and on to the rope ladder. As soon as I was on the ladder, our boat just dropped away from me. I was now clinging to a rope ladder on the side of a 100,000-tonne oil tanker in the Indian Ocean. If I had fallen off, that would have been it: no one would be able to retrieve me due to the difficult conditions. I'd have been gone.

I looked down at our boat then looked up again. It was a long way and I could see a group of men leaning over ready to grab me. I had never gripped anything so tightly in my life. I took it slowly and thought, "One step at a time." I had flashbacks to the precarious ladders that I'd crossed on Everest going through the Ice Fall. As I got closer to the top, I could feel my arms burning with lactic acid but it made me grip even tighter. Eventually I was pulled over the edge and initially fell onto the deck. I noticed an overwhelming smell of fumes and oil before getting up and seeing Ash. I hugged him tight and the crew walked us to a small room where we both sat down. I was absolutely pumped with adrenaline and had never experienced anything like that in my life. It was quite chaotic as the crew were all Indian and shouting different things in their own language.

I asked if we could see the captain to thank him so they escorted us out of the room to a lift. We all crammed in and it clanked noisily on the way up. I could see that Ash was clearly exhausted and once we knew we were safe, we both felt emotional. We walked out of the lift and stood in front of a massive metal door with the words "No Smoking" on it. We entered and it was like walking into a nightclub when people were allowed to smoke indoors! A friendly-looking Indian chap walked over with a cigarette in one hand and a beer in the other. With a beaming smile on his face, he said, "Wow, that was crazy, guys! Are you OK? I'm the captain and you're safe now. Anything you need, we will get for you!" This was probably going to be the highlight of their seafaring careers, rescuing two British adventurers in the Indian Ocean. He offered Ash and me a pack of cigarettes and a beer. We politely declined the cigarettes but cracked open a beer each. It was all a bit of a sensory overload. Just half an hour earlier, I was hanging off the side of the biggest man-made object I had ever come across!

The captain spoke excellent English, as did his senior officers on board. He told us that he was sorry but he was going to have to cut our boat away and get back on their scheduled route. He mentioned that if the weather was better, he would have used a crane to lift the boat on board but he could not deploy the crane in the current wind speeds – we understood. We stood out on the bridge that overhung the side of the vessel and watched as the *James Lewis* floated away behind us. It was a really hard thing to watch. It still hadn't really sunk in that only 24 hours ago, we were fine and on course, and now our row was over.

The captain said, "We will drop you off in Perth and then continue to Melbourne. It will take just under two days to get you back." I thought that sounded pretty quick. He went on to say that he'd been up all night planning our recovery and was going to take some rest.

Before that, the captain introduced us to his second in command, a younger officer, similar in age to me. He showed us to our rooms where we could shower and sleep. There was no way I could sleep: I couldn't even stand still, let alone sleep! Ash went to his room to lie down and I went back up to the bridge with the other guys on watch. The crew were very relaxed and extremely welcoming.

They all wanted to ask questions about our project, which I guess was understandable.

They explained what all the different buttons and levers did. The helm was a very small, half steering wheel which wouldn't have looked out of place on a computer gamer's desk. The officer on watch asked me if I wanted to have a go at steering. He took the auto pilot off and said, "Hold that heading if you can." I held the wheel straight and noticed that we had gone one degree off course; I corrected a little and nothing happened. "Not too much," he said. Sure enough, about 30 seconds later, it over-corrected. He put the auto pilot back on and said, "It's very difficult to manually steer, takes a lot of practice."

Most of the day had now passed: time felt like it was going extremely quickly. I thought I'd go and see how Ash was, but just as I stood up to go and see him, he walked through the door; he looked shattered and he'd apparently had a seizure in bed. We had already eaten earlier in the day but I asked if he needed anything. He assured me that he just needed to sleep. I checked on him later that evening and he was fast asleep.

That evening, I ended up drinking with the captain in his quarters. I told him about my time in India when I cycled around the world and he was impressed that I'd travelled extensively in his home country. He wasn't working that evening so was just enjoying a relaxing drink although, as the captain, he was never really entirely off duty. After a few hours, I left and went back up to the bridge. I think they were surprised to see me and asked why I wasn't sleeping. I spent most of the evening just chatting with the crew on watch. It wasn't until around 3am that I started to feel tired, by which point I had been up for over 48 hours. The adrenaline of being in a life or death situation will keep you going long past any point you thought humanly possible. I went back to my room and crashed out until 7am.

Ash was also awake so we both walked down to the mess hall where breakfast was served. All of the crew couldn't have been any kinder or more considerate. After breakfast, we sat up in the bridge and the first engineering officer asked if we wanted to see the engine room. We thought it was unlikely that we'd get a chance like that again so we followed him down. It was quite a sight: loud, hot and smelly, but amazing! The engine stands as high as a two-storey house. The engineer took great pride in showing us around and we only emerged from the depths of the ship about an hour later, both very dehydrated. It was blisteringly hot down there!

The rest of the day passed fairly quickly; we chatted with the crew and the captain arranged a team photo on the bridge. Every crew member stood with us and we set up our camera to take a picture. The crew members who worked below and on the deck appeared to be very excited that they were on the bridge, all taking selfies with us and their co-workers. I guess they didn't ordinarily go up there much.

That evening, I managed to get some sleep. The real world was waiting for us and it wouldn't be long until we were stepping ashore in Perth. The next morning came round and the captain was on the bridge in his uniform, as were the rest of the crew. In a really odd way, I was sad to leave the crew and the *Dubai Charm* but I imagine that the novelty would have long worn off after a few weeks at sea. We could now make out the coastline of Western Australia and even the high-rise buildings of Perth. The captain said, "I've spoken to the coastguard and they are going to send a police boat out to pick you up." We looked at each other and wondered what was waiting for us.

The next few hours passed quickly and it wasn't long before we were putting on our life jackets and shaking hands with the crew. We could see a small police patrol boat heading towards us. "There's your ride!" said the captain. I thanked him for everything, we were escorted out on deck, the gangway was lowered and we walked down it. There was barely a ripple in the water and it couldn't have been any calmer. The captain had slowed the ship down to no more than about four knots. The police boat came up alongside and we simply walked down the ladder then had to use the rope ladder for a few steps. It was a stark contrast to the way we'd boarded the vessel! Once we were both safely aboard the police boat, they accelerated away and we looked back, waving at the crew who were on the bridge waving back at us.

There were three, very friendly police officers on board, who asked us how we were and told us that there was a lot of media waiting for us. Initially, Ash would be checked over by a medic, before Immigration would clear us back into the country. We arrived back at the marina in about 15 minutes. The officer at the helm was on what looked like full power as the boat was literally jumping in and out of the water, skimming across the surface.

A medic was waiting for Ash, who was taken into a room for some tests and checks. I handed my passport to an Immigration officer. I walked out of that room into another and had to do a double take as I saw Kat there waiting for me. I'd messaged her earlier to explain what had happened but I didn't know she'd be there waiting for us. Ash was given a clean bill of health and an officer said to us, "OK guys, you're good to go, good luck. Oh, you'd better go out of the back entrance as there are media crews waiting for you outside." We got into Kat's car and as we drove out, the media were everywhere. When they saw us pull out, they were putting cameras up to the window and taking pictures.

Ash and I had already spoken about getting him on the first flight home. There seemed no point in him staying around for interviews. I also needed to get back up to Geraldton to see if I could organise some kind of recovery of our boat. Ash had found a flight on his phone for that very evening. I passed him my debit card and advised him to book it because his family were waiting for him. It was all very fast-paced again and we had no clothes apart from what we were wearing, so we headed to the shops to pick up a few essentials. He had a small bag with his laptop in and that was about it. I went into the airport with Ash and gave him a big hug and told him to let me know once he was home. As I watched him go through Security, it was like a film had been playing out in front of me and it was now coming to an end. I felt quite emotional.

Absolutely exhausted, we picked up some food on the way back to Kat's house. The next day, my phone was ringing off the hook, with calls from Euan and reporters wanting to know what had happened. Overnight, the news of our rescue had gone global. Euan advised me that it was essential to do an interview with one of the main media outlets in Australia as soon as possible, so I drove straight to the studios with Kat's brother, Hamish. The interview went really well and I was prepared for some tough questions regarding the cost of the rescue using taxpayers' money. I expected and almost wanted to be asked these difficult questions because I was keen to clarify that we hadn't used a single cent of public money. The *Dubai Charm* was able to come to our aid with no cost implications, as our position was very close to their scheduled routing.

There had naturally been some less than complimentary comments in the media, however there was also a lot of support for what we were doing. The interview was conducted by a well-dressed woman in her mid-thirties. She was kind, compassionate and complimentary of our efforts; she didn't ask one difficult question and she also gave our charities a good plug. We gave them exclusive interview rights and shared some footage from the rescue that had been taken by one of the crew members on board the *Dubai Charm*. It was quite dramatic and added to the story. Euan was absolutely right: the interview was very well received, so much so that I was inundated with further requests.

I had a message from John at *Max Marine* in Geraldton to say that they'd been looking at the tracker and our boat was drifting back to the coast, so there was a possibility of chartering a small vessel to retrieve it. With this in mind, I needed to get back to Geraldton urgently. I hired a car and drove up there that same evening. I went straight to their house and we started to hatch a plan. We put together a list of John's contacts who might be able to help and we worked out exactly how far away the boat was and what the weather was likely to do over the next week.

John started making calls immediately. Unfortunately, it wasn't good news: most boats that were capable of going that far out and towing back our boat were commercial fishing boats. The season was now coming to an end and the boats that John had in mind were now hard standing for the winter, having maintenance carried out on them. We found one owner who said he was prepared to do it but wanted over £20,000! John advised that this was probably a realistic figure to make it worthwhile for anyone who was willing to retrieve it. We didn't have that kind of money so it was becoming obvious that we wouldn't be able to even attempt a recovery. Our boat was now only a few hundred miles offshore, which in the grand scheme of the Indian Ocean, was very close by, but I wasn't able to do anything about it.

I was very sad and frustrated but spoke to my parents on the phone who told me I had at least tried and it was probably best to come home now. I knew they were right. I drove back to Perth the next morning and booked a flight back to London.

The time passed fairly quickly; Euan arranged some further interviews but in all honesty, I had lost all enthusiasm for them. I think Euan could tell I was feeling pretty low and despondent so he stepped in to do a few media requests on our behalf. My phone was ringing a lot but mostly from unknown numbers. When it was time to leave, I felt sad. I'd been very comfortable in Perth and it had a great feel to it. Both Ash and I felt eternally grateful to Kat and her family for their friendship and all that they had done for us, and I promised to stay in contact with them.

I wanted to take a different route home so I decided to fly via Hong Kong. I had never been there before so thought I'd take a look around. The flight I booked gave me 20 hours in Hong Kong, which was perfect. After a seven-hour flight, we eventually touched down in Hong Kong. I collected my bags and checked into a *Hilton* hotel at the airport. It was early morning as I'd been on a night flight so I grabbed a few extra hours' sleep in the hotel.

Eager to explore, I caught a shuttle train that took me straight into the city. I was amazed at the number of high-rise buildings, which looked mostly residential. Everything was so densely packed together! I arrived at the downtown stop as I wanted to head up to a famous viewpoint which offers stunning views over the city. Sadly, it was foggy so there would have been very little point as I wouldn't have seen anything. I walked around for quite a few hours, excited to be somewhere completely different. Ultimately, 20 hours wasn't really enough time but it gave me a feel for the place. I purchased a new shirt for the flight home and headed back to the hotel, showered and changed ready for my next flight.

Thirteen hours later and feeling pretty tired, I walked through Terminal 5 at Heathrow Airport. I saw my parents waiting for me. Sadly, it wasn't quite the triumphant arrival back in the UK that I was expecting but we were still alive, and for that alone, I felt very grateful.

6

The Amazon Jungle

The next few months passed fairly slowly. I was feeling low, demotivated, lethargic and was carrying a heavy sense of guilt on my shoulders about what had happened. I felt that I'd let a lot of people down. All of our sponsors and charities were very gracious and no one said anything in the least bit negative. We were extremely lucky to have had the support from the following companies: *Mattel* (Scrabble), *Cisco, River Island, Iridium, MMCG, Balmain, Centrix, Ofsure, Raymarine* and *Frontier Power*. Without their backing, the trip would never have happened.

One thing I had noticed was a significant increase in the number of speaking enquires that I was getting. I was expecting to lose a lot of speaking bookings after the row because in my mind, I thought I had lost all credibility but it turned out to be quite the opposite. My phone would often ring and I'd see a number I didn't recognise. "Hello, James speaking" I would say. "Yes hello, are you the James Ketchell who was rescued in the Indian Ocean?" Sometimes I'd reply, "Yes, there are not too many of them around" and we would get into a conversation! I wasn't expecting so much interest but it was good. Most of my income is generated from speaking and having spent most of my savings in Australia, this interest was a welcome relief.

What I thought was a particularly dark cloud of frustration and self-pity ended up having a silver lining. Of course I would have preferred it if the row had been successful and we'd both managed to make it to Mauritius, but I wasn't able to change the past. I would never have thought that anything good could possibly have come out of this situation at the time. However, with hindsight, there will always be something good that comes off the back of adversity.

I had been back in the UK for around three months and I was talking to Richard from *Kindled Spirit*. He was planning on organising a charity bike ride in India, which would be fully supported and pitched towards more of an adventure holiday. Richard had teamed up with a company that supported charities with endeavours like this. One of the employees was a guy called Phil who ran the operations and managed the third party companies delivering the experience in each country. He was a great guy, an ex-Royal Marine of almost 30 years, who had fought in the Falklands War at 18 years old, then half of his career was spent in the Special Boat Service. I liked Phil: he was a quiet, unassuming man who had seen and experienced things that you would only imagine seeing in Hollywood movies. He was motivated and had an incredible work ethic.

A few months after meeting Phil, an opportunity came up to go out to the Amazon jungle with him. I thought it would be an amazing experience, and when would I ever get the opportunity to visit the Amazon jungle with an ex-jungle warfare survival instructor again? Phil was heading out to meet a potential supplier who was planning to deliver some Amazon jungle experiences on behalf of a charity. We would also make some promotional videos whilst we were out there.

A few weeks later, we met up at Heathrow and flew to Sao Paulo; we had a few hours to wait then boarded a flight direct to Manaus. There was someone waiting to meet us in the Arrivals Hall who took us straight to an office that was occupied by the company we were meeting. I instantly liked Manaus: it had a certain quirky feel to it. I had read a few travel reviews and they weren't great but it felt a safe, yet quite exciting place to me. The city has a lot of history and the main lifeline was the Amazon River itself. The first time I saw the river, it was bustling with life and boats everywhere: small boats, big boats, even commercial ships would come hundreds of miles up the Amazon to deliver supplies.

We sat down and met with the company owner, a big guy who was dripping in jewellery, around his neck, wrists and huge gold sovereign rings on his fingers. He made a lot of effort with us; I guess he was grateful for the opportunity to do business with Phil and a company operating out of London. If everything went well, he would probably receive a lot of business via Phil. We spoke to our guide, a young man called Max, who was going to be travelling with us at all times. He was about 18, native to the jungle and had spent most of his childhood living and working in the Amazon as a tourist guide. He had also taught himself English, an essential skill for anyone wanting to work in tourism in Brazil. He always had a big smile on his face and both Phil and I instantly warmed to him.

We were shown to our rooms and unpacked our kit. Frustratingly, I'd had a few things taken from my rucksack, one of which was a hammock with a built-in mosquito net, an essential piece of kit for where we were going! There wasn't much I could do about it and Max told us that he had many hammocks so we didn't need to buy another one. We did however need to purchase a few other items so Max took us to a local hardware store. As we walked through the streets, it appeared that Max knew everyone, shaking hands with shop owners and other lads of a similar age to him.

"We need to purchase a machete and a few other bits," Phil said. We walked into a shop which had knives, guns and fishing equipment, floor to ceiling. We purchased two machetes and went back to the hotel. We separated out all of the items, some that would stay in Manaus and some that we would take into the Amazon.

The next morning, we were driven down to the river with Max. The plan was to take a large boat across the river, pick up some land transport then take a small boat for about an hour to our camp. It was about half a day's travel to get to our destination in the jungle. When we had arrived in Manaus the previous day, it was later in the afternoon and the temperature was around 35°, not as hot as I'd expected. I wasn't worried about the heat anyway but the humidity was something I had last experienced in Asia when I was cycling around the world. We arrived at the river with our kit and waited for our boat. It was incredibly humid and both Phil and I were sweating profusely. Max just said, "Wait until you guys get into the jungle!" with a smile on his face.

Later that day, after a ride in the back of a van that would almost certainly not be legal on UK roads, and a small, canoe-style boat with an outboard on the back, we made it to our destination. I was pretty tired and dehydrated. As fast as I could drink, it was literally just oozing out of my skin in the form of sweat, even when I hadn't really exerted myself. Phil had spent a lot of time in jungles and mentioned that it usually takes most people a few days – sometimes up to a week – to really acclimatise to the humidity. Nothing is done quickly; everything is slow and steady to avoid succumbing to heat stroke. We spent the first night in one of several small cabins with wooden beds. I slept like a log.

The following morning, both Phil and I were up at 5am, rewarded with a stunning view. It had cooled down significantly overnight and we looked out over the water. It was not the Amazon River now but one of the many thousands of beautiful, smaller rivers that feed into it. There were a few local people working in a kitchen which used a generator for power and, just off the kitchen, there was a communal hut with hammocks. The place was set up for tourists coming in and out for a few days at a time. Initially there wasn't anyone else there, so it was a good chance for Phil to have a look around. We were passed some coffee by one of the women working in the kitchen. I had never really drunk coffee before as I just didn't like the taste but I took it anyway because I didn't want to appear rude. This was different to any coffee I'd tasted before and it was incredibly sweet. I have no idea what else was in it but 15 minutes later, I had never felt more awake, refreshed and raring to go!

We spent the day acclimatising to the heat and humidity, just relaxing and reading. I was looking forward to the following day when we would be heading into the jungle on foot, walking in the day and sleeping in hammocks at night. The next morning, we had our rucksacks packed and headed off. Max really looked the part, wearing all military equipment; we joked that he just needed camo cream to finish off the look! It didn't take long before I was feeling hot and fatigued; it may sound simple to walk with a relatively lightweight rucksack through some trees but in reality, it really isn't. You cannot touch anything with your hands and everything is a potential hazard. Combined with the extreme humidity, I could now see why Phil had said that this is one of the most challenging environments in which he has ever operated. Nevertheless, it was fun and I was absolutely loving this unique environment and experiencing something new.

That evening before it got dark, we cleared an area in which to sleep and set up our hammocks. Phil explained that one of the benefits of being in the jungle was the amount of rest and sleep that you usually get. As soon as it got dark, we would be in our hammocks:

the jungle at night wasn't a place to be moving around. Phil talked me through different military tactics around jungle warfare which I found absolutely fascinating. He told me to take a good book with me when we were packing back in Manaus. I could now see why! It was around 8pm and, apart from the head torch that illuminated my book, it was absolutely pitch black. I would be there until 5am the following morning. Before I got into the hammock, I washed with wet wipes and changed into some clean underwear. My dirty, sweaty clothes were to be worn in the day and I'd always have some clean, dry clothes for the evening, after washing. It reminded me of being out on my Atlantic Ocean row, where having the discipline to follow a certain routine was also important, just as it was in the jungle.

I slept very well and woke up at around 4am, enjoying just lying there and listening to the amazing sounds all around me. The place was literally alive with noises and sometimes they sounded very close as if there was something right next to me. Max mentioned that there were jaguars around but told me not to worry as it was highly unlikely that we would see one. Phil also said to me, "No matter what happens, never scream or panic if you feel something brush up against you in the hammock."

At first light, we got up and packed away our kit. We had some food pre-packed for breakfast but would need to catch our lunch and possibly dinner too. We had a short hike through some dense jungle; Phil was clearing as we moved and Max was behind me. I sensed all this was just a bit of fun for Max who had spent the majority of his life in this environment. He would always make us aware of something if he needed to but he didn't really need to babysit us as such as we were pretty self-sufficient. It was more that Max was sharing his knowledge and he could see that I was keen to learn. This was a different experience for him from his usual work with groups of tourists.

We took turns in clearing the dense jungle and I was now trying to film what I could without the lens steaming up. Max loved being in front of the camera and the content was great too. We came to a clearing and Max told us that we would now embark on a river crossing. We used our rucksacks as floatation devices and kicked with our legs, using one arm to push ourselves forward. There was clearly a technique to this! Phil made it look pretty easy but I, on the other hand, found it tricky. The water filled my boots and I had to fight just to keep my head above water. Finally, I made it to the other side and was grateful to feel the ground beneath me. Exhausted, I walked up the bank, when Phil said, "Go back in James, that was a great shot of you coming out of the water." I laughed and did as instructed, which at least provided some temporary cooling off!

About an hour later, we had come back to our boat and headed out onto the river to find our lunch. By this point, I was pretty hungry. We were using bits of stick with a line and hook attached to them. Max took a bit of dead fish that was sitting in the bottom of our boat and attached it to the hook. He put it in the water, pulled it up and down a few times and within a few seconds, there was fish on the end of it. It was a piranha! Max carefully took the hook out and showed us its teeth which were razor sharp with serrated edges. "Don't let it bite you," he joked. Phil and I gave it a go. As soon as I dropped the bait into the water, there was something biting at it. The technique was to give the stick a sharp pull as soon as you could feel the bite.

Eventually, I caught one. Phil picked it up pretty quickly and after about an hour, we were catching loads. Max did have a fishing rod and managed to catch a few larger fish too. I said to Max, "What happens if we don't catch any fish, what else do we have to eat?" He replied, "There is no other food: we must catch some fish otherwise you will not have dinner. I'm serious." That would be quite a scary prospect for a lot of people but it was inspiring to see that Max was so confident in his surroundings. He knew that he could use his experience to survive in this environment and the river was literally a lifeline for the whole community.

That evening, we cooked our catch over a fire. To my surprise, the fish tasted really good, despite the bones. It was only my second night in the hammock but I felt remarkably comfortable and I was really enjoying the whole experience. I had acclimatised well and the heat and humidity wasn't affecting me quite as brutally as the previous day.

The next morning, it rained hard. We figured that there was no point in trying to stay dry as the humidity made you wet anyway. In the afternoon, we visited a local community living in the forest because Max needed to see someone there. I had images of being greeted by people who resembled something you'd see in *National Geographic* magazine. I was surprised to see them wearing jeans, Nike trainers and T-shirts; I even saw one guy working away on a laptop. Max said that he didn't know of any untouched tribes that were left in the Amazon. We stayed for about half an hour before heading back.

That evening, Phil and I were trying to get a fire going but were having difficulty because the leaves and foliage were wet from the rain. We were almost there several times then the flames would die out. Max watched and laughed at us. He said, "Guys, that's not going to work." He rummaged around on the floor and in the trees and pulled out some dry kindling that was a mix of dead leaves and dry bark. I guess he knew where to look and had done this many hundreds, if not thousands of times. He took our flint striker and instantly got a fire going, which was roaring within minutes. "That's how you do it!" he joked. This young man was impressive to watch in his own surroundings, where most people would be out of their depth within a few hours, wondering how they were going to survive.

Max was inspiring and made everything look effortless.

The next few days passed relatively quickly. Both Phil and I were really enjoying our time with Max and heading out on little adventures every day. Phil managed to complete all of the necessary assessments, whilst we also honed our fishing and survival skills.

It was now our last night in the jungle before we returned to the concrete jungle of Manaus. We met up with some of Max's friends and headed to a sand bar that was in the middle of one of the rivers close to where we were staying. "We are going for a barbecue and a few drinks," Max said. "This should be interesting!" quipped Phil. I didn't really know what to expect: it was obvious that fish was going to be on the menu. We arrived and a couple of Max's friends were there with a roaring fire going. We pulled our boat up on to the sand so it wouldn't float away without us noticing. The three of us were each handed a can of beer and Max would occasionally translate as Max's friends spoke broken English.

One of them went to their boat and pulled out a massive caiman, probably close to six feet long, which they had killed a few hours earlier. We got used to seeing these crocodilian-looking creatures everywhere and I was surprised to learn that they are apparently no real threat to people and the locals swim in the water around them. Max had never heard of them actually attacking a person, not even a child. He knew of injuries where people had been badly bitten trying to catch them but that was different. I had not seen one this big and up close before. Initially, I felt a little uncomfortable knowing that this animal had just been killed. Max told us that it was a normal thing for them to do and that the caimans needed to be culled anyway as there were so many of them.

After a few beers, we were all feeling pretty hungry, so the guys pulled the caiman off the barbecue and placed it on a sheet, along with some lemon and salt. Max cut sections of the meat out and passed them to us. "Squeeze the lemon over it and sprinkle some salt on it," Max instructed. Wow, it tasted amazing! It was white meat, a bit like chicken, slightly chewy but juicy and succulent at the same time. The lemon and salt just finished it off. There was more than enough meat to go round and what was left was taken back to the family of Max's friends. He explained that absolutely nothing is wasted here.

The sun was slowly going down. It was still hot but the intense heat from the day was fading away to a more comfortable temperature. The river was sparkling in the sun, there was wildlife all around us, birds were flying about and some pink dolphins even swam past us. I joked with Phil that if we could bottle this whole experience and take it back to the UK, it would be worth a fortune. We slowly ate and drank around the fire, just chilling. It was probably one of the most amazing moments of the whole trip and one that I will never forget.

The next day, we were up at 5am with our kit packed away and ready to start the journey back to Manaus. We arrived in the afternoon and were not flying back to the UK until the following day. Rather than sleep, we took a bit of a walk around the city with Max, before heading out for dinner in the evening with him and his family, as well as the company owner we'd met on arrival. It was a truly fantastic experience and both Phil and I had made a good friend in Max. I hope that one day I will get the chance to show him around London and the UK, which I guess would be equally exciting for him as the Amazon was for me!

Max accompanied us to the airport. We said our goodbyes and started our journey home. With the layover in Sao Paulo, we had been travelling for around 20 hours by the time we arrived back at Heathrow.

7

Atlantic Rescue

Over the next few months, life became quite busy for me. I launched my first book, *The Ultimate Triathlon*, and continued to do fairly well on the speaking circuit. I never really thought of myself as a motivational speaker, I just liked telling stories and sharing things I had learnt. People seemed to enjoy listening to them.

It's funny how things and people can come into your life for a reason and sometimes just at the right time. I was put in contact with a guy called Anthony, a London-based businessman who owned a very successful, high-end removals company. He didn't need to work as he had a great team running his business, but he did anyway. He was highly motivated, driven and had built up quite a business empire. I was introduced to him by another ocean rower, Charlie, who ran a company building ocean-rowing boats. I knew Charlie relatively well as he rowed across the Atlantic Ocean in the same race as me, and he had built our boat for the Indian Ocean row.

Anthony was looking for an adventure: he had met Charlie some years earlier and expressed an interest in rowing across the Atlantic. He didn't want to do it on his own, as he didn't have the time and also felt he didn't have enough experience. Charlie suggested that I could partner with him for the crossing and manage the planning aspects of the project.

I went to meet Anthony one evening at his house; he only lived about 40 minutes away which was quite convenient. I instantly had a good feeling: he was a warm, friendly guy and had a lot of enthusiasm for the trip ahead. We talked through lots of different options for a boat and what it was like out there in an ocean. Although slightly off topic, we spent a lot of time talking about climbing Mount Everest and my cycle around the world. I guess it was just a case of getting to know each other and I also met some of his family. It was understandable that they wanted to meet the guy who had the experience and was going to lead this crazy adventure. We spoke for a good few hours, as Anthony told me about his business and shared his story, which was inspiring to listen to. He was clearly a wealthy man but he was also modest and unassuming.

It was potentially an exciting project. Anthony could only take about a month off work because of all his other commitments. This would pose a bit of a challenge as most fast two-man crews very rarely cross the Atlantic in that kind of time! Then, if the weather was not favourable, it could easily end up taking 70+ days to make the crossing. There was a lot of uncertainty until Charlie suggested that he build a hybrid boat that could utilise wind as well as human power. Anthony was also a keen cyclist and preferred the idea of a pedalo design more than a specific rowing boat.

With this in mind, Charlie's team set about designing and building a pedalo. This was no normal pedalo that you'd see floating around the Serpentine with a swan's head mounted on the front of it! It was a state-of-the-art, carbon hull with a recumbent cycling position and also a rowing position, if we wanted to utilise it. The wind element was going to be generated via a kite. Anthony didn't want it to have a mast and sail otherwise he thought we may as well just sail across, which wasn't the plan.

Over the coming months, Anthony and I spent quite a lot of time together. We often went up to Burnham-on-Crouch in Essex where the boat was based, to test things out. Mostly it was just tweaking the drive chain and trying different propellers and positions on the pedal-powered part of the boat. We found that the best prop, after hours of testing, ended up being a model aeroplane propeller! The rowing set-up was easy and worked well. We still hadn't quite found the best solution for the kite set-up but different ideas were being assessed. I was made aware of a French engineer who made rescue kits for sailing boats. The concept behind it was that if a yacht lost its sail or mast, the kite was deployed off the bow of the boat, released from a winch. It would operate a bit like a large spinnaker sail, pulling the boat downwind. It didn't need to be manned or flown, it was simply released and would keep itself up in the wind.

I went over to Bordeaux for the day to meet the engineer; he spoke good English and was keen to help us with our project. After a tour of his workshop, there was just enough wind to test the kite, using a very small 25-foot yacht with no mast and outboard on the back. It was tied up on the bank of a small canal that led into a large lake. We headed out onto the lake and turned the motor off. I was extremely excited to see how this would work. He mounted the winch and pulled out the kite. There were two sizes: a small one and a large one, both of which had an inflatable bladder around the outside of them, to keep them afloat if they hit the water.

It was quickly apparent that launching the kite was the tricky bit! Once it was up in the air, to my amazement, it did actually work. It floated back down into the water a few times but that was due to the wind easing off. I tried to visualise this working in the real world environment: that is, launching off a tiny boat in the Atlantic Ocean. It was going to take some practice but I could absolutely see this being a game changer if we could find a way to launch it. There would be more than enough wind out in the Atlantic so that wouldn't be a problem.

Overall, the trip went well and I returned home, pleased that I'd made the effort to visit him. I reported back to Anthony and the team with pictures, and we decided to go with this as our kite solution.

Anthony and I got on really well and we were having a lot of fun together. I had to pinch myself that this was my job at times! One particular day, we went up to Essex for a meeting with Charlie. We were late coming back and Anthony had to get home so he didn't have time to drop me off. We went straight back to his house and he let me take his car home. He said, "Have fun, don't kill yourself and you can give it back to me when I see you next." It was a two-seater, supercharged, 5 litre V8 Jaguar with 500BHP – this car was a rocket ship. When you just touched the accelerator, it literally took off!

I ended up driving it around for almost a month: it sounded amazing and it was a lot of fun. One particular day, I remember parking it up outside my mum and dad's house. My mum said to me, "James, when are you going to give that car back? It was nice of Anthony to let you borrow it for a while but you've had it a long time. You are driving it around like you own it, but you don't. Don't you think that's a little bit sad?" I was taken aback for a moment: I could always rely on my mum to bring me back down to reality! She was absolutely right though. Driving someone else's sports car around, which they'd earnt through sheer hard work, didn't quite feel right. I returned it to Anthony the next day and went back to my old, beaten-up Mercedes estate.

The rest of 2015 passed fairly quickly. I had a trip to New York City just before Christmas with my parents, brother, his partner, Yaz, and their little boy, Max, which was amazing. 2015 had been quite a year: I'd been rescued in the Indian Ocean, launched my first book and had had a great experience in the Amazon jungle. Now I was about to embark on another Atlantic crossing in only a few months' time.

Anthony and I planned to depart in February, as opposed to December or January when most ocean rowers depart. By leaving slightly later, this would allow us to hopefully take advantage of some stronger winds that usually start to develop around this time of year. We were departing from Gran Canaria and Charlie was arranging the transportation of the boat out to the island. I planned to head out there a week before Anthony in order to make final preparations. Anthony was pretty busy so he was going to fly out a few days before we were due to leave.

I travelled out with a good friend of mine, Ian, who was going to give me a hand with various tasks but he would mainly be filming the preparations and taking pictures. We landed in Gran Canaria and jumped in a taxi. The marina was on the other side of the island, facing south west, in a lovely, little harbour town called Puerto de Mogan. We checked into our apartments and met up with Rich, who was going to drive the RIB (rigid inflatable boat) home off the island, via ferry, once we had departed. The RIB was going to be used for support as we planned to do some sea trials with the kite. The French engineer who sold us the kites and launch system was also coming out for two days to help with the kite set-up.

The week passed fairly quickly and we seemed to be on top of all the things that needed to be done, such as shopping for fresh foods and fruit and conducting different trials and tests. The one surprise was just how efficient the cycling mechanism was: we had a gearing system that worked really well. It turned out that the drive coming from the propeller was more efficient and faster than rowing, even though it was only designed for a model aircraft. I was able to get the boat moving at around two knots whilst rowing, however the recumbent cycling position was producing almost twice the speed, at just over 3.5 knots. Both tests were carried out on the same day in the same conditions, with another person on board to replicate Anthony's weight. It was very promising. The kites were not quite as encouraging. There wasn't really enough wind to get them up in the air properly and launching them was tricky, due to the limited space on deck. However, I was confident, that with the right wind and a bit of launch practice, they would be viable.

I would send a quick text message or some pictures to Anthony most days. He never asked me to but I did it out of courtesy and to keep him updated with developments. When Anthony eventually flew out, Ian and I went to the airport to collect him in a hire car. He arrived in the morning so we had one full day to prepare and then we would be leaving the next day. Everything was packed and ready to go; I was feeling excited and eager to get out there. Back at the villa, Anthony gave me a gift. It was a watch: not just any watch but a limited edition *Tudor*. I was extremely grateful for his kindness and generosity.

That evening, we all went out for our last meal then had a fairly early night. I was no stranger to being in this situation by now as it was going to be my third crossing of the Atlantic Ocean. Yet no matter how many times you do things like this, there will always be some nerves.

The next morning, we were up early and headed down to the marina office to complete various bits of paperwork which would effectively sign us out of the country. Rich and Ian were going to come out on the RIB to film and stay with us for an hour or so, then head back in. As we pedalled out, there were crowds of people waving and cheering, which was an unexpected surprise. The weather was great, with blue skies and a light wind pushing us exactly where we wanted to go. There wasn't enough wind for the kite so we agreed to leave that until we had the right conditions.

The first hour passed in the blink of an eye and before we knew it, we were about three nautical miles offshore, with Rich and Ian waving us goodbye. They turned the RIB around and opened the throttle, bouncing off the small waves as they accelerated back to the marina. Anthony was enjoying it; the boat was working perfectly and we got into a rhythm very quickly. Over the first three days, the winds were fairly light. Our progress was by no means slow but not what we ideally needed it to be. The first few days are always the hardest when at sea, be it sailing, rowing or even pedalling!

From day three, the winds started to pick up so it was now time to pull out our big guns – the kite! It was tricky because even though we needed the wind to keep the kite in the air and pull us along, it also made it very difficult to unfold and inflate, often causing it to flap about and get caught on something. After an hour of trying, unsuccessfully, we decided to try the smaller kite instead. This was considerably more successful! Within a few seconds of it being in the wind and in position, we had almost doubled our boat speed and were now moving along at between 4.5 - 5 knots, on a par with a small sailing vessel. At this rate, it would see us cross the Atlantic in around 25 days! The kite needed to be monitored all the time as sometimes it could fall out the sky and weave from left to right. The concept of what we were trying to achieve, catching the wind and increasing our boat speed, was working very well. For the next few days, we were regularly covering over 100 nautical miles a day.

We were getting progressively faster over the coming days and the wind speed was averaging around 30 knots. This caused the sea state to pick up quite considerably; at one point, we were moving along at eight knots, which felt pretty quick for our little boat. The challenge we had was that the wind direction was starting to shift and it was blowing out of the north more than the east, effectively pushing us south. We had already made significant southerly progress and ideally wanted to be heading more westerly. We adjusted our course but the kite was not as effective if it wasn't going straight downwind. To add to the challenge, the sea swell was now building quite substantially and was swamping us with large waves that were often breaking over the boat. This meant that we had to stay in the cabin with the hatch shut.

It didn't take long for the air to become stale so I opened up the hatch. As I pushed it open, I said to Anthony, "We need to be very careful when doing this in rough conditions because if a large wave hits the boat, the cabin will get drenched." Almost as soon as I'd finished the sentence, a wave crashed into the boat, literally soaking us. "You mean just like that?" Anthony said, laughing. He had a good sense of humour and found it funny, despite half the cabin being filled with water!

Anthony was very easy-going and we would often sit for hours in the cabin, chatting about all sorts of things, from business ideas to other adventures. Utilising the kite meant that we had a lot of spare time on our hands. Once the boat was moving at around five knots, we couldn't even utilise the cycling position either, as it would not make any difference to our boat speed.

Sitting in the cabin would actually become quite boring after a while. At night, it was also tricky to sleep because the auto tiller was in a compartment behind our heads, so every time the piston moved in and out, we could hear all the gears moving, surprisingly loudly.

We had plenty of food on board but I'd overlooked the fact that we wouldn't be burning as many calories if we were using the kite and not active on the bike or rowing. We were consuming less than half the daily intake of our 24-hour ration packs, which consisted of mainly dehydrated meals and snacks. We quickly discovered that I had a far sweeter tooth than Anthony!

The electrical system was working perfectly and overall, apart from the rough weather and slightly off-course southerly trajectory, things were going well. We had timed our departure to take advantage of the trade winds and they were really blowing, more so than I imagined. I was expecting and hoping for around 20 knots but we were experiencing 30 knots gusting 40 knots. This wasn't necessarily dangerous and, as long as the wind was blowing the right way, we would be able to take massive advantage of it.

On the other hand, I knew just how magical it could be on a day when the wind is calm and there is little movement in the water. It's absolutely stunning: the water is a beautiful deep blue and if you look over the side, there is an abundance of wildlife, fish of all colours and sizes swimming around, sparkling in the water. There were inquisitive, giant sea turtles that would swim right up to the boat, with heads the size of humans. Whales were a common sight on my first crossing of the Atlantic and I even remember one fin whale rubbing right up against the side of my boat. They are big and powerful and it was so close that I could hear it breathing. Sharks were also a common occurrence, re-enacting a scene from the famous *Jaws* movie, as they approach with a fin sticking up out of the water. I found this rather exciting!

These were all the things that I'd experienced in abundance on my solo row across the Atlantic and I really wanted Anthony to experience them too. At the very least, I wanted him to be able to go swimming once. It's an experience you never forget: looking down, you can see the water becoming a darker, deeper blue, three miles to the bottom. It's a mind-boggling concept to think you are never far from land, it's just the wrong way! When you look out over the horizon on a calm day and all you can see is a dazzling blue horizon, it's quite spectacular.

Unfortunately, Anthony and I were not enjoying the same experiences. It was now overcast and the ocean was an intimidating grey colour, nevertheless, our spirits were still high. We had been at sea for eight days and nights and were on course for quite a quick crossing, well within the 30-day target that we had set ourselves. The wind had now shifted and was blowing almost entirely out of the north. We didn't need to make any further southerly progress at the rate of over 100 nautical miles per day, so we decided to retrieve the kite, which would slow us up and hopefully the wind would eventually become more easterly and push us west. We received a weather report on the sat phone and the wind direction did look like it was going to improve, although we might have to wait a few days.

I deployed a small para anchor (known as a drogue) on the back of the boat, to slow us down and keep the boat going with the waves, which was a lot more comfortable. We also turned the auto tiller off to save the batteries and to give it a rest, which made things a lot quieter. It was almost silent and all we could hear now was the sound of the water hitting the boat. The wind speed had started to decrease which made things feel a little bit more relaxed.

Things can change very quickly at sea. Just 48 hours later, I was activating our EPIRB (the emergency position indicating radio beacon) as Anthony had developed a medical problem and we couldn't take the risk of staying out there in the hope that he would be OK. It was my job to assess the situation and make any decision around the welfare and safety of the people that I'm with. In this case, as always, health and safety came first. Anthony did say that I could carry on with the crossing if I wanted to but I didn't want to leave him on a commercial ship. I also knew just how dangerous the transition was going to be, having already experienced this less than a year before in the Indian Ocean. I was there to look after Anthony, who had been extremely kind and generous to me, and it wouldn't have been right to continue without him.

It was a case of déjà vu from the procedures in the Indian Ocean. I called Falmouth Coastguard Rescue who, within 20 minutes, had arranged for a vessel to come to our aid. It was still 12 hours away and would arrive the following morning. Anthony was fortunately stable, conscious and coherent. The wind speed had now dropped to around 20 knots and the sea had calmed compared to 24 hours earlier. This would prove to be very useful the following morning.

The vessel was a Chinese bulk carrier on its way to the UK, of all places! I briefed Anthony the best I could and explained how the transitioning would go and the things to be aware of. I noticed that he was surprisingly calm. I had deployed the para anchor and the boat was holding nicely into the wind. I'd already established communication with the captain of the vessel, which was over 200 metres long. I explained that he would have to position himself up against us as were unable to manoeuvre to him. I'll never forget his voice when he said, "Oh my God!" over the sat phone.

I knew what was coming and was very nervous but tried not to show it. We could now see the vessel over the horizon, heading straight for us. We were both on deck and I looked at Anthony, who still appeared to be very calm. He was well-educated, motivated and successful. He was also a very well-spoken man, having been shipped off to boarding school when he was young. I asked him if he was OK and I'll never forget his response. He looked at me and calmly replied, "Yes…but one would think that this is a rather precarious situation to be in." It made me laugh. It was indeed an extremely precarious situation to be in, which I knew only too well from prior experience!

I stared out into the ocean, looking at this vessel as it approached us, slowly getting bigger and bigger. It was actually smaller than the *Dubai Charm* that had rescued Ash and me but no less intimidating when it's coming straight at you. I had prepared everything the best I could and packed our kit into a bag. The vessel was getting closer but I could tell that it was not going to pass close enough for us to get a line attached. The captain said he would go around and come up on us again. We sat and waited whilst this giant, man-made floating creation of metal slowly came around on us. I looked up into the sky, just as I had done in the Indian Ocean, and whispered under my breath, "Please help us." Again, I have no idea who I was really talking to but a few minutes later, we were looking straight at the bow of this vessel on a direct course towards us. I was worried that we were going to go under it, but luckily it missed. We could now see the crew on deck and managed to get a line attached.

The adrenaline was rushing through me, yet at the same time, I now felt remarkably calm and focused. The ladder was dropped down to us and Anthony went up first. He was able to climb without any difficulty and he didn't look unwell but needed to get to a hospital to run some tests.

Once I saw Anthony climbing over the rails, I stepped onto the ladder. Just as I did, our boat was lifted up on a wave and I was knocked off the ladder. Thank goodness I just fell back into the boat with no injuries. Had I fallen in between the two boats, I would have almost certainly been crushed to death. I quickly got up and jumped back onto the ladder. Strangely, once I was halfway up and clear of our boat, I knew that I was likely to be OK. I hugged Anthony then realised I'd forgotten to bring the bag that had our personal electrical items in it. I looked over the side and thought about going back down but something inside me stopped me dead in my tracks. It was an overwhelming feeling of "What the hell are you doing, James?" and I decided it just wasn't worth the risk.

We were led away to a medical room where Anthony lay on a bed. An English-speaking crew member asked us for our documents, which we assumed meant our passports, so we gave them to him. He then asked us to turn out our pockets. He took all the contents, although we didn't have much apart from a phone and wallet. He insisted that we both wear an orange boiler suit, adding in a stern voice, "You must put this on." He then left the room, locking the door behind him. I was high on adrenaline and just pleased that we were OK. Anthony was visibly shaken and said to me, "That was bloody dangerous."

A few moments later, we were brought some bottled water and then locked back in the room. I sensed that something wasn't quite right and I began to feel uncomfortable. It felt like we had just escaped from Guantanamo Bay, dressed in our orange jumpsuits. Nevertheless, we were safe. About 40 minutes later, two crew members entered the room and said, "Come with us." We followed them through to the galley where some food had been prepared for us. It was a very different experience from the Indian crew of the *Dubai Charm*.

I asked if we could see the captain and they took us upstairs, onto the bridge. The captain could speak English: he had to, by law, but it wasn't great. We could see he was visibly stressed. He said, "We are max speed towards Canary Islands, a helicopter will come and get you as soon as we get close enough. Maybe two days' time. You can rest now." I asked if we could have our passports back, to which he replied, "When you go I give them to you, they are safe."

We were shown to individual rooms where I was unable to sleep, so decided to go back and sit on the bridge. I wondered if they would tell me that I was not allowed in but they were OK. Communication was difficult as most of the crew, apart from the senior members, didn't speak English. I stared from the bridge, looking out over the horizon; the situation felt very surreal but I was still overwhelmed with relief at the same time. Anthony came up to the bridge and sat down beside me. I asked him if he'd managed to get any sleep.

He said, "No, not at all. I couldn't stop thinking about how crazy that was. When I was lying on the bed in that first room we were in, I almost broke down but managed to keep myself together. Thanks for everything." I replied "It's OK. It's quite overwhelming and you don't realise how dangerous it is until you look back." I think it's a natural reaction to sit and reflect on things when you come off the back of any high adrenaline, life-threatening situation.

That evening, the captain spoke to me and explained that it was a very difficult situation for him when we first boarded because the company was asking him lots of questions about us both. I think he was worried that he was going to get in trouble for picking us up. I thanked him very much for his help.

The two days passed quite quickly and it was soon time to be airlifted off the boat. I was actually quite excited about this. There was a landing pad on the vessel but the plan was to hoist us off. Anthony and I were escorted onto the deck with a few crew members, with the helicopter circling above us. It was an impressive sight and the loud "whoosh, whoosh, whoosh" as it hovered over us felt exhilarating. I later found out it was an *Agusta Westland AW139* (Registration EC-LJA) and there are many photos of this aircraft online. We shook hands with the crew members before they stepped back.

A rescue swimmer was lowered down; as he was descending, he signalled to the pilot to bring him in closer and he eventually touched down on the deck. He was fairly young, perhaps a similar age to me, with a broad smile. "OK, I bring the basket down now," he said with a Spanish accent. Anthony was going to be put in the basket and winched up. The basket came down and I expected Anthony to get in and go first but the winch operator wanted me to go first. The rescue swimmer fitted me with a full harness and clipped me in, holding on to me initially, then letting go. It was actually very smooth and, as expected, the rotor wash of air was quite phenomenal and took my breath away it was so strong.

I was pulled into the aircraft and before I knew it, Anthony was at the door being swung in, still sitting in the basket. I peered over and saw the rescue swimmer coming up after him and the aircraft was already moving away from the ship. He jumped in and strapped himself into a chair and pulled the door across. We were each given a set of head phones so that we could now communicate without shouting. The crew all spoke perfect English. The captain turned around and said, "Gentlemen, I am the captain, welcome on board, the flight time will be about 1 hour 30 minutes to our first stop to refuel, then a quick flight to Tenerife." He was an Italian pilot who had moved to Spain to work for the coastguard and had only learnt to speak Spanish in the last 12 months. "Very impressive," I thought to myself.

We needed to stop on the island of El Hierro to refuel which took around 10 minutes. The last flight out of El Hierro was stunning, around the north of La Gomera, then over to Tenerife. The crew pointed out Mount Teide, which stands at over 12,000 feet above sea level and is Spain's highest mountain. There was a lot of cloud around it but the summit was poking out above it and was a stunning sight.

We landed at what looked to be a military airport, where an ambulance was waiting to take us to hospital. I had been chatting to the rescue swimmer for most of the flight back and we exchanged *Facebook* details before departing. We were also given a bag of clothes with a tracksuit each to wear. This was very useful as it hadn't yet crossed my mind that we literally only had the orange jumpsuits that we were wearing.

The ambulance crew were very friendly and also spoke perfect English. I guess they probably spend most of their time picking up drunk British holidaymakers. We arrived at the hospital to find it absolutely packed: there were people everywhere and doctors and nurses running around. Anthony was seen quickly and underwent some tests. A few hours later, he was advised to travel back to the UK for further tests. Still in our orange jumpsuits, we left and hailed a taxi, pointing to the hotel we had found close by online on my phone. We checked in, took a shower and headed over to the local department store where we purchased some extra clothes. Anthony booked a flight home for the next morning.

I was going to stay out for another day as we had been given a lead for a shipping company that might be able to help recover our boat. They were based in Santa Cruz where we were staying so I was going to see them the following day. I wasn't sure what to expect but we needed to at least try and see what options were available to try and recover the boat. Anthony remained upbeat and once again was very generous, telling me to spend whatever I needed to whilst I was in Tenerife, agreeing to reimburse me later.

8

Water in the Fuel

The following morning, I waved Anthony off as he departed for the airport in a taxi. I walked down to the shipping company's office in the afternoon and met with the owner, a well-dressed man who spoke perfect English. He was talking to different shipping agents to see if they had any vessels close by that might be able to recover our boat. They themselves were unable to help but were using their contacts to try and come up with a solution. The owner of the company informed me that he would keep me updated if anything materialised. I called Anthony and he agreed that it was futile for me to stay out there. I had just missed a flight that day so I booked one for the following day. That night, I went out and walked around on my own, contemplating everything that had happened over the last week and thinking about what I was going to do when I returned home.

When I arrived at the airport the next day, I was standing in the queue to board the aircraft when my phone started ringing. I looked down and saw that it was a Cape Verde number, so I answered.

It was a shipping agent who was offering his services to recover our boat. He represented a company which owned a tug boat that had the range and capability to take the job on. When I asked him about cost, I was surprised that it was half of what I expected it to be. Here I was, standing in the queue, about to board a plane, and now suddenly I'm talking to a man about heading down to Cape Verde as quickly as possible to get on another boat to head back out into the Atlantic on a rescue mission for our own boat! I asked him if he could put his offer in writing and email it to me. I couldn't really do anything else at that time so I carried on with my plan to come home. I could always fly back out to Cape Verde from the UK. I called Anthony and explained the situation and he gave me the green light to do it. I arrived back at Gatwick four hours later, went back to my parents' house and we talked through the possibility of flying out again the following day.

I spoke with the shipping agent again and he informed me that the price had now gone up, not by much, but because the boat was drifting further out, it effectively meant it would take longer to get to it. It was obvious that I had to make a decision quickly and the longer I left it, the less likely we would be able to get the boat back. I called the agent back and agreed to go ahead but also made it very clear that the price could not change again. I said in my sternest voice, "You cannot change the price again, you must stick with this one price, do you understand?" "Yes, no problem," he said. I also asked him to confirm the quote on email. We would pay half the money now and the other half upon successful recovery. My dad and I did some research on the company and the boat that we were going to effectively charter, which was a powerful tug boat called *Iron Bull*. The company was legitimate and this would certainly be the last and only opportunity to retrieve the boat before it drifted too far out into the Atlantic.

Anthony paid half the money for the recovery up front and I booked a flight. I had only been back in the UK for 24 hours and I was now on my way back to the airport. I felt that I needed to go along and oversee the recovery as we had a lot of valuable items on the boat, including the bag that I'd left with our personal belongings in it. I was travelling very light with just hand luggage: I'd packed a sat phone, an external power bank battery and a handheld GPS. I wanted to be able to have my own way of ascertaining our position and an independent means of communications whilst on the boat.

Just 24 hours later, I was sitting in *Hotel Pestana Tropico* in Praia, waiting to be collected. There are ten islands that make up the archipelago of Cape Verde and Praia is the capital city. The islands belong to the Portuguese but it didn't have a European feel to me. I was keen for us to get going as our boat was still drifting further out into the Atlantic. We knew the exact position of the boat as the tracker was still working, which meant locating it would not be a problem. I had deliberately charged the tracker before we left the boat, so I knew it had weeks of battery life left.

I met the owner of the company and the guy who had first called me when I was about to board the plane from Tenerife. He was well-dressed and obviously educated because he spoke almost perfect English. We went straight to the boat, which was indeed a large, powerful tug boat. It had recently been relocated from Tenerife to Cape Verde. The captain was Spanish but spoke sufficient English to get by. The rest of the crew did not speak any English and were probably just locals working as deckhands. There was also an engineer who stayed with the captain on board as a full-time member. "We go today," announced the captain. They were also conscious that the boat was drifting further away from us by the minute. It was around midday and the plan was to set off at 15:00 local time. We drove to the supermarket to collect food for the trip; fortunately, we had a chef on board who would be preparing food for us. I also took the opportunity to pick up a few tasty-looking snacks.

When we arrived back at the boat, I was shown to a cabin and 30 minutes later, we were casting off. It was all very calm to begin with as we left the harbour. As we turned west and the island was no longer there to protect us from the wind, it was just like someone had flicked a switch. The wind wasn't excessive but it was hitting us at a beam on a 90° angle, which caused the boat to roll excessively from side to side. This was not a good combination and felt quite unpleasant.

We put the latest coordinates into the chart plotter on board the GPS, working out that it was going to take us 2.5 days to reach our boat. It was over 300 nautical miles away from Cape Verde; although the tug boat had a top speed of around seven knots, it was by no means quick. It was designed to push and pull vessels and have a lot of power, like a tractor, which is not built for speed. With the boat rolling violently from side to side, I wondered how on earth we were going to even recover the boat. The tug boat did have a crane and, when I expressed my concerns to the captain, he told me that he planned to use the on-board crane to lift it up and lower it on to some tyres on the back deck. It all sounded good in theory but I wasn't sure how it was going to work in reality. Nevertheless, we needed to find it first!

As the evening drew in, the constant rolling started to take its toll on the crew. "Bleurgh!" I could hear, as another person vomited over the side. It was too hot and smelly with engine fumes in my cabin so I decided to bring a mattress up on to the bridge. It was a small wheelhouse as opposed to a bridge and the captain had the vessel on autopilot. I managed to get some rest through the first night but the constant rolling was starting to take its toll on me too.

The following morning, no one was really talking. The captain went below deck and when he came back up to the wheelhouse, he looked at me and said, "Everybody is lying down sick." I replied, "Yes, very difficult conditions." He had kindly made me a sandwich for which I was very grateful as I hadn't eaten for a while and was feeling exhausted and hungry.

I received a text message on my sat phone with the latest position of our boat, which had remained in the same position for 24 hours. I gave the coordinates to the captain who updated the chart plotter. We took turns on watch and stood at the helm as it gave us something to do. He would sit beside the wheelhouse door, smoking, and I'd try my best not to inhale the toxic smoke. He was actually very courteous and started smoking outside in the end.

For much of the day it was pretty boring. In the heat of the day, the boat stank of fumes and I wondered if it was this that was causing everyone to vomit. I lost count of how many times I heard that horrible retching sound. Even the captain had succumbed to it; whilst I was talking to him, he ran outside and vomited over the side. So far, I was the only person not to have been sick!

Later that day, the constant rolling of the boat from side to side became quite overwhelming for me too. I hadn't been feeling great so far but didn't feel sick. Whilst lying down on the mattress, I began to feel very hot and clammy, with that horrible feeling inside my stomach, the kind of feeling you get right before you're sick. Suddenly, it was like an auto response from my body. I jumped up, ran out of the wheelhouse and was sick over the side. Instantly I felt better but now I was dehydrated and knew I had to force fluids down. It was not a nice experience: someone had obviously not made it to the side in time and had been sick on deck so the smell was lingering in the air. Mixed with the fumes and the heat of the burning sun beaming down on us, it was almost unbearable but we had a mission, and that was to retrieve Anthony's boat.

As the heat of the day passed and the sun was now on the horizon, I started feeling considerably better. My appetite had come back so I ate some chocolate and other bits that I'd picked up in the supermarket. Apparently, our chef was seasick too and unable to prepare any food so this was the best that I was going to get. "Good job I picked this lot up," I thought to myself. I ended up feeling bloated and tired after I had gorged on comfort food, so I had a little nap. It was now dark but we had a red light in the wheelhouse that remained quite bright at night. I was woken up by the captain shouting down the stairs. It was absolutely pitch black and the red light wasn't on anymore. I also noticed that the boat felt like it was hardly moving at all. The side to side rolling had almost completely disappeared. It was actually very peaceful all of a sudden. I fell back to sleep but was woken again to more shouting and commotion. At this point, I started to wonder what all the fuss was about so I got up and asked the captain what was going on. "The engine has stopped," he said. "It's lost all power and we are now just drifting. The engineer is working on it now."

I didn't think much of it at first and actually went back to sleep. There was obviously nothing I could do and I thought they had it all under control. A little later, the red shining light came back on which woke me up and I could hear the engines running again. The rolling of the boat was now throwing me from side to side again, which was rather unpleasant. We were now back on course as opposed to drifting downwind.

A short while later, we lost the engine again. This time, it was down for a lot longer and I could see that the captain was anxious. Throughout the night, the captain and his engineer were working hard to fix the problem. By first light, we were on the move again but we'd lost about eight hours in total. It was less than ideal but it wouldn't stop us. However, later that morning, the engine stopped again. I was now starting to realise that this could actually be quite serious: every time the engine went down, the entire electrical system was rendered useless on the boat. There was nothing that would work, not even the steering; everything required the engine to be running. The captain knew that I had a sat phone and asked to borrow it to make a call. I presumed it was to the boss back in Praia who I'd met in Cape Verde.

I was unable to properly understand as they were speaking in Spanish but I could pick up a few words. Essentially, there was no backup solution! If the engineer couldn't get the engine running again, we would literally be stranded. There wasn't even a backup GPS on board so it was lucky that I had packed one. At least I could find out where we were and I had a sat phone plus a battery bank. It dawned on me that this was actually a very serious situation. I began to feel quite pissed off but didn't show it. I asked what was wrong and the captain just said, "A fuel problem." He was clearly very stressed.

A few hours passed and there was no sign of the engine being fixed. Albeit slowly, we were drifting south and further away from our boat. It was now the afternoon and the engine was still not running. We were almost 200 nautical miles from shore in the Atlantic Ocean, in a broken boat: this was less than ideal. I remained calm but my brain was naturally starting to wonder, "What if we get stuck out here? Who on earth is going to recover us? Will we just be left drifting around in the sea for weeks? Will they send another tug boat out to recover us?" It was hard to believe that this was really happening.

It wasn't until late that afternoon that the engine came back online. The captain and the engineer were having quite a heated exchange of words, which I couldn't fully understand but which I could hear down below. The captain then approached me and calmly explained the situation. For some reason, he was now calling me 'sir'. He said, "Sir, I am very sorry but we have to turn back. The engine may stop again at any moment and we cannot go further out into the ocean. We must get back to port. I am very sorry, sir." I wasn't sure what to say initially, so I just replied, "That's not good." He said I could talk to the boss about our boat and money. I wanted to demand that they kept going as we had paid for the recovery but I could see that we had quite a serious problem on our hands. If a bus broke down, the operator would send another and the journey would continue but there was going to be no replacement boat coming for us. I was in a very difficult situation but there was nothing I could do or say. I realised the gravity of the situation and of course, for my own self-preservation, I didn't want to get stuck in the Atlantic Ocean!

It was obvious that all the shouting had been about turning round and going back. The captain had been very apologetic; reading between the lines, I think he wanted to carry on with the mission but was basically told by the engineer that it wasn't possible. The captain turned the boat around and we headed back to port. Before I could really begin to think about what I was going to tell Anthony, the engine cut out again. By now, I also just wanted to get back and was very anxious about the whole situation. It took 30 minutes before we were on the move again. We eventually made it back to port the next evening. The engine stopped twice more on the way back. It turned out to be a fuel problem and water was getting into the fuel.

I had to call Anthony to tell him what had happened, despite feeling pretty bad about it. I called him from my mobile phone when we were back in port as I didn't want to be half way through explaining the situation and the sat phone to drop out due to poor signal.

I told Anthony what had happened and he laughed, "Bloody hell, you couldn't even make this up!" He continued, "OK, just come home now, there is nothing you can do about it. We will have to talk to the company owner. Just get on the first flight and come home – you must be exhausted." He took the news surprisingly well but personally, I was so frustrated about the whole situation. It just didn't feel right; I knew we wouldn't get any money back and I think Anthony probably knew that too.

That night, I went back to the hotel and booked a flight home for the next day. I arrived at Nelson Mandela International Airport the following morning, only to find my flight had been cancelled and I wasn't able to get on another one until the following day. There were people everywhere and it was just a chaotic mess. When I knew that I wouldn't be flying that day, I didn't hang around for the free accommodation that was being offered, I just went straight back to the hotel that I'd come from. I called Anthony and filled him in on the latest saga. He saw the funny side again and joked, "I think this trip is cursed!" I was beginning to think it was too. In hindsight, I suppose the whole experience, whilst unpleasant at times, was a pretty crazy adventure. But most importantly, whilst I don't want to go into details to respect Anthony's privacy, he had been given the medical all clear.

The next day, after two flights and a connection in Lisbon, I finally arrived back at Gatwick. My parents were waiting for me in the Arrivals Hall. "You haven't had much luck," said my mum. "I think that's an understatement," I replied.

9

Round Britain, One Way or Another

A couple of days passed as I watched the boat drift further out into the Atlantic, via the tracker. I felt a huge weight of responsibility that I'd been unable to recover it. About a week later, the tracker stopped reporting and so the boat was effectively gone – or so I thought! I managed to catch up with Anthony a few days later and he had fully recovered from the ordeal. He was always in good spirits; I never once saw him down or fed up, or at least, he didn't appear to be. I joked with him that he'd wanted an adventure and boy, did he get one! He had also raised a lot of money for a local charity, so the project was by no means a complete disaster.

Feeling pretty fed up, I needed my own break to take my mind off things. When I'd cycled around the world some years earlier, I'd spent time in Fort Lauderdale. It was a great place and I had an open offer to go back and stay with the same people any time I wanted. I sent them an email and they replied almost instantly, welcoming me with open arms. I booked a ticket immediately and, just a few days later, I packed my bike into a box, a few clothes and flew out to Miami.

The weather was cold, grey and wet in the UK and, although I had recently basked in sun in the Atlantic Ocean, it was nice to get back to a warmer climate. It was an exciting prospect: I didn't really have anything planned as such, apart from riding my bike and just hanging out. Instantly, I felt comfortable being back in the US. Daniel and Patricia had a beautiful, three-storey townhouse not far from an inland waterway in an area called Las Olas in Fort Lauderdale. The area was a modern, trendy and safe neighbourhood.

Within a day of arriving, I went straight out on my bike. Daniel had to go to work, so I went out on my own. I knew where I was going, straight out on the A1A, one of my favourite roads to cycle along. I had previously cycled the whole length of it from St Augustine to Miami in two days. This time, it was a more relaxed cruise; the road runs parallel with the beach right along the coast of the Atlantic Ocean and is home to some of the most spectacular properties I've ever seen! I stopped for an ice-cream and, seven hours later, I had cycled just over 100 miles. I was absolutely shattered, sun burnt, dehydrated, suffering with a headache but feeling absolutely amazing! It was just what I needed.

I had planned to spend almost two weeks in Florida but I didn't want to outstay my welcome with Daniel and Patricia so I booked a hotel and also spent some time in Miami. The first week passed quickly and I had cycled almost 500 miles. Daniel had joined me on a few rides but I was mostly riding on my own. I returned to Daniel and Patricia's house, with a few days left before I was going back to the UK. I had been talking to Daniel about buying a bike in the States as they were certainly cheaper out there. We looked at all sorts of options but I ended up purchasing a bike from a shop called *Downtown Bicycles*. It was a carbon-fibre BMC road bike and it really was a bit of a treat to myself!

On my return to the UK, I felt refreshed, re-energised and motivated, albeit a few thousand pounds worse off! I had been thinking, before the pedalo trip with Anthony and after the Indian Ocean project, that I'd like to have a go at rowing around Britain. As a solo attempt, it had not been achieved to date. I could charter a boat, which would reduce the cost significantly and it was something I could quite feasibly pull together in less than three months. I felt that I needed to do something on my own.

I spoke with Charlie who built the pedalo for Anthony, as well as the boat for the Indian Ocean row with Ash. He said I could charter his lightweight solo boat that he'd used to cross the Atlantic Ocean in a record time. It was a super lightweight, carbon fibre boat with the cabin at the bow. Charlie pioneered this design of switching the cabin from the back to the front, resulting in a significant increase in windage that would catch the boat. There were mixed opinions regarding this style but there were no two ways about it: it did have an advantage over the standard design. In my opinion, it was no different to a Formula One team coming out with a pioneering new design to make their cars go faster!

Charlie and I agreed on a fee for the boat charter and I set about fundraising. Rowing around the coast of Britain is a tricky task for a solo rower because you cannot just let the boat drift. The most dangerous place you can be in a boat, especially one that doesn't have an engine, is close to the coast. The tides and currents around Britain are strong and, whilst there is some beautiful coastline around Britain, there is also a lot of very unforgiving, rugged coastline on which many a ship has been smashed to pieces. Numerous crews had rowed around Britain but no solo rower had successfully managed to complete the feat. Charlie himself came close when he attempted it but ran out of time.

As a two-man crew, there would in theory always be someone on the oars rowing so the boat wouldn't be in any danger of drifting onto the rocks. This solo attempt was going to be a tactical row, utilising the tides that turned every six hours; when I needed to stop and rest, I would drop an anchor to hold my position. I really liked the idea and felt rejuvenated and motivated at the prospect of a new challenge. To the average person, rowing across the Atlantic sounded like a much grander feat than rowing around Britain, but the truth is, this would be a bigger achievement.

I started training hard in the gym and spent a lot of time researching the project, looking at tidal patterns, average wind direction (which would determine the direction in which I would attempt to go around Britain) and what kit I would need.

I liked the idea of being close to land because I'd mostly have mobile phone and data coverage, which would open up more possibilities of sharing the trip via social media. I was going to use the trip to raise money for *Over The Wall*, a wonderful children's charity offering camps and respite care for terminally-ill children. Gordon, who had very generously helped me and Ash in Australia when we needed some extra funds, kindly agreed to sponsor the charter fees for the boat, and I'd personally pick up the other smaller costs. I was grateful for his continued support.

It was now early May 2016 and I had about a month before I was due to depart for my *Round Britain Row*. An opportunity had come up to visit Canada and do a week of speaking in schools in Guelph, not far from Toronto. I had recently given a few online talks to an organisation called *Exploring by the Seat of your Pants*. They invite scientists and adventurers to tell their stories to children and share their passions and things they have learnt, via online classrooms all over the world. Joe was the founder and we got on well; he was smart, motivated, loved travel and was an excellent teacher. Above all else, he really believed that what he was doing brought value to the children and I absolutely believed it did too.

Joe was able to secure a grant which enabled me to travel over to Canada for a week. We planned at least two school visits per day, even three on one day. The idea was to maximise the speaking time on the trip and to reach as many young people as we could. It was a really full-on week but it was a lot of fun too. Meeting Joe and his family in person was a real pleasure. Every night we ate out at a different restaurant and I was taken to a baseball game to watch the *Toronto Blue Jays*, which was absolutely fantastic. To this day, I still get messages from children that I spoke to that week, who remember my visit and tell me what they are doing now.

Once I was back home, it was time to get serious. The row around Britain was happening and I felt like I was mentally in a good place. I had also managed to get permission to depart from St Katherine Docks, right next to the iconic Tower Bridge.

Two weeks before I was due to leave for the *Round Britain Row*, I met up with a guy at London Waterloo train station. He had sent me an email whilst I was in Canada, expressing an interest in meeting me to discuss an 'opportunity'. He had watched a podcast called *London Real* for which I was interviewed. It was hosted by an American guy called Brian, an ex-banker living in London, who had now built an online self-help business, running mentorship classes and interviewing different guests on his podcast. It was a lot of fun; he was a very switched-on chap who had a good interview style.

Back to the opportunity. I was in London for a few days so agreed to meet him. He was a smart guy, running a start-up business in the tech industry. We got chatting about what I was doing next and what the future might hold with my expeditions. He was telling me about a project to discover some long lost gold that he had been researching, and also informed me that if I was interested, and looking for a new project, I should start researching gyroplanes. They were apparently the only type of aircraft that had not been flown around the world, despite a few attempts. He described how one person had got very close, but had to ship his aircraft from Japan to the USA as he wasn't able to fly through Russia. I made a few notes and thought it sounded fascinating. I left the meeting feeling intrigued but didn't follow up on it immediately. My mind was very much focused on my row, which I knew was going to be challenging.

Everything was in place. I had already packed the boat with my ration packs at Charlie's workshop and all other essential items, apart from my personal kit. The boat was towed down to London, launched on the Thames and I rowed it down to St Katherine Docks the day before departure. The team at the marina was extremely helpful and didn't charge me any berthing fees, which was appreciated. I had booked a hotel right next to the marina so I could be there first thing in the morning. That evening, I spent some time double-checking everything; the boat was well packed and squared away. I went to bed that night feeling like I was ready but certainly nervous.

It was 25th June 2016 and I was setting off late in the afternoon in order to catch the high tide to take me out into the Thames Estuary. There were plenty of well-wishers who attended my send-off, despite the forecast rain. The charity came along in great numbers, as well as friends and family members. Even Anthony was able to make it along and show his support.

Charlie had come along to support the launch in a RIB which he and his colleague, Angus, were crewing. They kindly offered to take a cameraman, my dad and a few other people out on the water for the departure. As the gates opened from the marina to the River Thames itself, it started to pour down with rain. The boat was flying along with the tide but I knew that everyone else on the RIB was getting absolutely soaked! The cameraman got the shots he needed and, after a few passes and waves, they quickly turned back to the marina to unload the drenched passengers. That was it: I was now on my own.

Thankfully, after about an hour, the rain stopped and the clouds cleared, leaving a beautiful sunset over the city; the tops of the Canary Wharf skyscrapers were illuminated by the sun. The tide started to get stronger and at one point, I had eight knots of boat speed – of course, half of that was just the tide. It wasn't long before I was passing under the famous Queen Elizabeth II Bridge, which the M25 London orbital motorway uses to cross the Thames. It was now dark and the tide was out; it would only come back in and slow me down. I had covered some good mileage and decided to drop the anchor for the night. I found a spot just after the bridge where the water was calm and there was not a breath of wind in the air.

I had already decided that I was going to go clockwise around the UK so I kept to the south of the Thames Estuary as it opened out into the sea. The next day, I made it along to Margate where I anchored again, just off the beach. I could smell the fish and chips! The nerves from the start had well and truly gone now, the boat was performing very well and my rowing position was comfortable.

Over the course of the next three days, I made very slow progress around the headland to Ramsgate and down to Dover. I was a little bit anxious about entering the Port of Dover due to the large ferries coming in and out but I called them on the radio and they sent a pilot boat out to escort me in. I dropped an anchor behind the shelter walls in the harbour. I was going to be there for a few days as the wind had picked up, blowing fairly hard from the south west, so I wouldn't have been able to make any progress against it. I was relieved to have made it into the safety of the harbour; I felt like the first little phase had been completed and London was a long way behind me now. The wind was set and looked fairly consistent for a good few days.

I passed the time, just chilling out. Occasionally, some flat water rowers would come over in their boats to say hello. My website and twitter handle were emblazoned down the side of the boat, so every now and then, I'd get a tweet from someone wishing me well.

Although it was frustrating to be sitting in the boat not going anywhere, I was quite happy. I had only completed a very small portion of the row so far but was feeling confident. Having already had the two previous projects not quite go to plan, I was sure I was going to do this. After all, lightning surely can't strike three times, can it?

Yet, just three days after arriving in Dover harbour, I was lying in bed in the local hospital with a terrible pain in my abdomen. I had been feeling extremely unwell and tired. Without going into too much detail, my urine was a colour I had never seen before. I had spoken to a doctor on the phone and he confirmed that I needed to have some tests run. This of course meant that I had to leave the boat. I called the port authority on the VHF radio and they brought the pilot boat over, where I disembarked and was taken straight to an ambulance. The boat was sitting on an anchor and was absolutely fine where it was.

It was all very surreal: I couldn't believe this was happening! I knew I wasn't well and wanted to understand what was wrong but sadly, this was one too many setbacks for me to take. When the nurse told me that it looked like I had a bladder infection, I'd already checked out mentally and have no recollection of what she said after that. I was in the hospital for about twelve hours, until I was allowed to leave. They had given me some painkillers which had made some improvement but the pills couldn't help with my completely shattered enthusiasm and low mental state. I got a taxi back to the marina and informed the port authorities of the situation; they were very accommodating and helped move the boat into a pontoon at the local yacht club. I called Charlie and told him the news but reassured him that the boat was safe. He sounded genuinely gutted but said he thought I still had time to carry on and start again from there.

My parents also tried to encourage me but I'd completely lost it, mentally. I felt like this really was the end of my career as an adventurer. I posted a picture that I'd taken in hospital to let people know what had happened. I was overwhelmed with good wishes but as some people pointed out, everything I was touching or doing just appeared to be jinxed!

I made a decision that I wasn't in the right place mentally to carry on: the charity, friends and sponsors were disappointed for me but were understanding at the same time. My brain was in overdrive and I was on a wild roller-coaster ride of emotions. I really didn't know what to do. I felt incredibly despondent and started to become quite bitter and angry. "Why have I had this run of bad luck? I'm a nice guy, I don't deserve this. I've never wronged anyone so why is this happening to me?" I thought to myself. I could not let the fact that I had already achieved some impressive feats make me feel entitled. Looking back I probably was, and that was a mistake: no one should feel entitled to anything.

I was in a place in my head that I wouldn't wish on anyone. I'd fallen into a pattern of time-wasting, negative thoughts and worrying about everything that was out of my control. When I was young, I would deal with my problems by simply switching off and spending all day in bed. I was starting to do the same again, which was particularly destructive and damaging behaviour. It was a very bad habit that cost me many opportunities in my younger days. Luckily, all bad habits can be broken and it had been many years since I had behaved like this. That fire in the belly that defined me was no longer there. Ultimately, deep down, I knew that nothing was going to bring me peace but my own mind and having the ability to leave the past behind and move on was now essential.

Thankfully, there was still one little spark of light burning inside me that said, "This isn't you James, you are better than this."

One of the happiest times of my life was when I cycled around the world. The endorphins that were coursing through my body from the constant exercise made me feel great every day. I had so much energy, despite cycling over 100 miles a day for half a year. I used to jump out of bed before the alarm clock had even gone off! Every day that I was on the road, nothing would ever bother me; I felt calm and had clarity in my thinking. After I'd cycled 100 miles, sometimes more, I felt amazing, no matter what the weather was doing or how dirty the hotel was.

I knew that I needed to get some focus back and I had to keep moving. When I was descending Everest with my Sherpa, Dorje, I didn't know that I had pneumonia. I have never been so close to dropping down dead but somehow, I made it down. It was the concept of just keeping moving, albeit one slow, small step at a time, and the help from Dorje, that got me off that mountain alive.

I had forgotten that, despite these recent setbacks, I was a strong person when I needed to be. Every difficult situation that I'd ever been in was overcome by not doing anything special, but by just continuing to keep moving.

I knew this row was over but I needed to get myself moving again. I decided I needed to get back on my bike and would cycle around the coast of Britain instead. Of course, I recognised that it didn't have quite the same kudos as rowing round, I just knew I needed to do something. I also thought I owed it to myself to continue doing the things that made me happy, content and true to my character. Adventure and motivational speaking has given me a lot to be thankful for, despite some well-meaning people telling me to give up on these silly adventures and go and get a 'real job'! Ironically, some of these very people have been let go from jobs they never wanted to do in the first place. So if you can fail at something you don't even want to do, you may as well have a go at something you do want to do!

Whilst the bike I already owned was a very good one, it was not suitable for touring around Britain. I'd always wanted a titanium bike: I had my eye on a particular brand made by a small UK company called *Vaaru Cycles*. They produce titanium frames and build beautiful road bikes. I searched on eBay and found the model I wanted in the exact size that I needed, a 57cm frame. I couldn't believe it! At that moment, I thought, "This was meant to be." I didn't haggle on the price but called the guy that day and told him that I'd come and collect it immediately, despite having to drive half the length of the country.

It was now August 2016 and I was determined to try and at least salvage something of my coastal project, not just for myself but also for the charity, *Over The Wall*. The CEO, Kevin, had been ever so good to me; I had previously taken some high net worth individuals on a Three Peaks charity trek on behalf of *Over The Wall* and Kevin totally understood what I was about and knew I was usually hustling for project funding. He had always tried to help me and would often introduce me to new contacts, which not many charity CEOs would do, so it meant a lot to me.

Their office was based on the south coast, just outside Portsmouth, on Langstone Technology Park. I had been there many times and this was going to be the start and finish of my ride. I did some research on the route and mileage; I was surprised to see that there were many different opinions on the actual mileage of the British coastline. Whichever one was right, it was undoubtedly quite considerable! I wasn't going to follow rivers inland but I would use bridges to take the shortest distance between two land masses. A quick calculation told me that this was still going to accumulate 3,000 miles at the very least, even cycling as close to the coast as I feasibly could.

I had packed fairly light, with a similar set-up to my world cycling kit. I was using frame bags and a large saddle bag for most of my kit, with a roll mat attached under the handle bars. I was fully equipped to sleep out as and when I wanted to, with a sleeping bag, bivvy bag and roll mat. It was a pretty slick set-up.

I was waved off by the charity employees on a very warm, sunny, mid-August day. It didn't take long to ride around the Portsmouth sea front and up to Southampton, finishing in the New Forest on my first night. It had been a while since I had ridden back to back days of 100 miles plus, so I knew I had to break myself in gently.

A few days later, I found myself in Devon staying with a friend and his family. Pat was a writer and had written a few articles about my previous adventures. I was feeling tired when I arrived but tried not to show it as their children were excited to see me and show me their cycling skills in the garden.

I had been to Devon a few times but I'd never realised just how lovely the area really was. I was approaching Plymouth and didn't want to stay in the city so I Googled some local B&Bs in the area. I found one called *The Ivy Barn* where I was warmly welcomed by the owners. They showed me to my room and locked my bike away in a secure shed (that was the only problem with having a nice bike, I was always worried about leaving it anywhere!). The next morning, I walked into the breakfast room and the host said to me, smiling, "I think you've forgotten to tell us something." I was totally perplexed. At first I thought, "What have I done?" then realised that, apart from going to sleep and having a shower, I hadn't done anything. I wondered if perhaps I'd got grease on the sheets without noticing? "You didn't tell us you're a celebrity adventurer. And now you're here, telling us you're doing a little charity bike ride, eh?" she said, with a smile on her face. "Oh yeah, well I'm not really a celebrity," I said, awkwardly. "Right, here's your bill," she added. But before I could say anything, she tore it up with enthusiasm and said, "It's an honour to have you here, you are not paying for anything!" It really was a lovely thing to do and it was greatly appreciated. Her husband cooked an amazing English breakfast for me, with extra portions. "You'll need the extra fuel with all the hills around here," he joked. I left that day feeling great: the sun was shining and it was a lovely way to start the day. If you ever find yourself on the south coast of Devon and need a place to stay, be sure to visit Nicky and Rik at *The Ivy Barn B&B* in Holbeton.

Over the next five days, I passed through Cornwall, reached Land's End and was cycling up the North Devon coastline. I was joined by my super-fit friend, Sean, who was living down there at the time. He had inspired me to cycle around the world, after I joined him for his last day when he returned from cycling around the world himself. We had also kayaked the length of the River Thames together.

When I reached Bristol, I met up with a friend called Sarah, who let me stay on her couch. She was an avid horse rider and a keen triathlete, so cycled into Wales with me. She was also keen to cycle in Scotland and I told her that she was welcome to join me. I knew she'd have no problem riding the hundred miles a day that I was aiming for.

The cycle was going well. Devon and Cornwall were a baptism of fire due to the extreme, undulating terrain but I'd now found a rhythm. I was dropping body weight by the day and it was getting easier and easier. Ian, who'd come out to film me and Anthony in Gran Canaria, was living in Cardiff at the time, so I met up with him. Over the two days that he cycled with me, we made it up to Aberystwyth before he needed to catch the train home. It's always a pleasure cycling with Ian; he is just a very easy-going, thoughtful person.

It only took two days to get round to Liverpool, then the route took me up in to the Lake District, whose coastline I was able to ride in one day. That evening, I met up with an old work colleague called Graham; he was also a keen cyclist and all-round fit guy who worked in the outdoor trade. He cycled into Scotland with me the following day, then returned home.

I had two days to make it to Glasgow, which was fairly straightforward. Sarah had decided to cycle around the top of Scotland with me. The first day she joined me, it rained hard all day as we cycled to the beautiful, iconic Loch Lomond and up to Fort William. Despite the rain, it was actually quite a fun day. The weather improved over the next four days and the cycling was absolutely amazing. We would sometimes ride for hours without seeing another car on the road and most of the traffic was tourist sightseeing. We made it round to John O'Groats for a picture at the famous landmark. It was all downhill from here! Of course not literally. Sarah managed to get a bus down to Inverness and flew back to Bristol.

There are many things I like about cycling but one particular thing is the people you randomly meet out on the road. When I cycled around the world, I lost count of how many strangers I met out cycling. I would get chatting to them and to this day, I am still friends with many of them. Just as Sarah was leaving, we randomly got cycling with some lads from London who had travelled up to Scotland to cycle the very route that Sarah and I had just cycled together. It's called the North Coast 500: it starts and finishes at Inverness and is a 500-mile circuit. I cycled with these guys, who were fit and good fun, down to Inverness. They weren't carrying as much kit as me so I had to work very hard to keep up but they pulled me along nicely.

Over the next week, I made my way back down the east coast of England, cursing the headwinds at times but cheering with joy when I was being blown along. The rest of the ride was fairly uneventful but strangely, I did meet another cyclist who was cycling around the coast of Britain. We rode together for two days which took us down to Kings Lynn, where he had a rest day and I carried on. Over a leisurely two days, I had arrived back at the Queen Elizabeth II

Bridge as I now needed to cross the River Thames. It wasn't long ago that I was rowing underneath it.

I was now retracing the coastline that I had started to row around. As I passed through Dover, I made a point of cycling to the marina. How different things were now! I was back to my usual self and the disappointment of the row had passed. I dread to think what would have happened had I not made the effort to get on my bike and try to at least salvage something from the failed project. I would probably have achieved nothing and would still be moping around feeling sorry for myself.

Whenever you face some kind of crisis or difficult situation, I cannot emphasise enough the importance of just keeping moving. Work through the problem, keep trying and, more often than not, things will come good. The worst thing you can ever do when you are facing some kind of difficulty is to just stop.

On my last day of cycling, I stopped in Chichester to meet James, the owner of *Vaaru Cycles*. He had contacted me as I was halfway through my ride. I liked James and we had a lot of similar interests: he was the same age as me, really passionate about bikes, as well as being an engineer and skilled paint sprayer. After a fantastic pub lunch, which James wouldn't let me pay for, I had only a short ride to the charity office, where I had departed from a month earlier. I had raised at least some money for the charity and, most importantly, I had got back on the horse (or bike, in this case) after three back-to-back failures, and that's what was important.

When you are achieving your goals, paying your bills, enjoying good relationships, life is easy and anyone can feel motivated. You only really find out what you're made of when things start to go wrong. If you're not getting the results you were expecting or think you deserve, you can start to feel resentful and angry, sometimes feeling that it's someone else's fault and that you have been wronged.

That's when you find out if you're the person you think you are. There is usually a big difference between the person you think you are and the person who you really are. But it's never too late to change, no matter how many times you have started and failed.

Luck has a habit of finding people who don't give up and continue to keep trying. I'm sure you've heard someone say, "They were just lucky." But you have to be on the field in order to score a goal! It's the same in life: you have to keep showing up, day after day, and the most important time to do so is when you don't feel like it. When you look closely at the people who 'got lucky', nine times out of ten, they will have done three or four times the work compared to the people who are complaining. Does that mean they still 'got lucky'? I'll leave you to think about that.

The rest of 2016 passed by quickly and before long, 2017 rolled around. I had big plans and I was feeling motivated, continuing to enjoy my cycling.

Cycling around Britain had raised a modest amount for the charity and was the boost that I needed to get fit again. There is something about riding a bike that just makes me feel good, from a physiological point of view. It must be the endorphins it releases but I'm convinced it's more than that. Whenever I'm going through a phase of riding my bike a lot, I'm usually in quite a proactive place in my life and generally feeling good; less positive things tend not to play on my mind quite as much.

After returning from the ride, I was fit, lean and at a good weight. I decided that I would continue to push my cycling more seriously, whilst improving my diet and getting sufficient rest. My local bike shop, *Hoops Velo*, had always been good to me and I knew the staff well. I now had two excellent bikes which they helped me rebuild: the carbon BMC, which was going to be used for racing and my titanium road bike. I had been doing some rides with a guy called James who was a nice guy and an extremely fast rider. He was cycling full time and sponsored by *Hoops Velo*. James said that I should have a go at criterium racing, where a group of riders race around a fairly flat track for about an hour and the winner is the first across the line after a certain number of laps. This race took place every Tuesday at Thruxton Race Circuit, a well-known racing circuit in Hampshire. I knew I stood a chance of doing fairly well and I was able to race in the Cat 4, which is effectively for new racers. It was my first race and James came along with me. As I drove into the parking area, I noticed the car behind me was my girlfriend at the time, Laura. She had driven all the way up from Taunton to watch my first race, which was a lovely surprise.

James told me not to sit on the front of the group for long as I would expend too much energy and needed to save it for the last lap, which would usually be a sprint to the finish line. I felt good and found it hard to hold myself back but knew I had to. It did come down to a sprint finish and I finished just outside the top 10 from a field of around 35 riders. I had absolutely loved it and continued to race through the summer of 2017.

Above: The James Lewis being lowered into the Indian Ocean

Below: Ash and me waving goodbye to friends, family and scouts at Heathrow Airport

Above: News crews interviewing Ash and me before we set off

Overleaf: A passing ship on the Indian Ocean

Below: Ash on the oars for our first press day in London

Above: Phil and Max in the Amazon jungle

Below: Me after shooting a scout video

Above: Testing the boat in Gran Canaria

Right: Anthony spinning the pedals

Below: Being airlifted off the Chinese bulk carrier

Above: Half way around Britain at John O' Groats

Below: Making my way out of London on the River Thames for my Round Britain ro

10

Earning My Wings

I had been thinking a lot about the chance meeting I'd had at Waterloo station and the prospect of flying around the world, especially in a gyroplane. I think most people are aware of the famous *Little Nellie*, built and flown by Wing Commander Ken Wallis in the James Bond film, *You Only Live Twice*.

An autogyro, otherwise known as a gyroplane, would look like a small helicopter to the untrained eye; it is, however, more like a plane than a helicopter. The rotor is not powered itself but it spins by air passing over its rotor, as a result of forward motion which comes from an engine that provides the thrust. This is usually found at the back of the aircraft, although some earlier models had the propeller at the front and designs have varied over the years. The free spinning rotor provides lift once it reaches a certain speed, known as 'autorotation'.

The concept of flying with a rotary wing was first discovered and pioneered in 1920 by the Spanish inventor, Juan De La Cierva, not long after the Wright Brothers' first flight. It was developed over the years and has proved to be quite a capable machine. It was used for delivering air mail in the US and was even used to calibrate radar during the Battle of Britain, as no other aircraft could fly at the slow speeds required to carry out the calibration without stalling.

With the birth of the helicopter, the autogyro slowly faded away but in more recent times, it has enjoyed a resurgence as an incredibly popular form of recreational flying. It was fascinating to research this machine and I was learning a lot. Many fixed-wing aircraft, some helicopters and even hot air balloons had flown around the world, but to date, no gyroplane had officially circumnavigated the globe.

I continued my research and decided to get in contact with Norman Surplus who had attempted to fly a gyroplane around the world some years earlier. He flew from Northern Ireland to Japan where he was denied permission to fly through Russia. He needed to route through Russia in order to cross into North America. He spent three years trying to enter Russia, going back out to Japan every summer, where he had stored his aircraft. Eventually, he came to the conclusion that he was unable to gain the permission he needed, so decided to ship his aircraft to the west coast of the US and fly it home from there. It must have been very frustrating but it is a remarkable story of determination. Norman had flown a very long way and set numerous records, however he had not officially 'flown around the world' because he had shipped his aircraft from one continent to another.

I'd contacted Norman as he was clearly well-qualified to advise me if I decided to attempt this mission. I flew over to Belfast to meet him in early May 2017. His aircraft was stored in a barn on a farm, and he just used a small field to take off from and land in as there was no airfield close by. He patiently answered all my questions, shared his route with me and showed me bits of kit that he'd used, as well as telling me what he would do differently. I flew home that evening feeling motivated and excited. It was the encouragement I needed, although it was something I was still thinking about. I was unable to fly and had no finances to purchase an aircraft, let alone fly one around the world! But I did have energy and enthusiasm and that alone can take you a very long way. The rest of May passed quite quickly. I was busy with speaking engagements, riding my bike and spending time with Laura.

On 24th May 2017, Laura and I attended a fantastic event at Buckingham Palace. I was asked to give a short speech and present certificates to a group of young people who had achieved their Duke of Edinburgh Gold awards. The event was hosted in the gardens. It was a glorious day, the sun was blazing down and there was not a cloud in the sky. I'd had the privilege of doing the same thing the previous year at St James's Palace, so I had a pretty good understanding of how the day would go.

In early June, I headed to my local airfield at Popham, located on the outskirts of Basingstoke. I had always remembered Popham Airfield as I was taken for a flight as a child by my next door neighbour on more than one occasion. I can recollect visiting Popham on a 'fly in' day, when pilots fly in and take kids for rides. I flew with a guy in a motor glider and, to this day, I still remember him turning the engine off. I think I was around 12 years old at the time. I had always had an interest in flying but thought that it was something for people who had lots of money and were very intelligent. I felt a long way off on both of those attributes!

I decided that I should have a trial flight and see how I got on. A guy called Steve was the gyroplane instructor out of Popham so I called him and booked a flight. I remember turning up at Popham, ever so excited. I met Steve and instantly felt at ease; he was laid back with a happy, cheerful disposition. We had a pre-flight brief in his office, he told me what to expect, what not to do and a few things I needed to know. He asked me if I wanted to sit in the back or the front. "Of course in the front!" I said. This meant that I had to do a few things that he couldn't do from the back seat, like pre-rotate the rotors.

I pulled the lever on the stick which, to the untrained eye, would look like a brake lever. The rotors above our head started spinning up as I was looking down Runway 26. The aircraft was loud and vibrating and I could hear a "whoosh, whoosh, whoosh" from the rotors spinning above my head. "OK, let go of the pre-rotator," Steve said over the radio. Flying from the back seat, Steve had full control. The engine roared into life and we hurtled down the runway. I was quite taken back at the acceleration, which was quicker than I had expected. "We are now flying," Steve said.

We were only a foot or so off the ground but the grass was whizzing by underneath me. I looked at the airspeed indicator in front of me and could see that we were doing over 100 miles per hour (mph). Suddenly, with no warning, we shot up into the air and it felt like I'd left my stomach behind. "Wow, this is amazing!" I shouted to Steve, as we started to climb higher. I was actually a little nervous to be honest as I felt incredibly exposed looking out over the edge. Steve gave me control of the aircraft quite soon and explained how to keep it in balance with the wind by using the rudder pedals.

"OK, I have control," I heard Steve say, then he really started to show me what the machine could do. He pulled the power right back, which felt like he had just stamped on the brakes, and I could feel the harness holding me back. It felt like I was at the top of a roller-coaster looking over the edge, just before you hurtle down the track, except we didn't hurtle anywhere, we just stayed in the same position. Steve explained to me that we were now just gliding. "It's not possible to stall a gyroplane," he said. That's the major advantage over a traditional fixed-wing aircraft.

We landed about an hour later. I must have had the biggest grin on my face because the whole experience had been amazing. I knew then and there that I wanted to learn how to fly a gyroplane. At the time, I didn't say anything about flying one around the world!

I was now obsessed with everything that related to flying. I knew that getting funding for this project was going to be the hardest part, by a long way. I had saved up enough funds to learn how to fly but not to purchase an aircraft or even get close to purchasing one. I wanted to take it slowly to begin with and initially didn't tell too many people about my plans to fly around the world.

Laura was very supportive but unfortunately, we were spending less and less time together as we both became busy and had our own goals and ambitions. We ended up going our separate ways, which didn't bother me too much to begin with as I thought it would enable me to have greater focus on my goal. However, it didn't take long to realise that I missed her company; sometimes you don't realise what you've got until it's gone!

I contacted Steve a week or so later to make enquiries about starting my training to acquire a gyro license. It transpired that he was pretty busy, which was no surprise as he was one of the most experienced gyro pilots around, and his customers would travel far and wide to fly with him. He advised me to contact one of his colleagues at another flying school close to Oxford, Chiltern Park. They were all part of the same group, *The Gyrocopter Experience*. It was run by Andy who set up the flying school after retiring from the RAF. There was another gyro instructor working out of the airfield who was called Clive. Steve suggested that I start my training with Clive and, when Steve had the capacity, he would continue with me at Popham.

I spoke with Clive who was more than happy to help and said we could start as soon as I wanted. It was now July 2017 and I had picked up some work from a friend, helping out as support crew for a charity row from Barcelona to Ibiza, so I was going to be away for just over two weeks. With this in mind, I decided to start my flying when I returned.

Crews from the US and the UK were rowing as four-man teams from Barcelona to Ibiza, then another crew would take over and row back to Barcelona. I was going to be on the support yacht for the crossing and, in the ports, I would help the crews out with general preparation and advice. It turned out to be a lot of fun.

When I returned, I got straight into flying with Clive. He was an experienced instructor and was also easy-going. We got on very well, had a lot of fun and it didn't take me too long to start getting the hang of flying. I think I still had fairly good balance and coordination from my motorcycle racing days, which was useful.

Things were starting to come together: the flying was progressing and I was in contact with Norman. He introduced me to Eddie, who ran a company called *General Aviation Support Egypt* (GASE) with his friend and colleague, Ahmed. Eddie used to be based in Egypt, hence the name, but was now based out of Warwick in the UK. He was a real aviation enthusiast and, although he wasn't able to fly himself due to a medical condition, flying and supporting pilots was in his blood – he loved it. He had helped Norman and many other pilots complete long-range flights all over the world and sometimes complete circumnavigations. Eddie was extremely supportive, had a lot of experience and many contacts.

We met up and it didn't take long to broach the obvious challenge: there was no point in flying all the way to Japan, just to get stuck there and find myself in the same position as Norman, unable to continue. Eddie explained that things had changed over the years and he was now able to get me through Russia. This was reassuring to know, as the question was surely going to come up when speaking to potential sponsors. I came away from the meeting feeling great and, within a few days, Eddie had sent me through various route options and ideas to be thinking about.

Not long after meeting Eddie, I was introduced to a guy called Kip who was living on the outskirts of Bristol, renovating an old Dutch Barge. He was in the process of completing his gyro instructor certification. I drove down to meet him and we chatted about the potential challenges of my trip. Kip was very supportive and we agreed to go flying together at some point in his gyro.

I needed to pass some ground exams in order to progress my flying, covering meteorology, air law, navigation and a technical exam. Kip mentioned that he had been designing some material around this and he spent many evenings with me going through the presentations. It really helped and, slowly but surely, I started working through the exams. I didn't want to 'just' pass, I wanted to fully understand everything, and more!

Kip and I flew a couple of times together, which was always fun. He was a very experienced pilot, having flown Hawks and Jaguars in the RAF and spent many years teaching young officers to fly. I had potentially planned to do my training with Kip and be his first student, but he needed a bit of time to get his school going. I wasn't really able to wait as I needed to get as many flying hours as possible under my belt. I was getting on well with Clive and, after 10 hours, I was about ready to fly solo. Just at this time, Steve contacted me and said he had space for me to come to Popham if I wanted to carry on with my training there. I really enjoyed flying with Clive, it was simply just more convenient at Popham as I only lived 15 minutes away. Clive was very understanding and joked with me on my last day flying with him, "Now Ketch, remember I took you on your first international flight… the Isle of Wight!" He did indeed and I still remember it vividly to this day.

Flying continued with Steve and the intensity was stepping up, even after just a few lessons. We were flying around the circuit at Popham doing touch-and-go landings. Flying around the circuit means following the direction of the other airfield traffic, landing and taking off on the same runway. By this point, most of my landings were fairly good; there was the odd heavy one but by and large, flying the machine had pretty much 'clicked' for me.

It was a calm, clear day. We had just landed and taxied off the active runway. "OK, just put the brake on and turn the aircraft off," said Steve. He then jumped out of the back. I wondered what on earth he was doing and thought perhaps he had dropped something. He then said, "OK James, conditions are good for you to go solo now. Just remember what we spoke about when I briefed you." At that moment, I felt my heart rate go up considerably! I knew what I was doing and was quite confident but as a student, it's knowing that you have an instructor there as back up that gives you that confidence a lot of the time. I took a deep breath and thought, "OK, I've got this, I've done this many times now." I slowly went through all my checks, lined up, spun the rotors up and accelerated along the runway.

Steve wasn't wrong about it now being a bit lighter: I was off the ground in almost half the time it usually takes. I flew the circuit and it wasn't long before I was on my final approach for Runway 21. Steve was standing by the clubhouse with a handheld radio, listening to my radio calls as I announced my position in the circuit. No doubt he was praying I didn't prang his aircraft! Thankfully, as I remember, it was a fairly smooth landing. "Well done, sir" came over the radio from the clubhouse operator, who congratulated me on my first solo flight and landing. I exited the runway and heard Steve say, "Very nice James, do you want to carry on and do a few more?" Of course I said yes! The nerves had passed and I was now flying on my own. I taxied back to the hangar with the biggest smile on my face. However, there was still a long way to go before I was ready to take my test and I still needed to make several solo cross-country flights.

Steve and I continued to work through the rest of the syllabus fairly quickly. I asked a lot of questions. I imagine on many occasions, he probably thought, "Just shut up and fly" but he always patiently answered anything I asked him, even if it was the third time he explained something to me. It didn't always come easy; Steve was such an experienced instructor that he made everything look so simple. I wanted to be as slick as him on the radio but I knew that would be impossible for a beginner, reminding myself that everyone has to start somewhere.

We completed a couple of mock flying tests, which Steve was happy with. Then we booked the test, so it was now the real deal. I was nervous the night before but thought to myself, "Whatever happens, just stay positive." As Steve had taught me to fly, he would not be able to be the examiner, so it fell to Steve's business partner, Andy, who ran Chiltern Park. Andy was a very experienced gyro instructor. I had never flown with him before so I looked at this as a chance to show him that I was capable and had the airmanship skills required to obtain my licence.

We checked over the aircraft first and I explained all the pre-flight checks that I had carried out and why we needed to do them. "OK great, let's go flying," he said. I remember Steve telling me not to do anything differently than I have ever done before. Andy would give me instructions and I would just follow them. I remember taking off and climbing out of the circuit. Another aircraft that was joining the circuit was flying towards us, so I pointed out to Andy that I had seen it but we didn't need to make any course adjustment. He later joked with me that at that point, it was a pass, as I had almost immediately demonstrated that I had situational awareness after taking off, a critical skill for flying. Of course I hadn't really passed at that point, as I still needed to complete the tasks set, but they were not too difficult, to be honest. We were on the way back to the airfield and the only manoeuvre that we had not carried out was the forced landing. Just as I was thinking, "I wonder when he is going to do the forced landing?" Andy cut the throttle. It was all very calm: I still had plenty of height, turned the aircraft into the wind, made the dummy Mayday calls, selected a field and even made an S-turn to lose some height. Andy was happy and said, "OK that's good, head home now, mate."

I knew that I must have passed, providing I didn't crash on landing. It was a smooth landing and we parked up back at the hangar. I didn't say anything initially and there was a moment of silence before Andy said, "Mate, that was absolutely brilliant, you have passed, really nice flying, James." Steve took a picture of me and Andy next to the aircraft, shaking hands. I had been a little anxious that morning but bizarrely, once I was out there, I really enjoyed it and wasn't at all nervous. It felt more like a lesson than a test and I wanted to keep flying. Although I had passed my basic flying test with Andy on 30th October 2017, the truth was, the real learning was just about to start. I only had 47 hours of flying under my belt since the first time I sat in a gyroplane.

11

Global Ambitions

Steve and Andy represented *Magni Gyro* in the UK, an Italian company that had been producing the finest gyroplanes since 1980. Both Steve and Andy were now aware of my quest to fly around the world. We arranged to fly out to Milan to meet with the Magni family to discuss the proposed plan. I had only recently passed my test and now I was going to meet a family who has been building gyroplanes for almost as long as I've been alive, to inform them of my plans to fly around the world. I arrived feeling quite nervous as I wasn't sure what to expect. We were met at the airport by Chiara, the Sales and Marketing Director and the founder, Vittorio Magni. We arrived in the small town of Besnate and went straight to the factory, where I met Luca, his brother Pietro and the rest of the team.

After some introductions, I gave a short presentation to the Magni family, which was received very well and they seemed to believe in my vision. I was unaware of this but the family had a motto…*Magni Gyro, Makers of Dreams*. I spoke about dreams and goals in my presentation which I think, looking back, must have resonated with them.

We carried on with a tour of the factory, where Chiara explained the history and talked about some of the old gyros which were on display. The history was fascinating and it didn't take me long to realise that I really wanted to work with these people. I was aware that I'd be carrying the weight of their family history on my shoulders, which was a big responsibility, however it felt right. They immediately welcomed me and from day one, they believed in me. They could have been more cautious and thought, "Well, you don't have any flying experience, this could all go horribly wrong." But they didn't. When someone or, even better, a collection of people, believes in you, it's incredibly empowering.

It was coming to the end of 2017 and I had this grand plan but I didn't have any sponsorship. I was continuing to fly as and when I could but trying to live and juggle the finances was tricky. I flew with Steve and Andy when they had the spare time to take me and they also gave me 'mates' rates', which was a big help. The challenge I had was financing this project.

Everything was coming together with Eddie from *GASE*. We were going back and forth with each other most days, discussing various routing options. He spent a lot of time putting together an itinerary that he knew would work well, taking me through the following countries: France, Italy, Croatia, Greece, Crete, Africa, Jordan, Saudi Arabia, Bahrain, UAE, Pakistan, India, Bangladesh, Burma, Thailand, Malaysia, Singapore, the Philippines, Taiwan, Japan, Russia, USA, Canada, Greenland, Iceland, Faroe Islands, Scotland and finally back to England.

There was plenty to think about and in the beginning, I was just one person spinning many different plates. One of the first tasks I set about was establishing a timeline, working back from the date I planned to depart. It was critical that I had a departure date fixed and I could work back from that.

It all sounded fairly straightforward on paper but in reality, there was a lot more to it. I had to be aware of weather, such as the monsoon season in India and South East Asia, as well as any political instability in certain countries that could jeopardise the project. Eddie had a very good handle on airspace restrictions, or 'no go' areas. I also had to consider how I was going to film and document everything on my own, or even if I would be allowed to film in some countries.

I had to start looking at how I was managing my time. Funding was by far my biggest undertaking, from a logistics and sponsorship perspective, and it needed to be managed in a more structured way. Just as I had done on all of my previous expeditions, I broke the tasks into key pillars with subtasks. It's typically referred to as outcome-based project management, which looked something like this:

Finance

This was always the top priority and I had to determine how much I thought the project was going to cost and implement a detailed budget, including purchasing the actual aircraft, fuel, accommodation, fees, servicing and any further training required, to name a few. All of these things had to be factored in, even if I wasn't sure what the actual cost would be. I then had to work out a plan for obtaining the funding: where was it going to come from, by when did I need it secured, how would I approach potential sponsors and what the different sponsorship packages might look like.

Technical

This was about the aircraft itself, what navigation kit I would require, safety equipment, clothing for different flying conditions, camera and laptop set-up, audio recording whilst flying, sat phones and tracking devices. I also included the route in this section, figuring out where I would stay, establishing contacts or seeing what accommodation

I could secure in each country prior to my arrival.

Media

My mission was to inspire a million young people around the world to pursue their own goals and dreams. I had to consider how I would achieve this, how it would be measured, who would organise the school visits and who would take care of the press. I had to be sure that I could deliver on the commitments and expectations I had made with sponsors. I also needed a strategy to maximise charity donations.

Skills

Did I have sufficient skills and experience to fly around the world? Who would be a suitable flying mentor? Did I have enough time to build my skills and what was the plan to obtain them?

I had spent many weeks designing and tweaking a business proposal for the project. It was fundamentally four simple elements and it has never failed me when it comes to securing sponsorship. I call it 'The Four Ws':

1. What am I doing?
2. Why am I doing it? (this one is the most important)
3. What can I give?
4. What do I want?

I worked on this business proposal until I thought it was good enough, remembering it was never going to be perfect. Preparation can often become procrastination which I have seen many times when advising other people and I didn't want to fall into the same trap. The most important part was proactively sending my proposal out to potential sponsors. I tried various approaches, sending it far and wide, to literally thousands of people, which did result in securing some funding. However, the tactic that probably yielded the best results was developing contacts and being introduced to potential backers. This meant I wasn't going in to a meeting cold – an introduction from a trusted source is invaluable.

This was how I met the first sponsor of the project: Jonathan Goldstein believed in what I was doing, why I was doing it and committed to helping me. Without his support, I don't think the project would have got off the ground. Jonathan ran a property development company in London and I met him through a connection with the charity, *Over The Wall*. He bid on an auction that was raising funds for the charity to complete the Three Peaks challenge. I was the person organising and leading the expedition. I think that Jonathan may have thought this was a good team-building weekend away for his staff. When they perhaps didn't share quite the same level of enthusiasm, he decided to invite his family along instead!

I remember the weekend well. I had some support from a friend called Rob, an ex-military guy and keen outdoor enthusiast, who I'd worked with some years ago. We also had another one of Rob's friends join us to assist with driving and general support. It was a tough weekend that I don't think they will forget in a hurry either. The weather was atrocious and the torrential rain and high winds certainly added a different dynamic, making it memorable for everyone. Whilst walking on the trails, I was chatting with Jonathan and his family about my plans to fly around the world and to try and speak in schools in every country I visited. He liked the sound of the project and said he would look into how he could help me. True to his word, he absolutely did follow through and I will be forever grateful for his backing.

Jonathan's support made the voyage viable and the project was now officially on. I let Steve and Andy know, who were keeping the Magni family updated back in Italy. I still needed further funding before I could place the order for the aircraft but it was now becoming more real. I was running on adrenaline for a good few days after learning the news.

When you are chasing something hard and making a monumental effort day in, day out, and for the most part, not really getting anywhere, you just have to persevere and eventually you will secure a win. It's an amazing feeling: it makes me feel alive, like I'm really achieving something. I also enjoy the thrill of the chase, identifying the right people, targeting them and proactively approaching them, trying new methods, constantly learning, honing my pitch with every phone call or email. Proactivity pays off, there are no two ways about it. How much it pays will depend on many variables, but if you put yourself out there and simply do not stop, you will eventually get what you are looking for and you will inspire people around you.

2018 was passing quickly. I was busy on the speaking circuit and when I wasn't speaking, I was spending my days at a co-working space in Basingstoke. I liked the discipline of getting up every day and going to a place of work. Looking back, it was the discipline and routine of getting up and simply turning up every day that kept me going. I'd often stay there until almost midnight and would get kicked out by Security. I made a lot of things happen from that office; often the biggest opportunities came from a time when I least wanted to do the work but I did it anyway.

Eddie had introduced me to a long-range helicopter pilot, Peter Wilson, who had just returned from flying around the world in a *Robinson R66*. Peter was a very experienced pilot, who conveniently lived fairly close by. Eddie thought he would be a good source of knowledge and support for me. There are many people who have thousands of flying hours around their local area but very few have flown around the world. Peter had also flown the first solo helicopter flight around Africa from London to Stellenbosch return in 2016, so he was very well-positioned to offer some guidance.

Peter was full of energy and enthusiasm. I instantly liked him: he was motivated, driven and was an absolute wizard with Excel spreadsheets. He had worked hard his whole life, building a successful business and had retired even harder. We met up many times, flying together regularly. Whilst I wasn't flying a helicopter around the world, the radio procedures were the same, so I would often operate the radio as we flew together, chatting. I wanted to get as much practice as I could.

It was now April 2018. My proactivity was paying off slowly but surely and my network of contacts was building. I was talking to more people and my pipeline of possible sponsorship from companies who had expressed an interest was expanding.

I had been introduced to a lady called Georgie, who had worked in the finance industry in the city for most of her career and was now moving into coaching. We met up a few times and I gave a talk at her old school. I was grateful that she went above and beyond trying to help me; she was well connected and introduced me to many different people. She even recruited the help of her brother, Tim, who also worked in finance. He thought my project would be something of interest to his boss so he kindly wrote an introductory email and it wasn't long before we got some positive feedback.

His boss was called David and he'd set up a company called *R3* and spent a lot of time based in New York City. I was not looking for a crazy amount of funding and really wanted to get in front of him. The only challenge I had was finding a space in David's very busy schedule. I knew I needed to see him whilst it was relatively fresh in his mind. He did agree to meet and passed me over to his PA to arrange something. I think the earliest date she offered me was two months away and she joked that, if I was in New York, I could see him almost any time.

It was a bit of a crazy idea but I quickly searched for flights to New York. Surprisingly, they were much cheaper than I'd thought. I emailed his PA and confirmed a date. I had very little money at the time and my bank account was running on fumes but something felt right. So I booked the cheapest hotel I could find and flew to New York the following week. I arrived and went straight to David's office from the airport. He was extremely personable and very complimentary about my accomplishments. We spoke about my flying project but I didn't want to force it upon him. He asked me what I was doing in New York. I replied, "Seeing you! I just arrived and go home tomorrow. You didn't have any dates available in London and I only have a certain amount of time." He looked at me for a while with a smile on his face, then said, "You are f**king crazy!" I laughed in response.

Some months later, David did sponsor the project and I learnt that it was actually his own money. I'm convinced that flying to New York to see him is what got that over the line. At times, it may not feel like it but people do appreciate it when you go the extra mile.

Another opportunity came up from a private philanthropist who wanted to underwrite the cost of the aircraft. I thought it was too good to be true. I still hadn't met him in person but I informed Andy and Steve that I thought we were potentially in a position to move forward with the aircraft build. The *Magni* factory runs flat out almost all of the time. *Magni* are very popular aircraft and scheduling a build can take some time. I was aware that it usually took at least three months from initial order to delivery. I had secured funding from Jonathan and, with the new offer of support, I took the risk and gave the go-ahead to proceed with the build. However, I was writing cheques I couldn't cash and I would learn the hard way.

I was so caught up in so many tasks, running all over the place, that I momentarily forgot about the aircraft until Andy called me to ask where we were with the finances. I needed to find out when the funding would be ready as we now had an aircraft that we needed to pay for. I spent a week trying to make contact with the philanthropist, to no avail. I was totally financially exposed and very anxious: I didn't have the money and should never have assumed that it was pending. When it comes to sponsorship, the deal is not done until you are looking at the funds in the project bank account. I received a call that I will always remember: "James, I'm sorry, I know you have been trying to contact me but I can't sponsor you any more (silence for 30 seconds). Sorry, I wish you well." As you can imagine, I didn't really know what to say and my heart sank.

It was my fault. I hadn't taken complete ownership of the situation and I should have managed the risk better and certainly qualified the opportunity more thoroughly. I was annoyed at myself and felt stupid. You only find out what someone is really like when you have to tell them something you know they won't want to hear. I was nervous about telling *Magni,* however, Luca couldn't have been more understanding. I had been on the phone for less than a minute, explaining the situation, when Luca interjected, "James, no worries, everything is OK, we sell that aircraft to someone else and build you a new one when you are ready." At that point, I realised they really were an amazing family and were absolutely the right people to be working with.

I was relieved that the aircraft could be sold to someone else and that my situation wasn't going to cause a problem. I was starting to feel overwhelmed and instead of focusing on one task at a time, my mind was just shutting down. I felt that I had bitten off far more than I could chew. I wondered if I should back out, return the funding that I had already received and just walk away. If I was ever going to do that, now would be the time. I could use the excuse that a major backer had pulled out and I had to postpone the project. It was only my mind talking: in my heart, I knew I wanted this and I also knew it wasn't going to be easy. If I had pulled out at that point, I would have regretted it for the rest of my life, and the one person you can never truly hide from is yourself.

I took a week off from working on the project to sit back and reflect on how far I had already come. I hadn't really had any major setbacks so far. I had sailed through my flight training much faster than the average student and I had already secured sponsorship from companies who were excited to work with me. I was lucky to have Eddie working on all the permits, we had a great route, a fantastic plan and in the grand scheme of things, I was doing incredibly well. But the brain is a funny old thing; it often overlooks the success in life and it's all too easy to find yourself dwelling on just the negatives.

I had to take a step back to see this and when I really thought about how far I'd come, I began to feel motivated again and put any thoughts of giving up behind me. Your mind can be your greatest ally, but for a lot of people, it is their greatest enemy and holds them back. I'd seen this first-hand and at times, I was susceptible to succumbing to this great enemy myself.

I had support from a lot of people and didn't want to let them down. I came back to the project with renewed energy and determination. I got straight back into it, following up leads and sending out sponsorship emails to companies and individuals who I'd not spoken to before.

12

Kindled Spirit

L ife can be strange at times. About a month after having to inform *Magni* that I didn't have sufficient funding, things started to happen that I wasn't expecting: emails that I had sent out months ago were leading to some interest in the project. An old boss, Dave Park, from my previous work life made contact with me; he was a great guy who rallied support for me when I rowed the Atlantic. Almost immediately, he was able to secure some funding from the company he was working for, *Fortinet*, as well as one of his customers, *Exclusive Networks*, in addition to making a personal donation. Another company, *Unaterra Global*, run by another David, came on board with assistance.

It was as if someone was looking down on me and thinking, "You really do want this, don't you? OK, you can have it!" I am not a religious person but I do absolutely believe in a higher power. Many times I have found myself in difficult situations, wanting to find an easy way out but have carried on. And every time, I have pushed myself, doing just that little bit more, hanging in there just that little bit longer, working through the challenge to get to the other side, and almost immediately, something amazing materialises. I think that's too much of a coincidence. These things have only happened when I have been right on the edge, about to stop and give up, but have made the conscious choice to keep going.

I now had sufficient funding to progress with the aircraft manufacture. I paid *Magni UK* and, a few weeks later, we headed back out to the factory. I cannot tell you how good it felt when I watched the first part of my aircraft being cut out on a CNC machine, the carbon fibre instrument panel. Luca and I had a photo taken together with it and I also signed my name on the engine that was going to be used for my aircraft. I will never forget that day!

It was now early June 2018. Peter and I had been regularly flying together in the *Robinson 66* G-DIGA helicopter. We flew up to Wrexham to meet one of Peter's sponsors, *Aircovers*, a small family business run by John and Sasha, who were friendly and enthusiastic. They supplied the best covers in the business, custom-made for military and civilian aircraft all over the world. Peter had informed them about my plans to fly around the world and they kindly offered to make a cover for my aircraft, which was greatly appreciated. John and Sasha also arranged for a local school to come along and sit in the helicopter; a lucky few were even taken for a quick spin with Peter.

It was a busy time for me. A few days later, I found myself standing in front of 500 people, speaking at an Awards Day at a lovely school in Surrey called St. Edmund's. I got chatting to the Marketing Manager, Emma-Jane, who was a vivacious person, always smiling. She wanted to find a way for the school to be involved with my trip and, true to her word, she did. She continued to lobby for me, making an introduction to her husband who worked in a senior position at a company called *Tealium*. The company was doing well and the founder was an American guy based out of San Diego. He was an ex-fighter pilot in the US Marines and flew F16s out of Miramar, which any *Top Gun* fan will recognise. Apparently, when he was told about my attempt to fly a gyroplane around the world, he said, "Jesus, if he is crazy enough to have a go at that, we will sponsor him!" I met him a few months later and I gave a keynote speech for the company.

I was soon heading back to the *Magni* factory in Milan. My aircraft had been built in half the time we had expected and I now had a production company that was interested in making a documentary about my project and following the journey. They were called *Film Farmers*, a young, dynamic and talented company. They had already produced some good content and the owner, Tom, thought he could probably secure a commission from a broadcaster.

The aircraft was only a day away from its first test flight and Luca asked me if I wanted to fly in the back. Obviously, I jumped at the chance! We thought it would make good content for the documentary as well. The first day was spent filming with *Film Farmers* in the factory. It proved to be a great location, with lots of interesting things to film: carbon fibre moulding, welding, CNC machines, paint spraying and engine test runs. I felt incredibly happy and could now really see the project coming together.

The following day, the aircraft was strapped onto a trailer and we drove to the *Magni* flying field for its maiden flight. The weather was perfect: no wind and beautifully warm. A small amount of fuel was poured into the aircraft, then Luca and I jumped in. I was dressed in just a shirt and jeans and wanted to get up into the air, just to cool off. The gyro fired into life and we were soon taxiing to the other end of the airfield. Before I knew it, we were lined up and then hurtling down the grass runway. There are very few people who know the limits of a *Magni Gyro* as well as Luca and he was only too willing to show me! I never knew it could do half the things that Luca was doing. We swooped over the guys filming a few times on the ground;

at one point, they leapt to the ground as we flew over them!

We landed five minutes later. Luca said, "It's good but it could be better, so we make further adjustment now." Up we went again, turning, climbing and descending our way around the sky. We had to stay below 500 feet AGL (above ground level) as we were not far from Milan Airport and had to fly under their zone. Luca was happy and on the last landing, he turned the engine off in the air and we just glided in. It all went silent apart from the "whoosh, whoosh, whoosh" of the blades above our heads. A perfect landing again from the master.

I was chatting with Steve at Popham a few days later and he informed me that 'G-KTCH' was available as my aircraft registration. Of course it was an absolute no-brainer and was meant to be. Things just kept getting better!

The team at *Magni*, Steve and Andy pulled a lot of strings to get the aircraft assembled quickly and fast-tracked its arrival back to the UK. It needed to have a CAA (*Civil Aviation Authority*) inspection but as expected, there were no issues. *Magni* knew that things were financially difficult for me and realised that I was not their typical customer, hustling for sponsorship to procure the machine. Luca pulled in a few favours from some of his suppliers, including *Beringer*, who supplied the wheels and brakes, as well as *Trig Avionics*, who donated a transponder and radio, all of which amounted to a good and gratefully received saving.

I remember the day that G-KTCH arrived at Popham. It was early August 2018 and I just couldn't stop looking at it, touching it, cleaning it and generally absorbing its presence. I was now the proud owner of an aircraft! How crazy was that? If someone had just cut a cheque for it in the beginning and I hadn't had to go through all the ups and downs of securing the funding, I don't think it would have meant half as much as it did.

I was chatting with my good friend, Richard Cribb, who runs *Kindled Spirit*, an anti-trafficking charity that supports young girls in India. He asked how I would feel if we called the aircraft *Kindled Spirit*. I liked the name: it had a record-breaking feel to it and it just felt right, so I agreed it would be called '*Kindled Spirit*' for promotion but for aviation purposes and radio comms, it would still need to be referred to as G-KTCH.

I was due to leave in November 2018 and it was starting to dawn on me that there was still an awful lot to do in less than three months. Steve suggested that I speak to Mike Pearson, the Airfield Manager at Popham, just to make sure he was happy for me to put out a public invitation and hold a press day. When we met, I instantly liked Mike and he couldn't have been more supportive. I updated him on the whole project and explained how difficult it had been just to get to where we were now. He kindly offered to help cover the cost of a marquee and said that ultimately, anything I needed on the day, he would organise.

I was also looking for some help with various admin tasks and Mike introduced me to Jude, who was brilliant. She had finished and moved on to what she thought was the next logical thing to be doing before I'd even asked her! She was also a pilot and did some freelance PR work for the *Royal Aero Club*. She was just the additional pair of proactive hands that I needed.

Everything felt right about Popham. I walked away from an almost fully-funded, six figure support package from a major finance company to underwrite the whole project because they wanted me to start and finish in Manchester. That put me in a tough position as I really needed the funding but it just didn't feel right. I had to trust my intuition that I was doing the right thing. There was also another reason why I wanted to leave from Popham. The airfield itself is still owned by the Church family. Charles Church was a very successful property developer and sold many high-end houses around the UK. He also had a passion for aviation but tragically, he was involved in an accident in 1989 whilst flying his *Spitfire* in Hampshire and was killed. Although I never met Charles, I had a gut feeling that he would have liked what I was doing and been very supportive too.

I was spending a lot of time organising and not as much time practising my flying as I would have liked, but it was a necessary evil. There was a lot of responsibility on my shoulders: I'd been given substantial sponsorship funds and people were watching me.

I was now in the process of putting together a more solid media plan and followed up with a contact that my first sponsor, Jonathan from *Cain international*, had put me in touch with. Emma was the CEO of a major PR firm in London called *Newgate Communications*, typically working in the commercial property sector. They had a good understanding of sponsorship and, although they represented one of my main sponsors, they also appreciated that I had others to consider as well. I will be eternally grateful for the support that Emma decided to give me: it was all pro bono and added an extra workload to an already packed list of clients that they had to service on a daily basis.

Emma introduced me to Guy and Louise who would implement the media campaign and work with me on an almost daily basis as the project got going. The first task was to organise the press releases. Both Louise and Guy advised me that the press moves very quickly so we didn't need to be contacting anyone just yet. I knew I had absolutely fallen on my feet with the support from *Newgate* so that freed up some of my time.

I was now fascinated with the weather, watching it every day, trying to notice patterns and see how the weather actually compared to what the forecast had predicted. I wanted to start flying in conditions that pushed me a bit more; it was all pretty easy flying around in light winds with perfect visibility but it was not going to replicate some of the conditions I would inevitably face whilst flying around the world. I noticed on the forecast that there was a day approaching that was quite windy. There was no way that Steve would have been teaching students in that wind, so I asked if he would fly with me to give me some high wind flying experience, which he thought was a good idea. It was blowing pretty hard at around 40 knots. The sound of the wind whistling through the trees made it feel a lot stronger and, apart from the staff, there was no one at the airfield, let alone flying – just me and Steve getting suited up. I was actually quite nervous.

The plan was to do a few circuits and practise landing in high winds. We lined up on the runway and had plenty of time as no one else was around. Instead of using the pre-rotator, the rotor started spinning up just by the wind alone, so I gently let the stick come back which would cause the rotors to spin up even more. I gradually fed power in to get us moving down the runway and within what felt like seconds, just the wind and our forward motion had the rotors spinning up nicely. I pushed the throttle forward and up we went. The wind instantly got under the gyro and pitched the nose up; our ground speed was very slow at 25 mph but we had over 80 mph indicated air speed. I was holding the stick hard: I'm not sure how Steve knew but he said, "Just relax, let the aircraft do the work."

As we flew downwind of the runway, the aircraft accelerated with the wind behind it. The ground was hurtling past below me and we were literally being blown all over the place. I was nervous and didn't feel in control. We made a turn onto the base leg of the circuit and it felt even worse! At 800 feet, it was certainly gusting harder than 40 knots. I remember shouting down the radio to Steve, "We must be right on the limits, Steve!" He replied, "Take your hands off the stick." "WHAT?" I shouted. "Just take your hands off the stick, NOW!" he replied with more authority. At first, I kept my hands close to the stick but eventually put my hands up to show Steve in the back that

I'd followed his command.

Something happened that day… every time the aircraft pitched, rolled and yawed in every possible direction, it would stabilise itself, coming back to the same position. I started to realise just how amazingly capable this aircraft really was, and this was certainly the type of flying and learning that I desperately needed. After almost an hour of being thrown all over the sky, we landed and came in for a debrief. I said, "Wow, that was fun! I was a little nervous to begin with but that was amazing!" Steve chuckled and calmly said, "Yes, I could tell." He went on to explain that a gyro is probably the most stable aircraft in the world, which can be flown in almost any wind. The limitations are more to do with the pilot than the machine itself. I left with a new-found confidence, with a feeling that my flying had moved up a notch that day.

I had a photo shoot coming up with a friend and needed to get the sponsorship graphics and logos onto the aircraft, which had been produced by Martyn at *Camberley Signs*. I'd been side-tracked and ended up putting them on at about 1am in the hangar with the help of my brother, Jeremy. Once we had the graphics on, G-KTCH, aka *Kindled Spirit*, looked absolutely amazing. The gyro came alive and certainly looked the part! The photo shoot went really well and we captured some fantastic pictures.

It was now the start of October and I had about a month before I was planning to depart. I needed to head back over to *Magni* to collect a few things that they had made for me. I felt that I needed to be flying more on my own so I decided to fly G-KTCH to the *Magni* factory in Italy.

I was a little more nervous than usual but overall felt quite comfortable. Apart from a few weather delays through France, the journey was going well, until I passed the town of Valence. I needed to fly over some higher ground around 2,000 feet, as there was a nuclear power plant situated next to the river with a restricted zone around it. This wasn't a problem so I climbed up to around 3,000 feet. My ground speed was now just over 105 knots and I had a fairly strong tailwind. As I climbed up, I could see the town of Montelimar. I flew over the top of the hill and noticed a massive amount of acceleration, as if a rocket had just been ignited.

My ground speed on the GPS accelerated to 135 knots and I was losing height fast. The ground was coming up at me worryingly quickly and the aircraft was being thrown all over the place. It was only the training that I'd had with Steve a few weeks earlier that gave me the confidence to know that the aircraft could handle high wind. As I was descending fast, I applied full power and tried to slow the aircraft up so I was not driven into the ground by the downdraft. I was now climbing, so reduced the power and trimmed the aircraft (by taking the force off the stick). I was sweating and holding the stick for dear life. Every muscle in my body was tensed up and I knew I needed to relax. Montelimar had high ground all around it and is built in a valley next to a river; the wind was now funnelling through this area and was much stronger than before. I felt out of control and was trying not to panic. My eyes were drawn to the large, green, open space of the airfield, so without hesitation, I headed straight for it and no matter what, I was landing the aircraft there.

I set the frequency into the radio (I always keep a selection of frequencies of airfields that I'm passing written down) but had no reply. I was now turning into the wind and the aircraft came to a grinding halt. I had about 70 mph on the air speed indicator but could see below that I was not going anywhere. I slowly approached the airfield and the wind was straight down the runway so it wasn't too difficult to land. I needed to be so careful once I had landed: if I moved the stick in the wrong position and the wind got under my rotors whilst they were still spinning, it would simply roll the aircraft over and would no doubt completely write it off. I landed and was relieved to be on the ground! I taxied over to some hangars where I saw a small helicopter company with their doors opened. They spoke good English and commented, "A little windy today." "Yes," I replied.

I had some coffee and the owner showed me around some of the two-seater helicopters that they made. The company was called *Heli Tech* and their aircraft looked very well-engineered. He then took me over to meet a guy called Pascal who owned a French gyroplane manufacturer called *DTA*. Pascal spoke good English and shook my hand. He showed me his workshop and hangar and he also had a flight school and accommodation built inside the hangar. He said I could stay there if I needed to. I explained my plans to fly across to *Magni*, but had been struggling with the weather. "It's not a good time of year now, very few good flying days," he said. It was now starting to rain so I'd certainly made the right decision to land, and what were the chances of landing at a gyro school?

It was obvious that I wasn't going anywhere that day and I was quite restless for the remainder of the afternoon. The forecast had changed and was now showing rain for the rest of the week. I wanted to get to *Magni* but I could not sit there for days, waiting for better weather at a time of year when it's not particularly good anyway. It dawned on me that this was as far as I was going to get. I couldn't even fly home as I was now stuck in bad weather.

It was a bit of a logistical nightmare but I decided that I would get the train to Lyon, fly home, collect my car and trailer and drive back to pick up the gyro. I would then deliver it to Milan as *Magni* needed to fit something, then I'd take it home. I was quite disappointed about this decision but knew I had made every possible effort. I went to bed that night in the hangar's student accommodation, staring at the plywood walls, facing the stark reality that I wasn't ready to fly around the world. I needed more time to build up my experience.

The following day, I explained my revised plan to Pascal who was more than happy for me to leave my gyro there for a few days.

Within 48 hours of arriving home, I was on a ferry from Dover to Calais with a trailer that Andy had kindly lent me. It took me a day to drive to Montelimar. I dropped the trailer off that evening at the airfield and checked into a hotel. The next day, I collected the aircraft and Pascal helped me take the rotors off and secure everything to the trailer. I now had the best part of a day to get to Milan and a beautiful drive through the Alps. I arrived just before Luca was going home, so we had a quick coffee and a catch-up chat. Seeing Luca was always uplifting: he is an extremely positive person and fun to be around. I left the car and gyro on the trailer and gave the keys to Luca. They needed the gyro for a few days so I told them to just keep it for the week and that I'd fly back to get it. Luca dropped me off at Milan Malpensa Airport and l flew back home.

I now had the pressing matter of informing my sponsors that I had made the decision to delay my project until spring the following year. I was not ready to leave and I needed more time. I also needed to inform *Newgate Communications* who were busy priming their contacts for a press release. It effectively gave me another five months to build hours and gain further experience.

I emailed and called all of my sponsors. I was anxious about telling them that I had delayed my departure date, however, I knew only too well the importance of communication, so I hoped that by explaining my reasoning, they would understand. I remember talking to Fiona, who at the time was Head of Global Sponsorship for *DHL*. I had worked with *DHL* before on another project and Fiona had pulled a few strings for me this time round for which I was grateful. She thought it made total sense and thanked me for updating her. Every other sponsor agreed that it was the right thing to do and the more I thought about it, the more I realised that perhaps it was meant to be.

13

Things Happen for a Reason

It was hard to see at the time but I think the difficulty I faced on that European solo flying adventure was a turning point for the project. Initially I was having a bit of a wobble and that overwhelming feeling of "I've bitten off more than I can chew" came back. I really struggled mentally and I'm embarrassed to admit it but I was looking for a way out without losing my credibility. Thankfully, I had enough maturity and life experience to realise that backing out was never an option, so I was able to push on.

Anyone can make up a believable excuse to stop – that's the easy option – but it takes sheer determination to keep going. This was my career and my life: I had put everything into this and so far had left nothing on the table. Knowing that kept me going, but most importantly, I had the right people around me who continued to support and encourage me.

I had often highlighted to teenagers when I was speaking in schools, that the people you have in your life and who you hang around with are so important. "You are who you spend your time with,"

I told them. It was having the right people around me that kept me believing that I could do this.

Every now and then, I would hear of someone saying I had no chance of getting round the world with my limited experience. I'd come across these types of people before, who often weren't particularly experienced themselves. These people call themselves realists, but are actually quite negative and in some cases, can be quite argumentative. I had learnt over the years to never meet negativity with negativity, I personally meet it with extreme positivity.

The most effective form of learning is practice, not planning, and I had now identified that I needed more experience and had taken the appropriate action to gain further experience. I booked to go to Avignon where there was a *Magni* flying school run by a pilot called Jean Christophe. Luca knew him, he was an experienced guy and agreed to do some mountain flying with me. Before I could visit him, I needed to collect my aircraft from *Magni* as they had now completed a few outstanding actions.

My dad and I flew out to *Magni* and drove *Kindled Spirit* back on the trailer together. It was a big help having dad with me and between us, we drove almost non-stop from Milan to Calais. There was no way that I would have been able to do that on my own and it was more tiring than I thought. We made it back to Popham the next morning, both exhausted.

As I had decided not to depart until the end of March 2019, I now had time to take advantage of a fantastic opportunity to do some fixed-wing flying. A few months earlier, I was invited to give a talk at a flying club based out of Wellesbourne, called *Take Flight Aviation*, run by a guy called Mike and his marketing assistant, Hannah. They had a great little club with hundreds of members and agreed to give me some free flying instruction, which worked out at just enough to obtain my fixed-wing licence, in return for a talk to their club members. That worked perfectly for me and was a thoroughly enjoyable evening. A chap came up to me that evening and said, "Hello James, you don't have any idea who I am, do you?" I was actually puzzled and said, "Sorry I don't." He replied, "It's your old next-door neighbour, Bill, I took you flying out of Popham when you were a kid." "Bloody hell, yes I remember!" was my response. Bill wanted to congratulate me. I couldn't believe it! My first memory of Popham airfield was with him and his son, Jonathan, a very long time ago now.

I'd already had a couple of lessons with one of their senior instructors, David Donovan, who was an amazing guy and great fun to fly with. He had been flying for most of his life. In the day, he flew for a regional airline and in his spare time, he was an instructor with *Take Flight*. I informed David that I was moving my departure date back so we could continue flying and I'd put in for my test at the end of the year. Whilst it wasn't gyro flying, it was still flying and the more time I could spend in the air, the better. We racked up the hours quite quickly and it didn't take long before I was flying solo. I actually found the aircraft very easy to fly once I had built up a few hours and got some landings under my belt. David would always show me just how capable the little Cessna 152 really was, throwing it all over the sky and demonstrating stalls. It was thoroughly enjoyable.

December 2018 was an incredibly busy month. I managed to get out to France to fly with Jean Christophe for a few days, where we flew up to Gap in the Alps and to the Italian border. We discussed mountain flying and a few general things to be aware of. It was really just to give me some experience flying in mountainous terrain that I needed. I was chatting with Mike at Popham on a fairly regular basis and he advised me that he knew Geoffrey Boot who manages the records for the *Royal Aero Club* on behalf of the *Fédération Aéronautique Internationale* (FAI). I needed to see Geoffrey anyway, so the discussion couldn't have been timed better.

The *FAI* is the governing body for all aviation records. It was founded in 1905 when it became apparent that there needed to be a governing body to ratify and authorise claims when aviation records were booming in the early days of flight. The *Guinness World Records* do issue records independently from the *FAI* but they are usually issued with guidance from the *FAI*. It was critical that my flight met the criteria set out by the *FAI* in order to set an official *FAI* flight around the world and to be recognised by the *Guinness World Records*.

I was looking forward to meeting Geoffrey. *The Royal Aero Club* was important as they would manage my *FAI* records. Geoffrey held over 300 records and Mike spoke very highly of him. He also lived in a castle, which I thought was pretty cool! I drove to meet him in December and he was very supportive. We spent quite a while chatting about flying and some of my other adventures, as well as his own flying records. He also introduced me to Hannah, who worked with Geoffrey as his assistant within the various businesses that he owned and ran. All his work with the *Royal Aero Club* was voluntary. I gave him a copy of my book and then spent some time chatting with Hannah, before driving home. She was a great help and said, "All you need to do is get the papers signed, send them to me and I'll take care of everything." "Brilliant!" I thought.

2018 was coming to an end and what a year it had been. I was able to complete my fixed-wing training and passed my General Flying test on 28th December 2018 at Wellesbourne, with an instructor called Pete, who flew private jets for a living.

2019 got off to a good start. I was flying as much as I could, building up the hours. It was very cold flying an open cockpit aircraft in January but I figured it was all good training. If I couldn't cope with flying in the UK winter, how on earth would I be able to fly in Siberia and Greenland? I was experimenting with different clothing combinations and glove types. The cameras wouldn't last long in the cold conditions and no matter how many socks I wore, my feet were always cold. Steve was using an electric jacket that I thought might have some potential but in the end, I found a solution that worked well. It was made up of multiple layers of base clothing and then a large down jacket that I'd worn on Everest, plus a cold weather flying suit underneath. It was tricky to get into the gyro at times, as I was like a Michelin man sitting in the aircraft!

January and February literally flew past and I was still working through my 'To Do' list. I needed to collect my life raft from *Survitec* who had kindly sponsored my dry suit, life raft and flying suit. I was very fortunate to have been put in contact with a guy called Stewart, who provided safety equipment for the *BAE* test pilots. I was introduced to Stewart through a guy called Mark, who had been a Fast Jet pilot and was now in a managerial role within *BAE*. When I was explaining to Mark that I needed a good dry suit and life raft, he said, "Now that I can help you with," and mentioned Stewart's name. *Survitec* were based near Liverpool and we thought it would be a good idea to do a test session with the dry suit and life raft in the pool. The suit was absolutely amazing: it was so buoyant that at one point, I thought about not even taking a life raft. I wanted to replicate the clothing I'd have on if I was to ditch, so I had all the underlayers on under the suit, plus my boots. It didn't let a single drop of water in – I was very impressed. The small, one-man life raft was tricky to get into but once I knew the technique, it was easy.

I had about a month left before I was due to depart on 31st March 2019. Eddie and I had been chatting almost every day and, every time I flew, I would call him from the aircraft. I had found a device that allowed me to connect my phone to my headset so that I could make calls from the air. Eddie was amazed at how good it was. He often asked me if I was flying or at home when I called!

There had been some troubles developing in Pakistan and it was obvious that tension was building. A military plane had been shot down and it was drawing enough attention that it was on the mainstream news most evenings. Eddie was very concerned that this was going to scupper our plans to fly from Khasab UAE across to Gwadar and Karachi in Pakistan. I did not have the range to cut these stops out and fly directly to India. If there was a problem here, it would cause a major issue. Eddie called one evening to say that a NOTAM (Notice To Airman) had been issued and Pakistan had shut their airspace to all traffic. Not even British Airways was permitted to fly there. It was on the news the very same evening.

I remember saying to Eddie, "We are stuffed, mate." He replied, "No we're not." Parts of Russia had been open for quite a few years now and a number of aircraft had flown from Japan into Russia, and onwards to Alaska. My Russian leg was going to be managed by Evgeny Kabanov who ran a company called *MAC General Aviation Services*. Evgeny was an experienced helicopter pilot himself and had flown extensively all over the country. Peter Wilson had expressed an interest in a VFR (visual flight rules) route across Russia and had been in close communication with Evgeny who had been working on this as an option to open up Russia to GA (General Aviation). Eddie wasn't sure if it was possible yet but we put the question to Evgeny. We received the good news that it was possible: it was a complete game changer.

There was a lot of uncertainty with routing through the Middle East, India, Asia and Japan. The weather posed a big challenge, as I'd needed to take into account the monsoon season, which comes and goes at different times across the whole Asia region. The bureaucracy in certain places would also inevitably make this route tricky, but I knew it could be achieved.

We confirmed with Evgeny that we wanted to move forward with this new option and he provided a complete route and a letter of invitation for me to obtain a Russian visa. There was now a lot of work to do: Jude had arranged school visits and Eddie had been utilising his contacts to line up talks as well. I wasn't just flying – I had committed to visiting schools en route. All of these meetings effectively needed to be cancelled, however Jude suggested that we do not cancel them completely but offer to do them online. That way, we were not completely letting them down.

This drastic route change did cut the number of countries that I would fly through by almost half, which was a shame as I was looking forward to experiencing the many different cultures and countries. However, when one door closes, another one opens and the opportunity to fly the entire length of Russia was simply amazing.

As this route was a lot more direct than my originally planned itinerary through Asia, I would need to fly additional miles in the US because I had to cover a minimum distance in order to set the *FAI* record. This was no problem as I had a soft spot for North America, having already cycled across the country twice. Eddie and I discussed the option of landing in every mainland state, so he set about looking at a possible route, utilising his contacts. I was very excited at the prospect of flying through Russia.

I also informed Guy and Louise at *Newgate Communications* of the new route, who were now working hard to pull together the press launch. We launched the project a couple of weeks before departure: any earlier and it would have been old news. I had been introduced to a photographer called Andrew Wilkinson; we did a couple of photo shoots at Popham and my goodness, I was blown away at just how amazing his pictures were. I don't really like looking at pictures of myself but he somehow had this ability to make me look really cool!

The press launch was unbelievable. *Sky News* came along and I presented down the wire live into the studio, giving a tour of my aircraft. Guy played the footage back and I was pretty chuffed with how it went. *Channel 5* came along and I took Simon Vigar flying, one of the news reporters. Simon had interviewed me the best part of five years ago when I returned from cycling around the world. He remembered the day and they even cut to some of that old footage for their gyro piece. We managed to get some fantastic air-to-air shots as well, thanks to Steve who had a cameraman in the back of his gyro, wielding a huge, broadcast-quality camera. The day couldn't have gone any better. I had now officially launched my campaign to become the first person to fly a gyroplane around the world and inspire a million young people along the way.

The story went far and wide around the world. *CNN* picked it up, as well as many other news outlets, thanks to the *Press Association* who put it out on their wires. It developed so much interest that the *BBC* wanted to come along to film and asked if we could do a live piece from the aircraft. They wanted to go live at 9am the following day and Steve was on hand to help. There were some low clouds that had formed close to the ground overnight but it was just good enough to fly a tight circuit above the airfield and swoop down in front of their camera. Some precision flying needed to happen in order to get the timing right: their reporter was in the back and he would broadcast from his phone. Just at the right time when we flew past, they would switch to the cameraman on the ground who was also broadcasting back to the studio.

Before I took off, Steve said to me, "If this cloud rolls in over the airfield and you get stuck, don't panic, you have over two hours' worth of fuel, just fly around until it clears, which it will do as it warms up. Remember, flying the aircraft always comes before any filming." He was absolutely right: it didn't go unnoticed that Steve always had my back and I really appreciated it. It's easy to get excited and carried away when you have done something many times before, but one moment of complacency can be potentially devastating.

Steve was on the ground with a handheld radio talking to the cameraman who was communicating to the studio, then he would give me the timings over the radio. We flew past the camera low and slow in order to stay in the shot longer. We landed and the cameraman said, "That was amazing – the timings were great and the studio loved it!" When we watched it back later, it was actually pretty cool: a live interview from a flying gyro!

I had to ask myself if this was really happening. Five months ago, I was looking for a way out, feeling completely overwhelmed and my confidence in bits. It's amazing what 'keeping going' can do! I couldn't have been happier and, most importantly, I felt ready.

The PR was an important part of the project, not necessarily for myself, more so for my sponsors, to prove to them that they had backed a credible and capable project. It had been a tough journey just getting to this point. All the travel I had been doing and the unexpected items that I needed to purchase meant that I had burnt through more cash than expected. I had a chat with my contact, Derek, at *Barratt Homes*, who spoke to David, the CEO, to see what they could do. They were very impressed with the media interest that we had recently generated, which was down to the hard work of Guy and Louise. Derek confirmed that they would provide some additional support, which really helped take the pressure off, financially.

I made a list of the people who I wanted to contact before I left and things I still needed to wrap up. I wanted to get in touch with Laura who I'd not spoken to since we agreed to go our separate ways. I realised that I'd been completely obsessed with flying and securing funding for my trip, so I felt I needed to apologise for being wrapped up in myself.

I had a few flights that I'd committed to giving and there was one flight in particular that I wanted to complete. My friend, Pru, was working on a book with a guy called John Wilkinson, who had a very rare and aggressive type of face cancer and had been battling the awful disease since 2017. Pru had told John about me and he wanted to meet me! So one afternoon, John came down to the airfield; he was a tall guy who towered over me. In his former life, he'd been an accomplished rugby player and corporate executive. His condition must have made things very difficult but he was remarkably upbeat and positive, which I found very inspiring. I asked if he fancied going flying and he was very keen. Unfortunately, the weather did not allow the flight that day, so I promised John that I would take him flying as soon as I returned. Sadly, John lost his battle with cancer and I was upset that I wasn't able to honour the flight that I promised him. He was however able to publish his book before he died, *Face Cancer*, and all net proceeds go to cancer charities.

I was in communication with Mike who was managing the logistics for the departure day at the airfield and organising the marquee and barbecue. He was a little anxious and pointed out to me that I had effectively invited potentially millions of people across the country to come to Popham for a free barbecue and to watch me take off!

Through the fixed-wing flying at Wellesbourne, I had got to know the owner of *FarmFoods*, a great guy who flew when his schedule allowed. He kindly put some funding into the project and agreed to sponsor the barbecue for 500 people – burgers, sausages, drinks and buns – everything we needed. The only challenge was where we were going to store it. I was running around doing various last-minute things and we needed to collect the food. Thankfully, Mike volunteered and drove to Sunbury to collect everything.

Even the night before my departure I was busy. It happened to be my dad's birthday so the whole family went out for a lovely meal in London. We had a great evening and I went to bed that night, happy in the knowledge that I had done everything I could to be ready. That was a good feeling!

14

Off Round the World

I was up early and the first thing I did was look out of the window. It was a good picture: clear skies and calm conditions, which would hopefully remain the case. I had been checking the forecast daily for the past week and, apart from the wind being forecast to pick up a little, it was going to be clear all day.

I didn't really know what to expect in terms of a turnout. I knew Steve and Andy had put the word out to other gyro pilots to pop down, even if it was just for a free burger! I had pumped quite a bit out on social media and had also invited the whole country via live TV only a few weeks earlier…so this was going to be interesting!

My good friend, Ian, had driven down from Cardiff and had kindly volunteered to film the departure. Ian and I drove to the airfield in the morning. It was quite surreal seeing a bright yellow AA sign featuring the 'James Ketchell Event'. Of course, I had to take a picture of it!

At the airfield, I had quite a lot to pack into the aircraft so I went into the hangar, pulled her out and started packing my kit, cameras, laptop and clothes away. I had tried to pack as light as possible but still probably had too much. I needed to get everything organised and my pre-flight checks completed before people started arriving. I wanted to be able to relax and have the chance to casually chat with people who had made the effort to come and see me, especially considering that it was also Mother's Day.

The next job was to taxi the aircraft up to the marquee, which was positioned just next to the clubhouse garden. We parked G-KTCH, aka *Kindled Spirit*, beside the marquee where we had a large banner with all the project sponsors' logos. It looked really smart. We suggested to guests an arrival time of midday, however there was already a crowd gathering by 10am.

The Mayor of Basingstoke kindly accepted our invitation and also agreed to say a few words. Luca and some of the Magni family had made the trip over from Milan. Richard from *Kindled Spirit* and a representative from *Over The Wall* were invited to say a few words too, along with Jonathan from *Cain Intentional*, Luca and finally, myself. It was now approaching midday so Jude started to usher people into the marquee. I had been busy chatting with friends and sponsors so was unaware of the number of people who had now arrived and were congregating in groups, chatting amongst themselves. I guess I was a bit wrapped up in the moment, so also hadn't noticed the rows of gyroplanes that had flown in to support me!

No sooner had the speeches finished, I was whisked off to the briefing room. Steve had arranged for a few other gyros to take off before me and fly in an arrow formation for a final fly past, before I broke off to the south to my first stop. Steve briefed everyone so that we all knew our roles. We left the meeting room and struggled to get through the crowd queuing for the barbecue: the idea of having free burgers and sausages turned out to be a major hit.

Mike needed to sign my *FAI* paperwork before I left: the first of many signatures that I would need. As I walked back to the aircraft, a few marshals pushed the gyro out from the fenced-off area to the apron, where I would get in and start it up. I was aware that time was passing and in order to stay on schedule, I needed to get going. Yet at the same time, I felt a bit guilty that I couldn't talk to everyone who wanted to have a chat. As if he was reading my mind, Peter Wilson said, "Get a move on, you're behind schedule!"

As the aircraft was positioned away from the crowd, I had a better perspective on how many people had actually made the effort to come and see me off. There were over 500 well-wishers and it was quite overwhelming. I thought, "Whatever you do, don't mess this up!" I put my helmet on and stepped into the aircraft. I attached my iPad to my knee board that was running navigational software and strapped my pilot notepad to the other leg. I switched the fuel pumps on and pressed the engine start button. G-KTCH roared into life, along with my heart rate! I let the engine idle for a few minutes before I released the brake and slowly taxied, waving at the crowd, recognising many faces. It would be impossible for me to list every individual but I cannot thank everyone enough who turned out to support me that day.

I taxied to the holding point for Runway 08. Although I was at maximum weight, the aircraft was off the ground in no time at all. I flew slowly at 60 mph at around 20 feet off the ground, waving at everyone as I passed. We all flew a circuit and positioned ourselves to fly over the runway in combination. I made my last call on the radio, "Golf-Charlie-Hotel, departing the circuit to the south, for a flight around the world."

I wasn't on my own for long. Peter Kosogorin had flown his gyro all the way down from Blackpool that morning, with his son. It was a big effort which I appreciated. I slowed down to allow Peter to catch up with me. We flew alongside each other for 15 minutes, taking photos and waving, before he peeled off and started his journey home.

I was flying to Goodwood Aerodrome on my first day, which was only a 30-minute flight. It wasn't long before I'd established communication with them and was on the final approach to land. The last time I was there was over a year ago when I flew my first solo cross-country qualifying flight. Ian was on his way down to film the following day and we'd booked a hotel for the night. I was unpacking my kit and saw Norman Surplus walking over. "That was a fantastic send-off," Norman said. "Yeah, I was really blown away," I replied. I needed to head over to the office to pay my landing fees, so we walked over together, to discover that the fees had been kindly waived.

Norman had no plans that evening, apart from finding a hotel. He wanted to see me off the following day, so I suggested he came back to the hotel where Ian and I were staying and have dinner with us. That evening, we all tucked into a large pub dinner, which was just what I needed after a day of running on adrenaline.

I was up early at around 6am and Ian was also up and making a cup of tea. I checked the weather, which was good and I had my flight plan ready to file for Le Touquet. We grabbed breakfast and headed over to the airfield. I had just pulled the aircraft out of the hangar and James, from *Vaaru Cycles*, had arrived to say hello and wave me off. He lived in Chichester which was only down the road but it was nice of him to pop along. I needed to put my dry suit on: even though crossing the English Channel was not a great distance, the suit gave me a bit more confidence over the water. I had two flights to complete: Goodwood to Le Touquet, then on to Alencon, where I had the first of my school visits.

Before I left, I thanked everyone for coming along and agreed to stay in touch with Norman. As I left the coastline, I thought, "OK, this is it." I could see that Eddie was tracking me and sending me messages via *Facebook* as I still had good phone signal.

It was a fairly quick flight across the Channel, at around 20 minutes. I was soon flying low-level along the coast and would be given clearance to join the circuit on a final approach to land on Runway 13 at Le Touquet. I wanted to get my dry suit off as I was overheating and needed to use the toilet urgently! Customs has always been very efficient and quick in Le Touquet and this time was no different.

It was good to see the guys from Popham – Harry, Alistair and Andy – who had flown across to meet me for lunch. We didn't have a massive amount of time so we ordered a taxi into town for a quick bite to eat. The sun was shining, people were wandering around, smiling and happy, and it would have been very easy to have sat there all day eating, drinking and watching the world go by. However, that wasn't possible and it was time to head back to the airport. I said goodbye to the guys and thanked them for coming over.

I took off to the south and flew southwest to Alencon; the sun was now low and I was flying straight into it but it was beautiful. The air was cooling which made for a very smooth flight and, although I had the noise of the engine, it felt quite peaceful. There was no controller at Alencon and no other aircraft in the circuit so I flew a direct approach and came straight in to land.

There was a small crowd waiting for me, including a few local news reporters, armed with cameras and microphones. Jude had been in touch with an English gentleman called David who was now living in Alencon. He organised visits between my home town of Basingstoke and Alencon, which are twinned towns. Jude had set up a two-day itinerary of school visits and a lunch meeting with the local mayor. The local aero club had kindly offered the use of their hangar to put the aircraft in for the duration of my stay. A few parents had brought their children along to have a look at the gyro so I got a little side-tracked from the packing up of kit and ended up letting kids take turns sitting in the aircraft. David politely reminded me that we needed to get back to the hotel so I took the hint!

We had a pleasant evening where I was introduced to some of David's friends over a meal. I retired to my room where I began to work out a routine for uploading my assets from the day, mostly video footage and some pictures. I needed to get cracking with editing a vlog and planned to upload a video at least every other day, if possible. It would prove to be very time-consuming but was by far the most engaging way to share the journey.

The next day I was up early again. We arrived at the first school, where I was welcomed with a large banner saying, "Welcome, Captain Ketch!" Everyone was very friendly and I gave the talk to the children, speaking slowly. David and the teacher would translate when necessary and asked the children questions to make sure they understood. I could tell that some of them understood when they laughed at my jokes. It was only a short talk, as I shared pictures and videos from past adventures and ultimately things that I had learnt which I thought may be of value to them.

David explained that the second school may be slightly different as it was a school for young people who were not suited to the mainstream school system. Some had been in trouble and were given the option of a young offenders' jail or attending this school, and many pupils had come from challenging backgrounds and circumstances. From what David had told me, I was really looking forward to meeting them. I wanted to tell my story but also highlight to them that, whilst I was never badly behaved as such, I did really struggle in school and into my early twenties. Never in a million years did I think that I would have accomplished all that I have, let alone now be flying around the world. I believe that everyone has varying degrees of potential but sometimes they just need a little help to bring it out.

The audience was a group of young adults, all living on site. We had two translators as I gave the talk and I was told that I had at least an hour. I could see by their reaction that they were generally engaged, even though only a few of them could speak English. I ended the talk and asked if there were any questions. Almost immediately, most of them put their hands up, asking all sorts of questions. The bell rang for the end of the session but not one person got up to leave. The support staff looked surprised: this was now their free time so they could have gone if they wanted to but they all chose to stay. The support staff communicated to David that they had never seen them engage with anyone like that before and that I had a gift! I often think about those young individuals and hope they are doing well.

The following day was a busy one. The press wanted me to make a couple of flights around the airfield so they could film me flying and landing. I had lunch with the local mayor, said a few words at a presentation ceremony and visited an English-speaking group.

I was due to leave on 4th April and only had a short flight to Troyes. However, I wasn't flying anywhere just yet as there was fog down to the ground. David and his wife had an apartment in a high-rise building with a fantastic view, which was the perfect place to keep an eye on the fog. I departed just after 1.40pm, by which time the weather was lovely, with just a few light, fluffy clouds higher up and bright blue sky. I was heading east, passing south of Paris whilst remaining outside their Class A airspace. I flew an almost straight line all the way to Troyes, just passing through some light rain about 10 miles from my destination.

I was familiar with Troyes as I had now been there a few times but this was the first time that I was staying overnight. Eddie mentioned that there was a hotel right next to the airport, which couldn't have been any easier. There was no hangar that I could use but that wasn't a problem: as long as I secured the rotors to stop them moving up and down in the wind, my *Aircovers* cover would protect the aircraft from virtually anything. I looked at the charts on my iPad and called Eddie to look at our options for the following day.

I had two days to get to Friedrichshafen where my aircraft was going to be on display on the *Magni* stand for the duration of the Aero Expo. I could have flown there in one flight but even if I broke the trip into two days, I was still arriving too early. We looked at Colmar as a stopover option, which was still in France but positioned right on the German border. I agreed with Eddie that it looked perfect, as it didn't have its own controlled airspace and the airport was small. We did wonder if autogyros were permitted to land there but Eddie found a handler who told us that we would be more than welcome and he would sort everything out, for a very small charge. Knowing that I was flying to Colmar the following day, I retired to my room where I had to fight off the sleep demons to stay awake, in order to process my video footage and reply to various emails.

I woke up at 6am with the laptop still on top of me with a dead battery. I only had a short flight ahead of me again so I didn't need to rush, but was still back at the airport for 9am. I paid my landing fees then walked across to the back of the apron to unwrap G-KTCH and get everything packed away, ready for another day. I took off and continued heading east.

Colmar was situated in a valley just next to the River Rhine. I climbed up to 4,000 feet above sea level but was only 1,000 feet above the ground. The views were lovely; I followed a road around to the north of Colmar to avoid having to climb higher and knew that I could land on it in an emergency. Before long, I dropped down the other side of the high ground. The airfield was only 627 feet above sea level and, whilst I was unable to contact the tower on the radio earlier as I was flying through the high ground, I was now in the valley and had a clear view. I called the tower and they asked me what type of aircraft I was flying. After confirming I was in a gyroplane, they replied, "You are not permitted to land here." I explained that we had a handler who had advised us that we could land and had made arrangements but he continued, "Autogyros are not permitted here." "What a pain in the arse!" I thought to myself. After a few moments, I replied, "Golf-Charlie-Hotel will be landing, I am low on fuel and have prior permission, we can sort this out on the ground, request join instructions." In response, a cheerful voice replied, "OK, no problem, Runway 19 no other traffic, you are clear to land."

Once landed, I walked into the small terminal building and wasn't sure what to expect. I didn't know if I was in trouble and would have to face the wrath of some airport official but nothing materialised! I paid my landing fees and the person on reception signed my paperwork. I walked outside and spotted a perfect hotel just 50 metres away. After an ominous start, it couldn't have been any more uneventful!

The morning rolled around and just like the day before, nobody raised any issues with my landing of the gyroplane. The place was virtually dead, apart from a few helicopter sightseeing trips that came in and out. I pulled the gyro out and taxied up to the pumps, refuelled, paid for it and was on my way. As I climbed out of Colmar, there was quite a bit of low-lying fog around. Luckily, I was able to get on top of it, whilst remaining in sight of the ground. In a matter of minutes, I was crossing the Rhine and flying into Germany. As I climbed up to 4,000 feet, the scenery was beautiful with endless green, rolling hills. Almost as soon as I crossed into Germany, there were noticeable changes: the houses and even the electricity pylons were different. There were a lot of large wind turbines positioned on top of the hills, although there was no wind at all for me. The conditions were perfect and the flying was so majestic, I deliberately slowed down to enjoy it. It wasn't long before I was tuning the radio in to the airfield's automated information broadcast to receive the airfield information and current altimeter settings.

As I got closer to Friedrichshafen, which sits on the north shore of Lake Constance, it was impossible not to be drawn to the beautiful lake, which was sparkling in the sun. It felt absolutely amazing to have arrived here and it was probably the best flight I'd had yet.

15

Friedrichshafen Aero Show

The Friedrichshafen Aero Show is the biggest general aviation air show in Europe and I had committed to *Magni* that I would be there.

I followed the instructions from the controller and parked up in the designated spot. As I was now in an international airport, I wasn't able to just randomly walk around on the apron. I was dropped off by shuttle bus, walked through into the terminal building and checked in at the *Ibis* hotel next door. *Magni* had arranged accommodation for the duration of the show so I only needed this hotel for a couple of days. I sat on the bed, then woke up almost two hours later – I obviously needed the sleep! The flying itself isn't necessarily physically demanding but it does require a lot of concentration. When you're flying somewhere new or over more challenging terrain, your body is running on adrenaline which keeps you alert. The only downside is that it makes you feel incredibly drained and tired when you stop.

The Aero Show was running from 10th to 13th April. Luca and the *Magni* team were arriving on the 9th, so I had a few days in hand to look around and relax. I knew the importance of keeping moving, so the following morning I went for a run. There was a road that followed the airport round to the other side where the exhibition halls were located. I ran around to them and could already see that it was getting busy with event organisers bringing planes in and generally moving stuff around.

Over the next couple of days, I took a short train ride into Friedrichshafen and sat in a few cafés by the lake. I could see this place being extremely popular in the summer months. The stunning, white-capped mountain tops of the Alps were looming in the distance across the water.

I also spent time catching up on admin. I was getting a lot of emails that mostly related to things that were lined up further along on the trip. I also heard from Norman who had been mulling over the idea of potentially joining me for my flight across Russia, since we had briefly discussed this at Goodwood. His aircraft had been collecting dust in a farmer's barn for quite a while and needed some essential maintenance work before it could be flown legally. I didn't have a problem with Norman joining me on this leg of my journey; I was very aware of his struggles and Russia was undoubtedly his nemesis.

Luca and the team soon arrived and I needed to move my gyro to the other side of the airport. This would be a two minute job at Popham but here, I needed to pass through Security and get clearance from the tower to cross the runway. An official guided me round to the hall where *Magni* had their display stand. I got out to push it but to my surprise, they informed me to taxi the gyro. Eventually I arrived at the hall entrance, shut the aircraft down and jumped out.

It was fantastic to see Luca and the team. Within an hour, Luca had pushed my aircraft outside into the car park and was giving it a thorough check. We needed to remove the rotors as we planned to fit a rotor hub cover, which improved the airflow and in turn would improve the efficiency, meaning I could fly at the same speed at a slightly lower power setting, saving fuel.

I knew it was going to be a busy few days: I had various interviews to give and people to meet up with. The first day, which is generally more of a press and trade day, was brilliant. I had arranged to spend a bit of time on the *Trig* stand with the guys who were very supportive of my endeavour and had kindly donated my transponder and radio.

The *Magni* stand was built and *Kindled Spirit* was now officially on display. The stand was quite large, with a couple of tables and chairs dotted around for guests to sit down and have a chat. I was taking a few moments to relax whilst things appeared to be fairly quiet, when I heard, "Hey James." It was Barry Jones. He was an accomplished military helicopter pilot, as well as an experienced gyro pilot and it was Barry who had pioneered the first official attempt to fly a gyroplane around the world. He also used a *Magni* M16. Unfortunately, his aircraft sustained serious water damage whilst on the ground in India during a monsoon and he was unable to continue. Barry was very experienced and I was grateful for his support. He emphasised the importance of safety and the need to recognise that if something doesn't feel right, to just turn around. "It's always better to fly another day than it is to crash," he said. I now knew quite a few military pilots and all of them endorsed safety above anything else. Barry had also kindly introduced me to a company called *Airbox Aerospace* who provide digital navigation software; I had used their intuitive software called *Runway HD* ever since I had passed my test.

There had been three serious attempts to fly a gyro around the world. Barry Jones was the first, then Norman, followed by a gentleman called Matt Haydock, who made it from Italy to Thailand, where he ran into some difficulties and was unable to continue. I have not had the chance to meet Matt but I was informed of some of the incredible flights that he made.

The next morning, the *Magni* team and I bundled into the van and drove to the show. They had kindly arranged for a show pass for Peter Wilson as well; he had a lot of people to see and I still hadn't really looked around the show myself yet, so Peter and I took a few hours out to visit some of the other stands. There were some fantastic aircraft, from private jets to small, one-man ultralights on display. If you loved flying, whether you're a pilot or not, this was the place to be! I was also in contact with one of Luca's friends and *Magni* owners, Christian. In his spare time, he raced *McLaren* cars and was able to secure some sponsorship for my trip. I was extremely grateful and made sure that I put the *McLaren* stickers on the gyro.

Later that afternoon, we met up with Evgeny from *MAK General Aviation Services* and Ahmed from *GASE* on the stand and got some pictures of the four of us standing next to G-KTCH. It was great to meet both of them here, especially as Evgeny would not be around when I arrived in Moscow.

By the time the last day rolled around, I was feeling pretty tired. I helped the guys pack down the *Magni* stand and a few hours later, we said our goodbyes. It had been fantastic to see everyone from *Magni*; they were so incredibly supportive and it really motivated me to try and push myself harder with my vlogs and social media, especially as I had so many kind comments from people following the vlog and wishing me well for the rest of my journey.

I was able to meet up with another gyro pilot, Geoff Porter, who had learnt to fly at Popham. He was now living in Chile with his wife and had been following my progress, kindly helping me out with a few things. He was looking to purchase a *Magni* and start a flying school. He had spent most of his working life flying helicopters and had just retired from commercial helicopter flying in the Falklands.

I was well ahead of schedule in terms of my planned arrival date into Russia on 1st May 2019 and my next flight was up to Leipzig.

I had really enjoyed my time at the show but it had been a week since I'd arrived and I was ready to get moving again.

I flew past some iconic German cities, flying to the east of Ulm, directly over Ansbach and skirting to the west of Nuremberg. It was then a direct run into Leipzig, where I was stopping for a few days to see one of my main project sponsors, *DHL*, who had arranged a tour of their global hub. Leipzig is *DHL*'s largest, global airfreight hub, and when I say it's a big place, I mean it's a very big place! I could see the bright yellow hangars and sorting facility almost 20 nautical miles out. I was excited to be flying G-KTCH into an airport of this size.

I arrived at a quiet time of day and was instructed to report at point "Sierra" about 10 miles south of the airfield. There were two main runways: the north runway was mainly used for the passenger terminal and the south runway was to serve *DHL*. I taxied to the hangar where G-KTCH would stay for the duration of the visit. This had to be an all-time record for the largest hangar a gyro has ever been stored in. I could have literally taken off and flown around inside, it was that big! There were numerous different *DHL* aircraft lined up having maintenance work carried out.

I was meeting up with Malcom from *DHL* and was also hoping to catch up with Fiona, but she was in Japan working on *DHL*'s sponsorship commitments for the Rugby World Cup. I was looked after incredibly well and was put up in a lovely hotel in the city. The next day I was back in the *DHL* hub, giving a talk to some of the day shift staff and then went back to the hub at 10pm to speak to the night shift staff. Afterwards, Malcolm gave me a tour of the sorting facility, which was unbelievable. There were conveyer belts everywhere, automated machines moving different parcels and forklift trucks bringing things in and out. The whole system was near logistical perfection; they even had a way to measure the efficiency of the work flow via a traffic light system!

When everyone is sleeping, these guys are literally keeping the world moving. It was now approaching midnight and the whole *DHL* hub was buzzing with activity. Freighters were landing almost every few minutes and the apron that was empty earlier was now packed with row upon row of aircraft. "This place goes crazy at night," Malcom said. I could see what he meant – it was literally dead during the day and had now come alive.

The following day was pretty easy. I had a talk lined up in a local school which went well. That afternoon, I had some free time and was in desperate need of a haircut and beard trim, so I went in search of a barber. I found a cracking little place around the corner from my hotel, which looked quite trendy. Upon walking in, they were so welcoming and friendly that I felt I was committed and couldn't really walk out again! The customer service was excellent but it ended up costing me almost 50 euros, which was a lot more than I'd usually pay but as they virtually scalped me, I'd have plenty of time to save up for my next one!

My plan was to fly east into Poland, to a small airfield in Miroslawice. I pushed G-KTCH out onto the tarmac; it was very hot and I wanted to get in and go, just to cool off. I taxied to the designated intersection as instructed by the controller, where I was told to hold. A passenger jet was taking off ahead of me. "Golf-Charlie-Hotel, line up Runway 08R, you are cleared for take-off, caution wake turbulence." It's not every day you hear this command! The large passenger aircraft in front of me would have disturbed the air, creating wingtip vortices and jet wash behind it, the amount of which depends on the size and weight of the aircraft. If I took off immediately behind the aircraft, it would have been extremely dangerous, so a separation of a few minutes is usually needed. The aircraft was well clear of me when I lined up, so I spun the rotors, gently accelerated along the runway, gradually sped up, before the front wheel was off the ground pretty quickly, then the main wheels followed. I stayed low and built up some airspeed and gradually climbed out. By the time I was at 1,000 feet AGL, I still had half the runway left!

The flight was easy as there was no airspace to pass through and nothing to fly around. I just followed the *Garmin* and enjoyed the ride. I joked with kids that *Garmin & Runway HD* were my sat nav for the sky! The landscape was pretty flat, with a lot of forest and beautiful, blue lakes. So far, all of my flights had been comfortable with no real turbulence. This was the first time it was actually quite uncomfortable as there was hot air rising around me which was causing the aircraft to move around a lot. I tried various things: flying higher, lower, faster and slower. In the end, I think it got to the point that I just didn't notice it anymore!

As I crossed the border into Poland, there was an instant change in the buildings and roads. The houses and buildings looked old and dilapidated, although these would probably be classed as rural, and the larger towns and cities would be quite different. About 40 minutes into Poland, I could see the small airfield of Miroslawice.

A young guy in his twenties came over to chat to me in perfect English and was asking me all sorts of questions, so I told him I was flying around the world. He was very excited by this fact, and in turn told me that he was a military helicopter pilot although, judging by his age, he couldn't have been doing it for that long. He kindly offered to drive me to a local hotel, so I packed my kit into his car, which was a fairly new American *Mustang*. He was eager to tell me that it was a 5-litre V8 with 400 horse power and he wanted to demonstrate its speed. There was no doubt that it was fast but I didn't want to die in a car crash whilst I was flying around the world!

I left early the next morning and was now heading to Nowy Targ to see a good friend of Eddie's, Gabriel, who was also a pilot.

We had been introduced at the aero show so, although we had only met a week earlier, it would be good to see a familiar face. The journey to Nowy Targ was stunning. The air was very smooth, which was a relief, as I didn't fancy a bumpy ride like the previous day again.

Nowy Targ is situated just to the south of Krakow, close to the border of Slovakia, with a beautiful mountain backdrop. As the higher ground started to rise up, I noticed a road that was heading for Nowy Targ, so I decided to follow it. The next thing I knew, I saw a little gyro whizzing towards me, with Gabriel in the back, taking pictures! I had already tuned into the Nowy Targ frequency and it wasn't long before I heard Gabriel on the radio telling me to follow him back to the airfield.

This little surprise, along with media waiting to interview me, had been organised by Eddie and Gabriel. It felt brilliant to be on the ground with so many friendly, happy people walking around with smiles on their faces. Eventually, we pushed the gyro into a small hangar and locked the door. Gabriel said, "I have one more surprise for you." His friend had a small, fixed-wing aircraft and had offered to take me for a quick spin to have a closer look at the snow-capped mountains. We weren't up for long but it was great fun.

The next morning, as I flew back out over the road that I'd followed into Nowy Targ, there was higher ground around, so I had to be a little more conscious of where the wind was coming from. Within half an hour, I was completely clear of any high ground and it was all flat. I flew north, passing Krakow to the east before picking up an ATC flight-following service. Fifty miles north of Krakow, I was passed over to Warsaw Information. The radio work could not have been any easier and the controller spoke perfect English.

I wasn't flying into Warsaw's main international airport but into Warsaw Babice, located to the northwest of the city. As I touched down, the front wheel followed just after but something felt wrong.

I had no steering and the aircraft was shaking; it didn't feel smooth at all. I was now trying to taxi and I had to carry a lot of power just to keep the aircraft moving. It didn't take me long to realise that the front tyre was punctured! I managed to get it parked up on the grass and stepped out. It was as flat as a pancake.

Gabriel had kindly made an introduction to Matieuz, a young captain working for *Ryanair*. I made contact with Matieuz who was unavailable, so he arranged for his relative, Grzegorz, to come and meet me. He talked to the security guard and came through to the airfield where we shook hands. I was unable to speak Polish and he didn't speak English but this posed no real problem. Grzegorz passed me his phone so I could talk to his wife, who spoke perfect English, and she translated that Grzegorz would take me to a hotel and help with anything I needed. Grzegorz was an aviation enthusiast and keen photographer, so he was taking plenty of pictures whilst I was chatting to his wife. I explained to her that I needed to try and fix the puncture but I didn't think this would be too difficult. We grabbed my kit and headed for a hotel that Eddie had found. He had this knack of finding excellent hotels at a discounted rate, which really came in handy.

The next morning, Grzegorz picked me up and we returned to the airfield. He was chatting to a few pilots and mentioned that we needed to try and get my tyre fixed. They advised me that there was a mechanic who lived onsite just next to the tower. As soon as we got on to the airfield, I could see the rotors on G-KTCH moving up and down, which should not have been happening. I thought that perhaps the rotor tie had come off, although I remembered tying it down tightly. To my surprise, the rotor tie had actually snapped! I pulled back the cover and noticed that the stick retainer had also been snapped by the force of the rotors moving up and down. I now needed to fix the stick retainer as well: another job to add to the list.

To be fair, they were all very simple tasks and if this was all that I needed to fix on a flight around the world, I was very lucky.

The stick retainer would be easy to sort out but I wanted to focus on the tyre as I wouldn't be going anywhere if that wasn't sorted. The mechanic came over to look at the gyro. I had my small bag of tools and was ready to drop the front wheel out but we needed something to prop the front of the aircraft up with, so the mechanic came back with a car tyre, which we positioned under the front of the aircraft. I also tied the rotors down from the front and back to make absolutely sure that they didn't come loose and start bouncing around in the wind that had picked up overnight and obviously caused the rotor tie and stick retainer to snap.

After a few minutes, the mechanic had removed the front wheel and taken it back to his workshop. The front wheel splits in two which made it quite easy to get the tyre off. It had quite a large cut in it. It's hard to know where it happened but that didn't really matter, I just needed to get it repaired. Grzegorz and I drove around to a couple of different garages that fixed car tyres, but we had no luck. It was also a bank holiday so most of the garages were closed and the only one that was open told us it couldn't be repaired. It wasn't looking good.

Whilst we drove back to the airfield, I looked at flight options on my phone. The only viable solution I could see to take control of the situation was to fly to Milan and get Luca to swap it out for a new wheel and tyre. I could do this in one day with no real problems and, although it seemed a drastic solution, it meant that I could get it sorted and move on. If it hadn't have been a bank holiday, I might have been able to ask *DHL* to ship me a new one.

The mechanic did suggest some possible temporary repair ideas but I think by this point, I'd pretty much decided that the best way to sort this out was to go to Milan. Grzegorz dropped me back at the hotel; before leaving, I explained the plan to his wife over the phone, who confirmed that Grzegorz was happy to pick me up and take me to the airport the following day. It's funny how people show up in your life when you need help, almost as though our paths were meant to cross. That evening, they took me on a sightseeing trip around Warsaw. It was brilliant to see all the different types of architecture and it felt quite a cosmopolitan city.

The following morning, I was up bright and early and went for a run around a beautiful park next to the Vistula River, close to my hotel. It was a great way to start the day and I felt amazingly refreshed, energised and ready to go!

Grzegorz picked me up and took me to the main international airport. Unfortunately, I hadn't been able to find a direct flight so the only option was to fly from Warsaw to Milan Malpensa via Frankfurt. I was a bit anxious that Security might stop me, carrying a wheel and a tyre, but thankfully they didn't. Once I'd arrived at Milan Malpensa, I called Luca to let him know that I was waiting outside. It was a beautiful day, well over 30°C in the sun. Luca picked me up and we drove to a local aviation museum where *Magni* had an aircraft on display and we grabbed some lunch.

Having sorted out a new wheel and tyre, Luca dropped me back to the airport and told me that if I needed anything else to call him immediately and he would arrange it, no matter where I was. I sat looking out of the window, day-dreaming for most of the journey back, reflecting on the fact that I was so lucky to have great people around me. It made me want to complete this huge undertaking even more. I arrived back in Warsaw with my new front wheel and tyre in one hand and soon, a cold, refreshing beer in the other!

Back at the airfield the following day, the mechanic fitted the new wheel and repaired the broken stick retainer cable. Matieuz also got in touch and asked if I wanted the use of the hangar, courtesy of the *Warsaw Flying Club*. This would work well as it would keep the aircraft out of the wind. The *Aircovers* protection was brilliant and effectively meant that I could leave the aircraft out in any weather but where a hangar was available, it made sense to use it. This was now working out to be quite convenient: I had arranged to meet Andy Jones in Estonia to service the gyro, however I now had a good support network in Warsaw, the facilities of an aero club and a large hangar at my disposal, so we decided that Andy should carry out the service here instead.

Grzegorz and his wife kindly let me stay with them for a few days until Andy arrived, to help keep costs down. It was greatly appreciated and they were brilliant hosts. Everything was coming together and falling into place. Andy was arriving the following day, I was still ahead of schedule and I'd been lucky enough to meet some fantastic people who were giving me a tremendous amount of support.

16

Moscow

It was great to see Andy as the last time I'd seen him was at Friedrichshafen. The set-up we had was perfect: a large hangar to work in, we could come and go as we pleased in Andy's hire car and we also had the fantastic support of Grzegorz and his wife. Andy got straight on with the 100-hour service. It was all easy stuff for him but as this was the last service before I flew the whole way across Russia, he was taking a little more time to check things over. Changing the oil and fitting new spark plugs were first on the list of many tasks. Whilst Andy was servicing G-KTCH, I was filming, taking pictures and editing footage on the laptop. A Polish journalist who was reporting for the local radio station came to interview me and she also interviewed Andy, asking questions about what he was doing. As it was going to be broadcast on the radio and not TV, she asked Andy if he could bang on the aircraft to make some noises: the look on his face was priceless!

Andy made fantastic progress on the service and there were only a few things left to do the following day. We went out that evening and explored Warsaw old town, had a fantastic meal, washed down with a beer and even some chocolate ice-cream. I had many things racing through my mind and seeing Andy helped me to stay focused.

I had just learnt that Norman's motive for flying with me across Russia was in fact to link it with a previous journey he had flown more than four years earlier, in an attempt to try and claim the record I was working towards! I was initially perplexed as to how he thought he could do this.

I had no issue with Norman flying with me as we got on well and I thought that, by accompanying me on part of my challenge, it might help him bring some kind of closure to his journeys. However, it was now clearly an attempt to claim the record before I could.

Norman was aware of the importance of setting the speed around the world record as that was the only way to gain an official *FAI* record at the time. The *FAI* have three classes of 'around the world' records in the rotary class: speed around the world, a circumnavigation via antipodes and a circumnavigation via the poles. To be officially recognised by the *FAI*, just crossing all lines of longitude was insufficient; the criteria for one of these records had to be met.

I had not seen this coming and spent some time trying to calmly and quietly think the situation through. I pondered over why Norman would do this. I had shared the many struggles with him about achieving the sponsorship to make this trip happen and he was well aware that my campaign was financed and underpinned on the basis of setting the first circumnavigation. His attempt to chase a record in this disjointed way was not in keeping with the spirit of adventure, in my opinion. But it quickly became apparent that there was really nothing I could do. Having an argument over this would have achieved nothing, so at this early stage, I decided to let it go and focus on the things within my control. I had seen many people fall apart over the years as they worried about the past or future, driving themselves insane over things they cannot control. If I have no control over a situation I will simply let it be and go with the flow, and turn my attention to the things within my control.

The next day, Andy finished off the service and I visited a school in Warsaw where my talk was very well received. I'd never intended to stay there for almost a week but Warsaw had been amazing. Grzegorz and his wife came along to wave me off. I said goodbye to them and thanked Andy for coming out to help me. I was now ready for the vast journey across Russia, with a freshly-serviced aircraft that flew like a dream.

All my communication channels were established with Eddie, the tracker was on and I was ready to depart. The next flight was to Kaunas in Lithuania, flying an almost straight line the whole way there. For the first six miles or so, I was flying over a built-up, populated area, which always made me feel slightly nervous as there are very few options to land if a problem occurs. Once I was clear of Warsaw, it was fields all the way which made for nice and easy terrain. I thought about all sorts of things when I was flying. This particular day as I was flying over fields and forests, I was thinking about all the Polish pilots who bravely volunteered during World War Two. Without their assistance, it's highly unlikely that the British would have won the Battle of Britain. Many of them may well have come from some of the farms and homes I was now flying over.

Kaunas was an easy stop; the airport was a large, international airport but it wasn't particularly busy. I was parked on a stand next to a *Ryanair* aircraft, which was quite a picture! Eddie had booked me into a small, budget hotel next to the terminal, which was very convenient. The only downside being that there was no restaurant so I headed over to the terminal building and bought some snacks and supplies for the evening.

The following morning, I was up bright and early: the sun was shining and the birds were singing. It was my last flight in Europe before I headed into Russia. There was no wind at all and the conditions were near perfect. I was initially routed to the east of the city, flying across a beautiful lake, then I was given a direct heading. The flight would take me over Latvia and into Estonia.

As I flew over the dense forests of Latvia, I couldn't help but think back to the time that I was at St James's Palace in London, a few years earlier. I was handing out awards to young individuals who had earned their Duke of Edinburgh Gold awards. Prince Philip was meeting the young people and asking them questions. He was briefed on my background and when he came to shake my hand, he said, "Ah, you like rowing, climbing and cycling, don't you? Have you ever been to Latvia?" I hadn't then but I was now flying over it. He was an incredibly sharp man and had an outstanding knowledge of geography as we chatted about some of the countries I'd been to. I like to think that Prince Philip would have approved of my mission.

I arrived in my last European country, Estonia, on Sunday 28th April 2019. My European leg was now complete! I didn't have a permit to enter Russia until 1st May so I had two full days before I would depart. Jude had been in contact with the *Estonian Aviation Academy* to line up a visit with their students. It was organised by the Head of Marketing and Communications, a guy called Illari. He kindly came out to the airport to meet me, despite it being a Sunday. He was a nice guy and very excited that I'd stopped by and was giving a presentation to his students. Illari took me to a local hotel, which also had a spa with a massive swimming pool, sauna and jacuzzi. "I'm certainly going to use that!" I thought to myself.

Illari picked me up the following morning to give the talk. The academy was a well-equipped facility, which had a nice feel to it. There were over 100 students in the room and I had a large screen to showcase all of my pictures and videos. I spoke for just over an hour and answered many questions, after which we all went outside and took some pictures next to G-KTCH. The students were fascinated by the aircraft and some of them were training to be commercial pilots or aircraft engineers.

That evening, I crashed out when I returned to the hotel. Illari had invited me back to the academy the following day but I wasn't feeling too well. I felt drained, exhausted and generally quite anxious about the impending flight to Moscow, so I spent the day relaxing at the hotel spa.

The next day I was up very early: it was time to fly into Russia! I was extremely excited but also a little nervous. There was no particular reason to be nervous because everything had been arranged and the flying was the same, although the flights would be slightly longer. I guess it was just the uncertainty of the unknown.

I set off from Tartu and within an hour, I was on the ground in Pskov. As I crossed the border, there was very little change: the scenery and landscape remained exactly the same but the first thing I noticed was that the buildings looked older. I received a text from Eddie on the *Garmin inReach* saying "Welcome to Russia." As I got closer to Pskov, it was a lot more industrial and almost every building was grey in colour. There were quite a few chimneys with smoke bellowing out of them.

The controller at the airport spoke good English, albeit with a strong Russian accent. I landed and taxied to the terminal where uniformed personnel were waiting. I got out of the aircraft and smiled. They all stood and stared back at me. Along came an old, beaten-up white van and out jumped an airport representative who shook my hand and welcomed me to Russia in perfect English. He wanted to see my passport, which I handed to him. The place wasn't unfriendly in the least but it had quite a different feel to it; everyone was staring at me as if they'd been told not to take their eyes off me! A few of them started taking pictures, so I pulled out my phone and tried to take a selfie but someone quickly shouted, "No photos, no photos!" in a stern Russian accent. I was escorted into the building and passed through Security. This was a very old airport: I could see many different types of dilapidated aircraft parked up, both military and civilian, and the terminal was certainly not modern, although I'm sure it served the city very well.

I was handed over to another airport official and sat in her small office as she completed various bits of paperwork and asked me to sign some documentation. I had been on the ground for about 40 minutes now and wanted to get away as I still had two more flights before I arrived in Moscow. As soon as the formalities were completed, I was quickly whisked out of the building and back to the aircraft. I now had a short 25-minute flight north to Seredka for refuelling. It was a small strip run by a very friendly guy: it was like flying into Popham on a quiet day! After a quick turnaround and completing my *FAI* paperwork, I jumped back into the gyro and went through my checklist, which I now knew off by heart.

As I checked the parking brake was on, I pulled it up and heard a snap. I couldn't believe that the brake cable had broken! I now didn't have a functioning brake that I could use from the front of the aircraft, which meant that as soon as I started up, it would move. I worked out that I could reach my arm around and was just about able to use the brake from the rear seat which ran off a separate cable and still worked. It was a pain but nothing I couldn't get around with a little improvisation. I knew the aircraft would probably hold without the brake at idle as it was full with fuel and it was near its maximum take-off weight. There was nothing in front of me apart from the taxiway so I started it up.

The aircraft held fine, despite being on tarmac, so I eased more power very carefully and taxied out to the runway and turned it around, lining up on the centre line. I slowly span the rotors up but was struggling to hold the brake in the rear seat and feed the power in. I got the rotors spinning up to about 150 rpm (revolutions per minute) with the stick back, then let the aircraft start rolling. The rotors quickly gained momentum and were soon up to 200 rpm. As they passed 230 rpm, I applied full power and the aircraft really came alive. I knew I was going to be able to get off the ground but I would end up using a lot more of the runway. Eventually, I took off and was absolutely fine, although it may have looked to any observer like I was going to shoot off the end of the runway!

Evgeny had arranged for me to fly low-level the whole way to Moscow, which was fantastic. I climbed up to 1,000 feet and said goodbye to the guys over the radio who had been amazing. I was instructed to contact Pskov tower and spoke to the controller who routed me around the city; he also passed me my next radio frequency which I tuned in. It didn't take long before the controller from Pskov was gone and I was hearing broken transmissions for G-KTCH. All they wanted to know was my ETA at the next waypoint, which was all set up on the *Garmin* and therefore very easy for me to pass over to the controller. Every now and then, they would contact me and give me a new frequency. It was all easy stuff but it wasn't like Europe where I didn't need to talk to anyone and could fly wherever I wanted. The flights across Russia would be flown under full ATC control the whole way.

It was going to be a long flight to Moscow but the weather was good and the wind was coming from the side, which would become a tail wind later in the journey. For the vast majority of the flight, it was all relatively simple. I had some sweets that I was snacking on to pass the time and I also had a drink to sip on. The ground was all completely flat: some of it was farmed as I flew around populated areas but a lot of it was forest and grass lands. I was surprised at just how much dense forest I was flying over. I imagine that most of Europe was probably once like this but it had been farmed and populated over the centuries. This was completely untouched land, with the only sign of modern day life being the occasional set of powerlines running through it. As I came within 100 miles of Moscow, things started to change. Roads were becoming more noticeable and populated areas were more frequent.

Evgeny had arranged for me to have a helicopter escort into the airport from some of his pilot friends. They knew the waypoints that I would be flying to on my approach. I was scanning the horizon to look for the helicopter and eventually I heard them announcing my call sign. A few moments later, I could see two *Robinson 66* helicopters that had come out to meet me, which felt brilliant! The sun was starting to set on the horizon but there was still plenty of light left. They told me that I didn't need to do any more radio work and that they would speak to the controllers on my behalf, which was fine by me!

Moscow has a large motorway that runs around the city in the same way that London has the M25 orbital motorway. I was arriving from the north west and needed to fly round to the south east to land at Myachkovo Airport. All I needed to do was follow the two helicopters. As we approached the outskirts of Moscow, I could see the high-rise buildings in the distance. There were a lot of tower blocks and quite quickly it became very built-up and densely populated. We flew clockwise around the ring road and I managed to get some great pictures of the escorting aircraft. I had to put the fact that I was flying over a highly populated area out of my mind. It wasn't long before I was told to contact the tower at Myachkovo who were waiting for me. It was very simple: I was literally cleared to land and that was that. I had to be a bit mindful that I had no brakes but with the size of this runway, it was not a problem. I eventually taxied to the hangar, where I noticed a message from Eddie, which said, "Well done – call me when you can." We had been chatting in flight via the messaging system we had set up.

There was some media waiting for me, arranged by Irina, who helped out with communications for Evgeny's business, *MAC General Aviation Services*. It had been a long day but I was relieved and very excited to be on the ground. Irina was directing photographers and her husband Tim was also there. I had been on the ground no more than a few minutes when my phone started pinging like mad. A lot of people had been tracking my flight and were sending messages to congratulate me on a massive day and having officially arrived in Russia! The heliport hub was on the other side of Moscow so it wasn't long after the gyro had been unpacked and secured in a hangar that we were flying back. Irina told me to sit in the front and relax; by the time we made it to the heliport hub, I'd almost flown a complete circle around Moscow city. What a day it had been: I was exhausted but knew I wouldn't be able to sleep, feeling as high as a kite with excitement!

I spoke to Eddie who informed me that Norman was stuck in Germany with technical problems. He estimated that Norman was about a week behind me so I told him I would stay in Moscow and wait. It made sense from a safety perspective to fly together across the vast expanse of Russia, then we would go our own ways once we arrived in North America. I now had a week to spend in one of the coolest cities I have ever visited!

The first priority was to fix the broken brake cable. I explained to Tim and Irina that I needed to get this sorted as a matter of priority. The next day, I was relaxing in the hotel when Irina called to say that we would all fly back to the airport from the heliport the following day with a mechanic to fix the brake cable. Flying the route took about 20 minutes whereas driving would have taken at least an hour, so I was very grateful for their efforts. The pilot didn't speak English and apparently ran a very successful car auto parts business. We piled into his *Robinson 66* and headed back over to the airport. Replacing the brake cable wasn't particularly difficult, I just had to remove a few things to get to the master cylinder. One of the local mechanics had a spare cable, which he kindly gave me. There were a couple of mechanics milling around; once they realised what I was doing, they all picked up their tools and carried out the replacement work for me, which was greatly appreciated. I used the time at the hangar to give the aircraft a thorough inspection and clean and also repacked some kit neatly away. I'd now been in Moscow for two full days: the most important job had been taken care of so it was time to check the place out.

Jude had lined up a talk at the British School in Moscow and Irina came along with me. The headmaster was British and had been living and teaching in Moscow for quite some time. It was a thoroughly enjoyable afternoon. I made a list of all the things that I needed to pick up and wanted to see whilst in Moscow. Irina's husband, Tim, had some time off work and helped me out with purchasing an Internet dongle so I could get mobile data on my phone. Google Maps is extremely useful when exploring a foreign city.

Irina, Tim and some of their friends escorted me on a day trip around the city. It was brilliant to be standing in the famous Red Square, which is probably Moscow's most popular tourist attraction. Moscow has been the capital of Russia for over 800 years and I was now standing in the centre of it. The different architecture was amazing, particularly the glistening, rainbow domes of St Basil's Cathedral. The multi-coloured, onion-shaped domes were designed to make the building look like the shape of a flame on a bonfire. Irina explained that according to legend, Ivan the Terrible, who'd had it commissioned in the 1500's, thought it was so beautiful that he ordered the architect to be blinded so he would never surpass the creation. "Hopefully it was just a legend!" I said.

The Kremlin and Lenin's Mausoleum were also on my list of things to see. We headed into an old-style department store and I joked to Irina, "We could be in London." It was all very cosmopolitan and there were a lot of foreign tourists walking around; in fact, I heard more English-speaking conversations than Russian! I noticed an ice-cream stand which looked pretty good so Irina kindly treated me to a chocolate ice-cream. I probably looked like a big kid walking around eating ice-cream but I didn't care – I was having a great time!

I was in Moscow at an opportune time as it was a public holiday and a military display was taking place throughout the city. Hundreds of tanks, rockets and all sorts of military might were paraded through the streets in a show of power. I thought this was really quite an interesting spectacle but Irina and Tim explained that a lot of locals were not keen on it. The display was, after all, showing off tools of destruction and death. Tim mentioned that he would rather see a display of diggers and trucks: tools of construction not destruction! It was a valid point but the parade was quite a sight, nonetheless.

Over the next few days, I filmed various vlogs, caught up on emails and generally made sure that I was fully prepared for the flights across Russia. Evgeny had supplied the entire route with every waypoint, which I had input into *Garmin Pilot* on my iPad and on the *Garmin 795* that I was using in the aircraft. Tim updated it to include the complete Russian database, which was very useful. Irina took my clothes home and washed them – they even came back ironed and folded – what a star she was!

It was now 7th May and Norman was finally on his way to Moscow. Apparently, he had flown through some quite serious weather and I could see that he was relieved to be on the ground. We had 19 flights to go before we would be in Alaska and a lot could happen in that time. I still had to fly a lot of miles in the US and get back across the Atlantic via Greenland and Iceland, so there was a certain urgency to get moving. I wondered how many days Norman would need to rest after a big day of flying but I was very impressed when he said he only wanted to take one day off to look around. I think he was also aware that I had been waiting there a week for him already.

We were soon ready for our flight to Choboksary. My time in Moscow had passed quickly and I couldn't thank Irina and Tim enough for looking out for me. I'd felt very relaxed in Moscow and made a promise to myself that I would definitely return, however, I was now champing at the bit to get moving again.

Above: Departing Popham Airfield on the first day of my flight around the world

Below: Ahmed, Evgeny, Peter and me at the Friedrichshafen Aero Show in Germany

Above: Large areas of forest en route to Bratsk in Russia

Below: Speaking to kids in Krasnoyarsk, Russia

Above: Flying through the mountains leaving Providenyia

Left: Enjoying the open cockpit flying in Siberia

Below: The Diomede Islands crossing the Bering Straits and International Date Line

Above: Norman and me hiding from the rain in a public toilet after emergency landi

Below: Taking off the day after the emergency landing

Above: San Francisco Bay

Below: Cruising over the Hollywood Hills

Above: Meeting up with Bob in Phoenix

Below: G-KTCH evening flight en route to Oshkosh

Above: Flying around the Statue of Liberty

Below: New York skyline

Above: Low level flying on the east coast of Greenland

Below: Team Magni celebrating the finish at Popham Airfield

17

Heading East to Yakutsk

Norman and I had an early breakfast and headed to the heliport. I was absolutely raring to go: my aircraft was spotless, everything was packed meticulously in its place and the adventure was moving into unchartered territory!

It felt absolutely brilliant to be back in the air again. Our flight plan was filed under my aircraft so all the radio calls were to G-KTCH, which was all very easy. We had our chat frequency of 123.450 set as the first channel so we could talk to one another easily and the main working frequency would be on the second channel set to dual watch. As soon as a controller wanted to pass information to us, I'd quickly switch over and action the call.

We were given permission to fly low-level for most of the way to Cheboksary, which was stunning. The weather had now cleared, leaving beautiful, blue skies with the odd cumulous cloud around. Similar to the flight into Moscow, once we cleared the built-up areas, it was mostly fields and forests, but there was noticeably more farmed land around now. As we flew over the forest fairly low, we hit a large swarm of bugs. I'm not talking a few – my entire screen was absolutely covered with them!

Eventually I was talking to the tower at Cheboksary and given clearance to land. We had completed our first flight together. It went well and it was obvious to me fairly soon into the flight that Norman was laid back and fairly chilled when it came to flying. He had said to me when we first met that the actual flying is the easy part, compared to the logistical complexities of long-range flying. Having already flown through Europe, I was beginning to realise this for myself.

Evgeny had arranged for one of his friend's to meet us. Aleksandar was a local pilot, owned a *Cessna* and kindly allowed us to use his hangar. Both aircraft were filthy so I set about cleaning the layers of dead bugs off my screen and rotors. It was now early evening and a few locals had come to take a look at the gyros. They were very friendly but I think that was alcohol talking in some cases; at the point where one of the guys tried to hug me for the fourth time, I realised I needed to be a bit patient! There was a little boy hanging around who was looking at the gyros with his mum and dad. I pointed to the front seat, lifted him up into it and his parents took a few pictures.

The local guys invited us back to their shack for some vodka. Aleksandar thought it would be a good idea if we had just one glass of vodka with them, just to acknowledge their offer of hospitality . It was no problem because they were very welcoming, also offering us some snacks, but at the rate they were drinking and the amount they were pouring into our glasses, I would have been in a very bad way if we had stayed much longer! We thanked them and left. Unfortunately, I now had a splitting headache which was quite unpleasant, most likely caused by not drinking enough water and probably…almost certainly…the vodka.

The next day was fairly chilled. We had a tour of Cheboksary with Aleksandar, finishing up with some beautiful evening views over the

Volga River. We were staying outside the city in a small, B&B-style hotel and, as we left, the owner gave us both a souvenir. They were bright yellow ties, which we thought looked cool, so we decided to wear them despite looking a bit silly – but we didn't care!

The formalities at the airport were made a lot easier with Aleksandar's help. Our flight plans had been filed and the weather was clear, so we were good to go. We had two flights to complete so it was a much longer day for us. We wondered if we would encounter large swarms of bugs again but to our surprise, as quickly as they came, they were gone, apart from the odd one or two.

We landed at the grass strip in Pervushino, which is a small town close to the Belaya River. We knew that we needed to try and turn things around fairly quickly. We arranged to be refuelled and spent some time chatting and taking pictures. To my amazement, there was a small gyroplane school with two *Magni M24s*. I didn't expect to see them there but it was a great surprise, so of course I had to get some photos with them. After exchanging pleasantries, we were ready to depart.

Norman was a little concerned as he had asked for a certain amount of fuel and for some reason, his tanks had been completely filled, which meant his aircraft was a lot heavier than it needed to be. He lined up in front of me, spun the rotors up and accelerated along the grass strip. At the point that I was expecting to see him get off the ground, he wasn't even close. He kept going and eventually was airborne just above the ground; by now he must have been running out of runway or very close to it. It was a last-minute decision by the look of it but he landed again. Instantly he came on the radio, "I'm too heavy, I can't get off the ground." "No rush, take your time," I replied. I thought he would just empty some fuel but he wanted to try again.

I suggested that he line up in front of me and go again; I wouldn't take off until I saw he was OK. On the second attempt, he was able to get off the ground but was very slow. I could hear in his voice that he was worried when he told me that he wasn't able to climb and was only just maintaining his height. I span my rotors up and started my take-off. I was interested to see how G-KTCH would perform; interestingly enough, I was off the ground and climbing out without even using the extra boost setting on the throttle. I was also fully fuelled and weighed more than Norman. I was climbing out with ease, not even using full power, so I wasn't sure why he was struggling so much to get off the ground and climb. I quickly caught him up as he was flying slowly at around 65mph, which is the optimum climb speed for most gyros. He still sounded anxious on the radio. "That was silly: I honestly thought the aircraft was coming down and it was another Thailand all over again," he said.

Some years earlier on his first journey in Thailand, Norman crashed into a lake on take-off. There were a number of things which led to the incident and, by all accounts, he'd been quite unlucky. He spent months rebuilding his aircraft and was able to carry on, which was an incredible show of determination. The natural reaction when the aircraft is not climbing is to pull back on the stick but this will only make the situation worse as the aircraft falls behind the power curve and will descend even quicker.

Norman is a very experienced, long-range gyroplane pilot and it was his experience that saved him in Pervushino. I was just pleased he was off the ground and that everything was OK. We were now on our way to Koltsovo International Airport in Yekaterinburg. After an hour of flying, Norman's gyro had burnt off some fuel and was flying without any problems. It was strange how his engine rpm was so much lower than mine when we were at the same speed. In order to get to Yekaterinburg, we would be crossing the Ural Mountains. I was excited about this and didn't really know what to expect. Once we were clear of Pervushino, we noticed that the ground was rising but it was not as 'mountainous' as we expected. It was just higher ground and a very impressive landscape with thick forest as far as the eye could see. It was certainly not the place to have an emergency, that was for sure. There were absolutely no options to land but I was now used to this, as it was not uncommon to fly for hours over terrain that had no landing options.

Eventually, the controllers passed us over to the tower at Koltsovo International Airport and we were guided in. This was a large, commercial airport but it was surprisingly easy to fly in to. We were instructed to taxi to a stand and followed a 'Follow Me' car. Norman had managed to get our aircraft into a hangar for the night, which we shared with only one private jet. I was probably a bit over the top when it came to checking my aircraft. I was taking extra time to check things and look where I perhaps wouldn't ordinarily look. Having a problem out here would not have been easy to sort out so I was always trying to keep on top of my aircraft's condition, with thorough inspections and keeping it as clean as possible. I had finished inspecting G-KTCH and thought I'd take a look around Norman's gyro. I noticed that a carburettor nut was very loose; he tightened it up and thanked me for spotting it. He was also aware that he was getting through a lot of oil, so we topped it up and agreed that we would see what the levels were like after our next flight.

Continuing our journey east, our next destination was Tyumen. The terrain was now flat again with a mixture of forest and vast, green plains. We were lucky to have more favourable weather: clear skies, light winds and warm temperatures, which made the flying so much easier. We landed at Roshchino International Airport, which was not quite on the scale of the last airport but it was still fairly large. It took us a while to taxi from the far end of the runway to the apron. For some reason, we were instructed to park up at the other end of the airport, which could not have been any further away from the terminal building. We were literally parked with all the scrap aircraft in the bone yard! We weren't exactly sure why we were put here but in the grand scheme of things, it didn't matter.

There appeared to be a bit of confusion, as airport officials drove down to us and then drove away again several times. We asked about a hangar but the answer was a stern, "No, not available." We accepted that we were going to have to leave the aircraft outside. When we asked about fuel, they said that they didn't have a fuel truck with our specific fuel. We called Evgeny and passed him over to the airport official on the phone. Of course, we couldn't understand the conversation but Evgeny assured me that it would all be sorted. We were at least on the ground, so I unpacked my kit and wrapped G-KTCH in the cover.

A few hours had passed now and we still hadn't been picked up and taken back to the terminal. As the sun was going down, I managed to get a beautiful shot of G-KTCH but it was starting to get quite cold now and the novelty of standing around was quickly wearing off. Eventually we did get some support and were able to collect fuel. It was gone 11pm by the time we arrived at our hotel and of course, there was no food. We walked back over to the terminal, which was still open and managed to get something to eat. We toasted another successful day with a beer at almost midnight and watched the security guard escort a drunk man out of the terminal.

Thankfully, the next morning's procedures were a lot quicker. We were escorted to the aircraft and left to our own devices. The next stop was Omsk. We were pleased to take off and keep up the momentum of our journey across Russia. Conditions were good but we noticed over time that it was starting to become a bit bumpy and quite gusty. It wasn't necessarily helping us either as it was a cross wind. It was getting stronger as the flight went on, which now required two hand flying and just that little bit more concentration and effort. When we arrived at the airfield, the wind was blowing across the runway at an almost perfect 90 degree angle. If we were flying fixed-wing aircraft, we wouldn't have been able to land as it was gusting around 40 knots. Thankfully, we were able to descend vertically and land across the runway.

Norman went in first and touched down nicely. I was following and allowed plenty of space between us. It was actually quite tricky as I had to clear a small fence to get on to the runway but if I overshot it and needed to go around, there was a power line. Once I was committed, I didn't have the option of trying again. Norman was on the ground and I soon heard, "James, be careful with the stick when you are on the ground." He was right: if my stick position was not correct, the wind could easily get under the rotors and tip the aircraft over. I cleared the fence and gently touched down. I instantly pushed the stick forward into the wind and stayed there until the rotors had lost some momentum. "Phew," I thought to myself, "that was quite a technical landing with absolutely no room for error!"

It was good to be on the ground but it was also useful to have had a slightly more challenging landing as it keeps the focus and stops any complacency. It was a small, grass strip field but it had a lovely feel to it and there were quite a few private pilots waiting for us. They kindly arranged for our aircraft to be stored in what looked like a hangar but it had no front or proper flooring. I think animals had been using it, which was fine, as we were just happy to have somewhere to store them.

There was a little bit of cross wind around the following morning but nothing that would stop us taking off. We were now en route to another city, Novosibirsk. For most of the flight, we were threading between clouds and actively dodging heavy rain showers. Thankfully, it was clear when we approached Novosibirsk.

Sasha from *Aircovers* sent me a message a few days earlier to let me know that her brother, Quentin Smith, was in the area doing some helicopter flying. Quentin is a well-known adventure helicopter pilot, with many accolades under his belt. I'd forgotten about Sasha's message until a well-spoken British accent came on the radio, "Golf-Charlie-Hotel, good to see you made it, dear boy, we will be on the ground soon." I realised it was Quentin, also known as Q, and confirmed that we'd see him on the ground. Norman and I landed and not long after, Q swooped down in a *Robinson 44* helicopter. We sat around together and drank tea; it was the first flight where I'd started to feel the cold a bit more, so something warm was just what I needed. We said goodbye to Q and thanked him for dropping in. He was an interesting character: a well-dressed man with a certain suave, British eccentricity that few could match! I wasn't expecting him to make a standard departure and he didn't disappoint, putting the aircraft into a nosedive and swooping over the top of us, pulling up at the last minute to fly away into the distance.

We were making good progress and hadn't experienced any real delays yet. It would have to remain this way if we were to be in Alaska by 1st June, when our Russian visas were due to expire. We were aware that we were cutting it fine but all we could do was take it day by day and hope that we could keep moving forwards.

Over the next few days, we passed through Krasnoyarsk, where I gave a talk to some students at the airport. We also met a few *DHL* employees and chatted with a journalist. We really were lucky: every time we stopped somewhere, we were bestowed with wonderful hospitality. Our overnight stop in Bratsk was no different. I had received a message from Ivan who worked for *DHL*; I was really impressed that he was prepared to drive five hours just to meet me and take some pictures.

Bratsk was a short, gravel strip, run by a guy who lived on site and also worked as a commercial helicopter pilot. We were able to push the gyros inside the small hangar, where our fuel was waiting for us in jerry cans. Ivan took us to a local hotel and we headed out for dinner. I noticed a distinct change in this town. It didn't appear to be as developed and it felt like we had gone back in time about 60 years. The apartment blocks were very old-fashioned and there was not one modern car in sight. We stuck out like a sore thumb walking to the restaurant with Ivan, speaking in English. A group of young teenagers started following us and saying the odd English word. I had my camera with me so I filmed them for the vlog, which they appeared to like. Ivan explained that they wouldn't hear English spoken there, which is why it was interesting for them. We had a very pleasant meal then walked back to the hotel, where a stuffed bear sat proudly in the lobby.

We had two flights planned the next day, first stopping to refuel at a small town called Kazachinskoe, then on to Taksimo. The second flight would see us pass through some snow-capped mountains. It was going to be a big flying day and both of us were looking forward to it. We flew out over the frozen Angara River. We had made a lot of easterly progress and were now at the same longitude as Thailand but we weren't particularly far north. In fact, we were at a similar latitude to Edinburgh but it was getting colder; nothing uncomfortable yet but both of us noticed the drop in temperature. The flight to Kazachinskoe was uneventful and it wasn't too long before we were on the ground.

There was very little around and no sign of anyone when we landed. At first, we didn't think much of it as it was quite common to have to wait around for an hour or so. A few locals passed by and came to take some pictures. I had some small Mars Bars on me and gave some to a kid with his parents. A short while later, they came back and gave me a frozen salmon and a bottle of whisky that had been decanted into a vodka bottle. It was a very nice gesture and made for a few good pictures but I was slightly limited in terms of what I could do with it!

After an hour, we called Evgeny and asked if he knew what was going on. He advised us that the fuel was coming. Every now and then, the odd person would come over to take a look but it was generally pretty dead. We still had another flight left to complete that day and were getting hungry – or at least, I was! By now, a good few hours had passed and we both felt that our second flight was in jeopardy. Eventually, the airport manager and his son arrived with our fuel but we were now unable to make the second flight as we'd lost too much time. They chatted amongst themselves whilst watching us empty the jerry cans into the gyros. Randomly, the son did pull-ups on what looked to be a home-made bar! We were taken to a newly built log cabin for the night, which was nothing like the other local houses. The remainder of the evening was spent charging camera batteries and other electrical devices and editing footage. Having a routine every evening helped me stay focused and would always set me up for a better start the following day.

I was woken up by a banging at the door, followed by, "Get up, get up!" in a Russian accent. My bedroom door was flung open and there, with a cigarette in his mouth, was the airport manager. He shouted urgently, "We go, we go!" I looked at my watch and it was exactly 6am. I jumped straight out of bed and heard Norman shouting, "What are you doing?" Norman was not happy that this chap was repeatedly banging on his door so early, commanding us to leave immediately. I have to admit, I wasn't expecting this guy to just randomly walk into my room at 6am…he could at least have brought me a coffee!

I was up, dressed and packed in about 20 minutes. Norman, on the other hand, was not going anywhere. He was still in bed and he was not happy! "I'm not having this guy hurry us up at 6am when he kept us waiting for hours," he said nonchalantly. He had a point – but that was yesterday and it was now a new day. The guy came back and started trying to hurry Norman up again but he was still having none of it. I thought it was quite funny but at the same time, I didn't think it was very sensible as we were to some extent at his mercy. I made us some coffee and sat outside whilst Norman took a shower and got ready. Two hours later, we left the cabin. An early start was actually good for me as it gave me plenty of extra time to film cutaway shots of the beautiful landscape for my vlog. We laughed the experience off when we got back to the gyros, which had been guarded by a night watchman.

We were packed and off the ground quite quickly, heading for the mountains and the northern tip of Lake Baikal. The scenery was stunning and the snow-capped peaks looked amazing. We were able to follow a road and a railway line that ran parallel through the mountains. No sooner had we entered the mountains, it felt as though we were out the other side (the bigger, more mountainous terrain was to come further east). The view out over Lake Baikal was incredible. There was a vast, white frozen sheet of ice covering the lake, which didn't look to be frozen solid as we could see large cracks in it. It was listed as a UNESCO World Heritage Site in 1996 and is the world's deepest lake, at over 5,000 feet in places, and allegedly the clearest lake in the world. Ivan was telling us that it is held in high regard by the local people.

After passing over the small town of Nizhneangarsk, we eventually left the lake behind us as we flew up a valley and continued following the road to Taksimo. A few locals descended on the airport when we arrived, to take some pictures. An English-speaking controller had been flown in especially to talk to us over the radio for our arrival and departure, kindly helping us through the formalities. Our fuel was in a drum that needed to be pumped into the aircraft. Thankfully, we managed to get some help from a volunteer who had a hand pump that fitted to the drum and allowed us to simply pump the fuel in.

We had another big day ahead of us to Yakutsk, stopping at Olyokminsk to refuel. It was still mountainous as we departed Taksimo but it didn't take long for the terrain to flatten out again, with miles of trees. We flew up to join the Lena River that flowed to Olyokminsk. The runway was a dark red clay and, as we landed and taxied to the apron, I heard on the radio, "Golf-Charlie-Hotel, suggest hover taxi, suggest hover taxi!" I quickly found out why. My aircraft literally sank into the mud and I had to apply full power to get through it. Of course the controller didn't know that I couldn't hover taxi that slowly but she was trying to help me. Norman was behind me so had learnt from my mistake and managed to steer around it!

After a quick turnaround, we needed to get cracking as we had another long flight to Yakutsk. Our flight plan took us along the River Lena, which was spectacular. The sun was starting to set and the air was smooth which made for wonderful flying conditions. We landed at almost exactly 9pm local time on 21st May 2019. There was a group of journalists waiting for us when we taxied to the small terminal building; it seemed that our journey across Russia was generating quite a lot of interest. One of the journalists spoke excellent English and kindly offered to take us to a hotel that evening as we had landed at a small village outside of Yakutsk called Magan. It was one hell of a bumpy ride into the city as the roads were not that good. As we approached the city, we could see all the water pipes, which in most cities would be buried underground but here, that wasn't possible due to the permafrost. Steam was rising off the pipework and the roads were filthy with dust and dirt.

We arrived at the hotel and noticed two young lads violently fighting. There was a girl screaming for them to stop and an older man watching over them, carrying a large stick, but not making any attempt to break up the fight. "Welcome to Yakutsk," the journalist chuckled. They continued to scuffle and were repeatedly smashing each other in the face. I had a bit of a moral dilemma: at home, I would have attempted to stop them and asked the older guy what on earth he was doing just watching these young lads fight, but of course, I wasn't at home. They couldn't speak English and I certainly couldn't speak Russian, so short of physically stopping them and risking them possibly turning on me, my options were limited. As I tried to intervene, the older guy got right up close to my face, shouting in Russian and reeking of alcohol. My senses were sharp and ready but I could see this situation escalating badly if I got involved. I had a real problem with what was going on in front of me: from what I could make out, one of the lads was actively attacking the other whilst the older one was encouraging it. There is one thing that I absolutely despise and that is bullying. However, as quickly as it unfolded in front of us, it was over and they had disappeared.

We knew we were going to be in Yakutsk for at least a few days as the weather forecast wasn't flyable. We returned to the airport the following day to move the gyros into the maintenance sheds where there was plenty of room, alongside the snow ploughs and tractors. Later that day, the wind and the rain started to pick up so we felt lucky that we had been given a storage solution. We were able to get our visas extended because with the current weather delay, we would not have been able to leave Russia by 31st May. When it became obvious that we had fallen behind our schedule, we thought we might have to leave the country, re-apply for our visas and re-enter but thankfully this was not the case as Evgeny had pulled a lot of strings.

The next few days passed fairly quickly. We found a selection of coffee shops, one in particular which sold amazing chocolate cake, as well as an Irish bar, although they didn't serve Guinness! We hung out with the journalist and her friend for a few evenings.

We were even treated to an afternoon in some permafrost ice caves. We randomly got chatting to a group of French and American scientists one evening in a bar who were conducting field research work on the permafrost. They told us how the permafrost, which is a permanent layer of frost under the ground, is melting at an alarming rate and also releasing carbon dioxide into the atmosphere. When we asked what was causing it, they all said, "Global warming" simultaneously. They were all very passionate about the area and were keen to quiz us on our views from above.

We had been kicking around Yakutsk for a few days now and the novelty was starting to wear off. We had been watching the weather closely but we needed to be absolutely sure that we had two days of flyable weather with an acceptable cloud base to make it to Magadan through the vast mountain range. Eventually, a two-day weather window opened up. It looked like we had enough stable weather to make the flight to Tomtor then Magadan and we would reassess the weather from there. It was all systems go for a departure from Yakutsk on 28th May.

The day before we left, I was asked to give a talk in a local school, organised by Evgeny and the local authorities. The same representative who had assisted us with the visa renewal translated for me. We arrived at what looked like an apartment block, which was fairly run down with graffiti on the walls. From the outside, it didn't remotely resemble a school. We walked in along some concrete, walled corridors and through a small, wooden door. Inside, there was a group of children, probably around the ages of 10 to 13, all sitting quietly and waiting for us. We were introduced and I connected my laptop to a projector, whilst Norman took pictures for me. Even though I spoke through a translator, the look on their little faces and their eyes transfixed on the screen is what made it special for me. This is what my project was really about: connecting with young people, inspiring them and encouraging them to follow their dreams with confidence. I will always remember those children and I just hope they also have fond memories of when the crazy British adventurer came to visit.

18

International Date Line

The following morning, once in the air, we headed for our first waypoint east of Yakutsk, over the vast, flat terrain which was mostly populated with dense forest. We would see the beautiful, intimidating-looking mountains looming in the distance with their snow-capped peaks. There was a road almost the whole way to Tomtor that weaved its way through the valleys. The waypoints that we'd been given were fairly close to this so we agreed that we would follow the road for safety, ensuring that we always had somewhere to land if the weather deteriorated. As we entered the mountains, we lost comms with the controllers. I was using my sat phone to stay in touch and was also messaging Eddie who was relaying to Evgeny. Every now and then, we heard commercial traffic above us operating on the same frequency. Relaying to airliners was quite a common occurrence by now when we were out of range with the controllers. The most common were *American Airlines, Air China, Lufthansa* and the occasional *British Airways* flight, which would be referred to as 'Speedbird'.

We hadn't been in the mountains long when I heard "Golf-Kilo-Tango-Charlie-Hotel, *American Airlines* here, the controllers are trying to get in contact with you, we can relay," in a strong American accent. I relayed our position and ETA to the next waypoint and he passed back instructions. There was something pretty cool about being in one of the world's most remote areas and talking to an *American Airlines* pilot who was 30,000 feet above us!

The scenery was wonderful: the ground was a combination of lush grass, trees and gravel riverbeds that meandered through the valleys. On either side, towering mountains would rise up to around 5,000 feet with glistening, white snow caps. The road that we were following was over 2,000 km long, well-constructed and mostly gravel. It's called the Kolyma Highway but sadly also known as the 'Road of Bones'. A large proportion of it was constructed using forced labour from the government-run Gulag camps. The road is treated as a memorial, as the bones of the estimated 250,000 people who died during its construction are laid beneath or around it.

We were told that there were a couple of Chinese guys on motorbikes who had left Yakutsk a few days before us, riding to Magadan. We were actively looking for them but never managed to spot them. We landed on the small strip that was a mixture of gravel and grass. There was an old Russian helicopter which was intact so I guessed it was still operational. A large drum of fuel was waiting for us and eventually, a woman arrived with her daughter. They both spoke good English and took us back to our accommodation, stopping at the local grocery store on the way to pick up some supplies for the evening and breakfast. It was a small village, although they were in the process of building what looked to be quite a modern school (which they were keen to point out). The accommodation was very good considering this was a real frontier village – they even had satellite internet.

I woke up fairly early the following morning and went for a short run. To be out in the crisp, cool air, looking up at the blue skies and mountains that surrounded the village felt rejuvenating. Tomtor is located 30 km south east of Oymyakon, which is one of the coldest, permanently inhabited settlements on earth, with an average winter temperature of -50 °C. It was hard to imagine that extreme of temperature! I was running along in just a T-shirt and shorts, with sweat running down my face. I got back to the accommodation feeling great – I even did a few press-ups on the grass!

The flight to Magadan was a long one through the mountains. Much of the route was flying along massive, open valleys which made for stunning scenery. The weather was holding up well for the most part; there were occasional cumulonimbus clouds looming but we were able to avoid them. For most of the flight, we chatted between ourselves, confirming features on our charts and making sure that we were flying along the correct valleys. Jagged mountain tops scattered the horizon as far as the eye could see, which was a long way! We would sometimes see small, temporary settlements with diggers and heavy machinery cutting away at the rock; the area had a rich gold mining history, although it had declined over recent years.

I was receiving messages from Eddie on the *Garmin inReach*, who was doing a great job supporting us and putting out social media content. We were now 10 hours ahead of him, so he was staying up through the night to provide vital flight tracking monitoring.

As we approached Magadan from the north, clouds were building and more established rain had set in, thankfully not hard. Visibility was acceptable but it was certainly not weather we would ordinarily choose to fly in. We did expect some light rain and here it was, right on cue! We had descended due to the cloud and were unable to make contact with the tower at Magadan until we were on our final approach. The sky was now ominously dark but the runway lights were shining bright, which was a welcome sight. I was certainly ready to land.

We both taxied on to a stand and were met by one of the airport officials. Almost immediately, we began trying to secure a hangar for the aircraft; Norman and I were both hustling hard but we were having no luck. It was a little frustrating as we saw some buildings that I'm sure would have been able to tuck our little aircraft in somewhere but it was obvious that wasn't going to happen. We unpacked our kit and wrapped the gyros. The rain was no problem and my *AirCovers* cover had proved extremely valuable.

We passed through Security and the airport formalities were over relatively quickly, before being given a lift to the local hotel that most pilots use. It was surprisingly nice and I had an absolutely gigantic room, in fact, the largest hotel room of the entire flight around the world. It had quite a modern restaurant attached to it on the top floor and the food was delicious and most welcome. We were both tired, having flown two massive days through the mountains and we were pleased with our progress. We spent some time chatting and scrolling through the weather app, *Windy*. We were thinking about taking a day off the following day but the risk of getting stuck there was too great. The weather was flyable so we just needed to push on whilst we had favourable conditions.

The following morning, we were picked up by an airport official. Before heading back to the airfield, he gave us a quick whistle stop tour of Magadan. It was a fairly large port town located on the Sea of Okhotsk, with a population of around 100,000 people. The main industry is fishing and some food production facilities. We were driven down to the sea, to a metal statue of a woolly mammoth. The sculpture is called "Time" and is apparently a symbol of eternity and frailty of all life before the onslaught of time.

Back at the airport, our fuel arrived in jerry cans and we carried out our pre-flight checks. There was now a bit of a headwind building which would slow us down but would not be a problem later in the flight. We took off in formation, climbed out and flew along the now flat ground. The high ground of the mountains was off to our left and there were some mountains far off to our right but our days of flying through mountains were now behind us. It was all relatively low lying flat tundra, with a mix of grass, small trees and rocks. We could see snowmobile tracks in the grass but they soon disappeared the further away from Magadan we flew. We headed over a small coastal settlement on the Sea of Okhotsk called Takhtoyamsk but could see very little going on.

As we flew up the coast, it would prove to be some of the best flying of the entire trip. The wind had now completely died out and there was not even a ripple on the water below us. The air was super smooth so we slowed down to take pictures and film. There were occasional flocks of birds resting on the water and they would fly away when they heard us coming, sometimes getting quite close to our aircraft. Norman was flying just in front of me and I heard him say, "Bears! There are brown bears." I had my camera at the ready but was never quick enough to capture any. We did circle around once but it didn't feel right because the noise from our aircraft would probably scare them so we deliberately chose not to fly back over them. It was an incredible, once-in-a-lifetime flight and the conditions couldn't have been any better. We even saw an old aircraft wreckage on a flat piece of land next to the shoreline that had probably crashed many years ago.

Eventually we landed in Evensk, another coastal town on the Sea of Okhotsk. The end of the runway went almost right up to the beach. Once we had unpacked the gyros and covered them up, we were given a tour of the small settlement. I enjoyed walking along the beach: the sea was incredibly still and looked inviting with the sun reflecting off it but I can tell you, it would have been extremely cold! There were a few 4x4s that had huge tyres and high-lift suspension kits as they are used for driving out onto the tundra. They did look like a lot of fun!

Our accommodation for the night was in a small block of flats where Norman and I shared a room with a single bed on either side. All we needed was a bed and somewhere to charge our electronics so this was more than enough. We were given little plastic overshoes to wear on our trainers, to keep the floors clean. The small town of Evensk had a nice feel about it: the locals seemed very friendly despite not really being able to communicate. I think it was quite common to see foreigners passing through. We did get chatting to one Russian gentleman over dinner who was staying in the same accommodation. He lived in St Petersburg but was working for six months managing a small power plant that produced the electricity for the entire settlement.

The next morning, we were taken back to the airfield and dispensed our fuel from the drum into the gyros. We were getting pretty adept at that by now. The weather was excellent and I was looking forward to another clear, calm day. We took off and were immediately out over the sea, then flew back along the beach before heading north up to Markovo. The temperature was dropping and there were still areas of thawing snow and ice on the ground despite it being the end of May. A lot of the terrain would have potentially been possible to land on, which is always a bonus. We did see the occasional derelict radar antenna station that may have been from the Cold War era, some of which were really quite large. As we approached Markovo, the landscape had completely flattened out. The town is situated on the bank of the River Anadyr and we could see swamps, lakes and lots of smaller rivers that flowed out of it.

We landed in Markovo on Friday 31st May. Evgeny had informed us that we would not be able to carry on over the weekend as the airport was shut. It wasn't ideal but we were now coming to the end of our Russian leg and only had two more stops left before we reached the USA. We hadn't been on the ground long before we got chatting to the English-speaking controller who had been flown in especially to clear us to land. We learnt that rain was forecast over the coming days with a high possibility of flooding. This was potentially a serious problem as we didn't have the time to get stuck there. We immediately expressed our concerns, saying that we needed to leave the following day.

We were taken to our accommodation for the night, which was a small flat inside a larger block of flats. We were staying with the controller too and luckily the flat had three bedrooms so we all had our own rooms. The controller was a really nice guy who had come up from Magadan especially to clear us in and out of the airport. There was only one flight a week to Magadan so he would be there for the rest of the week and possibly longer if the water levels did rise significantly.

We went out to a shop to purchase our dinner as there were no restaurants. That evening, we sat and chatted with the controller, who discussed with his boss and the airport manager the prospect of us leaving the next day. Evgeny also pulled some strings which meant we were able to leave.

The next morning, there was no sign of the forecast rain as yet and, as there was no internet, we couldn't check the forecast ourselves. Eddie relayed that the weather looked good enough to get to Anadyr. We arrived back at the small airport where I noticed lots of little rivers and swamps close by, so I could see how easily it could flood.

Our fuel was provided in two, 200-litre drums. Someone would be benefitting from a lot of leftover fuel but it didn't bother me. As we were about to start fuelling, an airport official informed us that he didn't know if the fuel would be any good because it had been sitting there for a long time, which was really not what you want to hear when you are just about to put it in your aircraft and fly across frozen rivers! It really freaked us out. Evgeny confirmed that this was fresh fuel but the airport official was still saying something different. It was neither here nor there as there was no more fuel to purchase and we needed to leave pronto.

We checked in with Eddie back in the UK where it was still the previous day (we were now approximately 12 hours ahead of the UK). Norman and I both fired up our aircraft, which started first time. "That's a good sign," Norman joked. I already had some good quality *AVGAS* in my tank so knew that would help improve the quality of the fuel that was in question. We took off and headed straight out over the river and swamp lands. If we did have an engine failure, we probably wouldn't have died coming down in this terrain but I'm not sure that the aircraft would have been salvageable. After about 15 minutes in the air, we both tentatively joked that we wouldn't still be in the sky now if the fuel really was going to cause a problem. After 30 minutes of flying, we agreed that there was no problem and that Evgeny had been right. Evgeny always arranged fuel for us and had worked hard to make sure that everything was in place at each stop.

It was now a frozen tundra: miles and miles of ice and snow. The snow wasn't thick but there was a lot of it about. We approached Anadyr, the easternmost town in Russia, and flew over it as the airport is on the other side of the river. In order to get across to Anadyr, we were piled into a small minibus, which drove to the river bank. The river itself was frozen over but with large cracks and holes in the ice. In the dead of winter, it would be a passable road but now, the only way across was by hovercraft! It was quite exciting: we bundled in the small amphibious craft, the driver started up the engine and we instantly lifted up off the ground, hovering on a bed of air. We headed out onto the river and the machine rode over the bumps and holes in the ice with ease. It was an impressive little thing and was the perfect tool for the melting ice pack.

Once we arrived in Anadyr, we were driven to a hotel, probably the best one in town, certainly a world away from our previous night's accommodation! We needed to get internet connection so we could access the weather forecasts and make a plan for our final flights across to Alaska. After a day, we were up and running and starting to get on top of all the little jobs. I had been doing lots of filming so it needed to be backed up and edited. I also had commitments to make filmed messages for sponsors and schools.

We monitored the weather closely and found a suitable weather window from 6th June. It wasn't perfect but it would be workable: no rain, very little wind and good visibility. There was just the issue of cloud cover that we would have to negotiate en route.

I went for a run around the town most mornings. I was running around the harbour one morning and was chased by two dogs, only just managing to get away from them. It was at least a good sprint session I suppose… there is nothing like being chased by a couple of vicious-looking dogs to kick start the day!

Once my admin jobs were completed, there wasn't a massive amount to do, apart from a bit of shopping. We were also given a guided tour of a local museum which was interesting. The people of this region were clearly tough and hard-working, although in more recent times, most of the young people were moving away to the bigger cities where there are more opportunities.

We technically probably could have flown from Anadyr to Nome in one flight but it would have been pushing it unnecessarily so our plan was to depart Russia from Provideniya, a small settlement further east. We needed good weather for at least two consecutive days to make the crossing to Alaska.

After five days in Anadyr, we were ready to move on. We arrived at the airport after our return ride on the hovercraft, packed our kit into the gyros and began to put on our dry suits. The last time I wore mine was crossing the English Channel but now, I couldn't have been further away!

The weather was clear, albeit a bit chilly, but not as cold as I thought it would be. With all my cold weather kit and the dry suit, it was a bit of a squeeze getting into G-KTCH but it was very comfortable once I was in. On take-off, the air was cold and dense, giving the rotors and propellor plenty to bite into as they rotated. We were flying over the tundra to begin with but would soon be out over the ice-cold water below us. Flying over the water was something that I personally got used to very quickly.

As we left Anadyr, we did start to encounter some low cloud in front of us which pushed us a little further inland to try and fly around it. We were flying quite low and would occasionally see water being blown into the air: it was a pod of whales! They were very easy to spot as they cruised effortlessly through the water. I flew lower and circled one of the whales to get some footage, which came out fantastically well. I couldn't imagine how anyone would want to harpoon them and drag them onto a boat, butchering them on a huge scale whilst they were still alive, but commercial whaling still goes on to this day.

The cloud was starting to build and it wasn't long before we were completely on top of a thick layer of cloud. It certainly wasn't ideal but would be fine for now: the question was, what would it be like at Provideniya when we needed to land? The higher ground to our left was still very clear in the distance so we thought that this must be localised cloud that had established itself over the water. We were carrying enough fuel to enable us to turn back if we needed to, but we were no doubt in quite a serious position. If Provideniya was clouded in, we couldn't just descend through the clouds and hope to come out on the runway! With high ground around the whole airport, a manoeuvre like that without the correct instrumentation was unthinkable. Usually we chatted a lot over the radio but we didn't talk much for a while as we were concentrating and thinking through our options, hoping that our calculations around the forecast would be accurate.

Sure enough, as we got closer, we began to see small breaks in the cloud, which was a very good sign! We arrived over the port of Provideniya and made our descent to the airport. The forecast was almost spot on: we estimated the broken cloud base to be around 800 feet AGL which proved to be no problem at all. In fact, as we were on our final approach, the sun came streaking through. We had made it to the end of the world….Provideniya!

Almost immediately, a young official approached us who spoke English. He introduced himself and asked to see our passports, with a cheeky smile on his face, which was a pleasant surprise. I had quite a bit of adrenaline and excitement running through me and I had always wondered what it was going to be like here: it was certainly sparse! With no buildings around at all, it was obvious that the aircraft were going to be left outside, so we put our covers on and tied the rotors down. We were staying in the port settlement of Provideniya that was on the other side of the bay. It was used by the Soviet military and, at one point, had over 6,000 people living there. In the post-Soviet period, social and economic upheavals meant that the population had declined quickly. We were given a lift into the town in the back of a military-style truck that was used by the officials. I'm unsure as to why there was an entire team of people sent out to meet us but I guess it was all about the protocol!

After a short drive around the bay, we were dropped off outside our accommodation. We decided to go for a walkabout and it felt like we were walking through a film set. There were of course people living there, but you would think that the area had been abandoned for years as most of the buildings no longer had windows! When we went to a local café for dinner, I wasn't sure what to expect but was surprised to see the chef cooking on a barbecue outside. It looked quite modern, with a few locals sitting around eating and drinking. As you can imagine, everyone stared at us but not in an intimidating way, more out of intense curiosity. Some people smiled and waved, which was all quite surreal! Here I was, quite literally at the end of the world, eating pizza and drinking Coca Cola, surrounded by people just happily living out their lives. It really doesn't matter where you live on this planet: we were in a place that only a fraction of people on earth will ever have the privilege of visiting and we were warmly welcomed into their café and shown great hospitality!

I was still awake quite late as I couldn't really sleep due to the prospect of flying into the USA the following day. I was also overwhelmed at the realisation that we had flown the whole way across Russia in our tiny machines. It was really quite a feat. It's hard to articulate the sheer scale of the country without seeing it and travelling across it for yourself.

With all the excitement, I didn't have any problem getting up in the morning and got dressed in my many layers of undergarments to fend off the cold. Back at the airport, we had just put on our survival suits and life jackets when I was asked to go back up to the tower to sign a general declaration and write down some frequencies. Fully kitted up, I began to overheat in the small terminal building. However, I made sure I always did everything with a smile, no matter how frustrating a situation might be. I'd learnt over the years that, regardless of any language barrier, people can still pick up on your attitude, which can make a big difference to the outcome. I breathed a sigh of relief when I finally walked outside into the cooler air. "OK, let's fly to America!" I said.

The clouds had cleared a little and eventually we took off in formation, climbing through the clouds and making our way out to the Bering Straits. After about 10 minutes, Norman came on the radio telling me he had a problem. He had lost his pneumatic pressure that trimmed the rotor head taking the pressure off the stick. Without this, he had to take the full force himself which would not be possible to hold for long. We would have to go back, so I called the tower and informed them that we were returning. "Why are you returning?" the controller repeated over and over. I tried to explain but eventually just had to tell them we were coming back. Eddie was clearly confused by the trackers and wondering what we were doing.

Once back on the ground, the officials were asking again why we had come back, so we explained that Norman had a technical problem. All they wanted to know was how long we would be there! We couldn't see anything obvious that would cause a problem; I operated the pump on the stick whilst Norman swapped some pipes over and generally tinkered around. He was surprisingly calm as he methodically thought through possible problems and solutions. About 10 minutes later, the pneumatic system was working. We had no idea what he'd done but it was working so we took off quickly, eager to get going again. I can only imagine how worried Norman must have been but he held his nerve well.

It was now likely that Nome would be shut when we arrived although we would still be able to land. There would of course be no problem with light as it was light pretty much 24 hours a day now. We climbed above the broken cloud and made our way up the coast. We had opted to cross the famous Bering Straits, named after the Danish explorer, Vitus Bering, at the Diomede Islands. At the point of crossing, it was a distance of 57 nautical miles from Russia to Alaska. As we flew up the Russian coast, it felt incredible to be flying where no other gyro had ever flown before, and had certainly not crossed the International Date Line before! The International

Date Line marks the border between Russia and the USA off Alaska's west coast. The islands of Big Diomede in Russia and Little Diomede in the USA are separated by 2.4 miles of water, with the International Date Line running midway between them. Our plan was to fly in between the two islands.

It wasn't long before we could see the Alaskan mountains over the horizon, even though we hadn't yet ventured out over the water. We passed close to the settlement of Lavrentiya and could clearly see the building and runway that served the community. It was now time to coast out. That was it – the Russian mainland was behind us.

We would fly over Big Diomede that belonged to Russia, before crossing the International Date Line. I had heard all sorts of stories of rockets and missile launchers mounted on top of it but I can confirm that there was absolutely nothing! We flew pretty low to get a good look but saw no sign of anyone or anything based there. There is a small settlement that we noticed on the west side of Little Diomede that belongs to the USA. No sooner had we crossed the date line, the radio burst into life with the sound of the Russian controller who we had become accustomed to hearing: "Golf-Kilo-Tango-Charlie-Hotel, contact Anchorage control on 133.3." I repeated the frequency back and, just like that, Russia was now completed! I couldn't resist turning around and taking one last picture of Russia before we were gone.

However, we were by no means finished. We still had to get to Nome and the cloud was now developing below. We were very close to being over the Alaskan coast. We overflew the small airstrip of Wales and I managed to make contact with them on the radio. It was strange hearing an American accent! I asked if he could give us a forecast for Nome and he confirmed that it was completely clear, which gave us the confidence to carry on. The controller at Wales told us that we wouldn't pick up Anchorage control unless we were at

30,000 feet and not to worry about it. We were no longer under full radar control so could effectively do what we wanted. Norman and I spoke about landing at Wales for fun, but due to our late departure and the fact that his aircraft was still flying without any problems, we decided it was sensible to just carry on.

The mountains that we could see from Russia were now directly to our left as we flew down the Alaskan coast. Our route eventually took us over land and away from the sea. The cloud was breaking and clearing so we dropped down to around 800 feet AGL – our preferred height for flying. Eventually we saw a few minor roads and knew that Nome wasn't far away. I tried to reach them on the radio but the controllers had clearly gone home for the day (to be fair, it was almost 11pm!). We announced our arrival on the radio just in case any other aircraft were inbound or taking off. There was nothing, so we landed on Runway 28 and taxied over to some hangars. It was strange how when we were flying, neither of us felt the cold at all but as soon as we landed, it was absolutely freezing! Perhaps the adrenaline had worn off and we could now feel the cold or it was just colder on the ground than in the air. Either way, we had made it to the USA!

19

Alaska

Having landed, we got chatting to a couple of mechanics who worked for *Bering Air*. "Where have you come from, boys?" one of them asked. "England," I replied. "No freaking way!" We told them that we had just flown in from Provideniya and that we were very cold. "Come on in, then," they said, which was the invitation we were hoping for! We pushed the gyros into the hangar and immediately started to warm up. We knew we would be in Nome for at least a day or two as we had to sort out our US visas. We were able to get a ride to a hotel, courtesy of the mechanics who had just finished their shift. It was by now almost midnight but you would never have known because the skies were clear blue and it was as light as day!

I jumped in the front of a pick-up truck, instantly noticing an AR-15 assault rifle sitting there in between the passenger and driver's seat. "Bloody hell, we're in America now!" I joked into the camera as I was filming a vlog at the time. We were driven to a local hotel called the *Nugget Inn* and nearly had a heart attack at the price! There wasn't much we could do about it so we simply paid for the exorbitant rooms then went to the bar. I was ravenously hungry and luckily, we were still able to order food. I jokingly told the waitress that I'd have the biggest cheeseburger I could get my hands on, then realised that might be a mistake, considering we were now in America, the home of very large portions! We toasted with a beer and generally relaxed and enjoyed the moment. I think it was about 2.30am by the time we went to bed.

The next day, we had a walk around Nome, which didn't take long. We explored some of the gold mining machinery that sucks gold off the sea bed. I imagined many fortunes had been made and lost there. We looked at the finish point of the famous Iditarod Trail Sled Dog Race which runs from Anchorage to Nome, a distance of nearly 1,000 miles: it was a pretty brutal but amazing accomplishment. Nome is only accessible by air or sea as it's not connected to a road network, so travel is limited for the locals. I got a sense that many people have a lot of time on their hands and there was a surprisingly large number of people drinking in the streets. They were not causing any problems but there was a noticeably strong drinking culture.

We checked out the weather which was looking good for a flight the next day. Both of our gyros needed to be serviced fairly soon so that became a priority. Norman contacted a gyro mechanic called John, who had a lot of experience and had rebuilt Norman's aircraft in Thailand when he crashed it. He was qualified to work on both our gyros which are made by different manufacturers. We arranged for John to fly out to Anchorage, although it would be a week before he arrived. The local pilots advised us that we would have better weather if we flew the inland route to Anchorage because the coast can be very changeable and usually has a cloud bank that just lingers, so we took their advice. We decided on McGrath as our destination for the day and the pilots advised us that we would find accommodation there. I wanted to be sure so I called a local hotel, *Hotel McGrath*, who confirmed that they could gladly accommodate us.

It only took a few minutes to be clear of Nome and we made our way along the coast. There was a thick layer of cloud out over the sea but it was completely clear inland, so we flew slightly inland to be clear of the cloud below us, eventually cutting the corner off at Norton Bay which was around 25 nautical miles over the water. We then flew low along the coast at around 500 feet AGL to Unalakleet, where we made a direct routing for McGrath. As we flew inland, the ground started to rise up to rolling hills, until it flattened out as we crossed the Yukon River. We saw lush, green, untouched plains with smaller rivers that carved their way through the terrain, as well as lots of natural lakes. There was the odd rain shower around, which we were able to dodge, and we even spotted some lightning far off in the distance.

We landed in McGrath, which was a great little place with a lovely feel to it, situated on the banks of the Kuskokwim River. It was not connected to a road network, making it a completely self-sufficient town. It used to be a place where aircraft would refuel on their way to the Eastern front during World War Two. The owners of a small aircraft maintenance business kindly let us keep our gyros in their hangar. Jen, the owner of *Hotel McGrath*, gave us the keys to a house where we would stay just around the corner from the hotel.

The following morning, we both noticed that it was substantially warmer when we went outside. It felt like a hot summer's day: we couldn't believe it! McGrath must have had its own microclimate because it was literally in the twenties and was gorgeous T-shirt weather. We walked over to the hotel and were treated to the most amazing cooked breakfast. Jen informed us that she was not going to charge us a penny for our board and lodging, as it was her way of supporting us. It really was an incredibly kind thing to do. Norman and I weighed up how long we had to wait until John arrived in Anchorage and realised it made sense to stay in McGrath whilst we were in such a nice place. We informed Jen that we would stay for three or four nights but insisted on giving her a contribution each day for the food and accommodation.

We managed to borrow some bikes and started exploring; there was a dirt road that went for about 10 miles or so out of town and eventually just stopped. Within a day, we had seen everything there was to see, but it was an ideal place to be based. Internet connectivity was good at the house and I even managed to give an online Skype interview with *Sky News* one morning, which streamed absolutely perfectly!

One morning, I got up early and went for a run. I was probably about three miles out of town when I noticed a small, baby bear rummaging around in the bushes. I stopped to look then realised that I was on my own, at least 30 minutes away from anyone, and the adult bears must have been close by. So I slowly turned around and ran back – for some reason, my return journey was a little quicker than on the way out!

Whilst catching up with my admin, I learnt that Norman was not eligible to claim the *FAI* "speed around the world" record. It's funny how things work out: I had been so focused on my sponsorship commitments and things that I could control, I had almost forgotten what he was attempting to do. I was still a long way from home and couldn't afford any distractions. I needed to fly a lot of miles very quickly in order to stand half a chance of getting back across the Atlantic before I missed the weather window of opportunity. I had to keep reminding myself that no one had even come close to flying a continuous journey around the world in an aircraft of this type – this really was a pioneering effort!

Eddie had performed nothing short of a miracle to work out a route for me that took in all 49 mainland states, even looking at the best airfields in which to land and researching what facilities were available at each stop. Luckily, he had a good network of contacts and the plan was coming together nicely. We had been in McGrath for four days and decided it was probably time to move on to Anchorage. We had to find a suitable place for John to service both aircraft and were given a contact to ask for on arrival by the guys at *Bering Air*.

I had received a *Facebook* message from a British lady who was living with her American husband in Willow, which we would pass through on our way to Anchorage. She had seen my interview on *Sky News* and said that if we wanted to pop in, we would be welcome; it was perfect timing as we still had a few days spare before John arrived. I wrote back informing her that we would love to.

The next morning, we left McGrath after a fantastic few days. I left feeling motivated and full of enthusiasm, in stunning weather. We departed to the east and flew over the lush, green trees and scrub below us. Eventually the Alaskan mountain range came into sight, which separates the flat lands of McGrath and Anchorage. The range is home to the highest mountain in North America, Denali, otherwise known as Mount McKinley. Although it was a little further north of our route through the range, we could still see it towering above the other summits at over 20,000 feet. We had been advised of a pass to take through the mountains, called 'Rainy Pass', commonly used by light aircraft. Thankfully, it wasn't rainy when we passed through, quite the opposite. The conditions were lovely, making for a stunning and smooth flight as we passed through the valleys, looking up at the mountains, which had a lush, green base to them where the grass was growing. The views were simply stunning. At times, I had to pinch myself that I was really here doing this.

Eventually, the valley opened up in front of us, presenting a vast plain of trees and lakes. We slowly descended as the terrain lowered and we landed in Willow. We were given instructions to cross a main road, as our host's hangar was not located inside the airport grounds but on the side of a lake. Alaska is the home of float planes and it's where a lot of pilots go to obtain their float rating, which is understandable as there are lakes everywhere.

The road was quiet when we taxied across so we arrived at our host's without any problems and received a lovely welcome. We were in for a treat as they were cooking steak and baked potatoes; I was ravenously hungry so the meal didn't touch the sides! We slept in the hangar on blow-up mattresses. I placed mine right next to G-KTCH and slept incredibly well.

The following morning as we were getting ready to depart, our hosts warned us to be careful. They said, "Stay sharp and on the lookout, boys, there are a lot of planes flying around here – they pop up out of nowhere, usually from a lake!" They told us that there were quite often air to air accidents as so many small planes fly around the area. Flying small planes in Alaska is like driving a car: it's a completely normal thing to do and a lot of families fly and own planes. In the US, it's almost half the price of flying in the UK which probably makes it more accessible.

As we set off on our way to Merrill Field in Anchorage, we were told that it would be busy as it was the most commonly used airport for light aircraft. There was now a lot more going on via the radio and we had to really concentrate. Just before we turned on to our final approach, I heard, "Golf-Kilo-Tango-Charlie-Hotel, do you see the large runway off to your right?" "Yes sir," I replied. "Good – you are NOT landing there." It was a large military base and I believe they'd had foreign pilots land there by mistake so I think he was just trying to be clear with us. We needed to go to *Lake & Peninsula Airlines* to store the gyros. Within a few minutes, people had gathered to look at our aircraft. Arriving at a new destination in our open cockpit aircraft always drew a crowd, especially with the flying around the world element! We arrived in Anchorage on 14th June and John was due to arrive the following day.

We found a motel only a few hundred metres across the street called the *Mush Inn*, which was cheap but incredibly grim! It looked like we'd be staying in Anchorage for at least five days and the motel looked safe enough so we opted for this as our base for the duration of our stay. We did look at a much nicer hotel in a better part of the town but at almost $300 per night, that would have been reckless, when the cannabis-encrusted carpets and blood-stained bed sheets of the *Mush Inn* would suffice at $60 per night! I was almost getting high in my room on the first night because the smell of cannabis was so strong. I was moved out of my room on the second night as sewage was coming up through the shower plug hole!

We decided that the best way to get around was to hire bikes, which was a cheap and quite enjoyable way to check out the city. It wasn't a city in the sense of New York but it was still quite big. John arrived with a terrible cold but got to work on servicing the aircraft the following day. We booked John into a hotel around the corner from us, as there was no way we would have expected him to stay in our less than salubrious motel! My aircraft really didn't need much work. After an oil change, new spark plugs and a thorough polish, it looked like it had just rolled out of the factory. Norman's gyro needed a bit more attention. Within a few minutes, John ascertained that the propeller pitch was incorrectly set or had misaligned itself somehow. It was too coarse, which meant it was cutting into the air too much, which explained why he struggled to get off the ground but had a lower engine rpm than me when we were flying together in Russia. It's a bit like trying to pull away in a car in third gear; it would be very difficult but once it's going, it's fine. John worked extremely hard and fixed all of the issues. Spending time in the hangar was fun. "You are going to clean that bloody aircraft away if you keep going," John said to me, which made me laugh. To be fair, I did clean it a lot!

The days passed quite quickly and before we knew it, John had finished his work and was getting ready to go home. I didn't know John that well before he came out to Anchorage but knew him a lot better when he left. I was very grateful that he'd travelled all the way out to help us and really got stuck in when he arrived.

I received a lovely message from a lady called Kristen who worked as a pilot for *American Airlines* and was following my trip via social media. Kristen and her partner, Kent, were in Anchorage doing their float ratings and wanted to see if we could meet up. Both of them had so much positive energy, they were instantly very likeable. Kent was also a pilot for *American Airlines* and we agreed to meet up for dinner that evening. We had a great time chatting: they lived in New York about an hour from downtown NY and often flew their light aircraft along the Hudson River and around the famous Statue of Liberty. They told me that they would take me on the same tour and take some air to air pictures when I was passing through. At the time, it felt like an age away but it was something I was determined to do. It was a lovely evening and I was very grateful that Kristen had reached out to me. We were building quite a following on social media and I was receiving a lot of messages from gyro pilots asking where I was going in the US with offers of support.

It was now 21st June and we had been in Anchorage for a week. From what I had seen so far, Alaska was a beautiful place and one that I would like to visit again. Although I was still very much on schedule, I had an underlying sense of urgency to get going. My aircraft was freshly serviced, polished to perfection and ready to go! It didn't take too long to clear the built-up area of Anchorage and we opted to route through Alaska and Canada via an inland route, commonly referred to as 'The Trench' route. This would take us down to Seattle and back into the US. As stunning as it would have been, the coastal weather was too unpredictable and had limited landing options, so we decided on the safer option.

We followed Highway One all the way to Tok Junction, but not without a pit stop. I had drunk too much that morning and, no matter how hard I tried to ignore it, I could feel my bladder bursting. We overflew Tazlina airstrip, which was an uncontrolled, small, gravel strip; there was no one around so we landed for five minutes. Eddie was wondering what was going on as he looked at the tracker so I told him I needed a toilet break! It was now considerably warmer and I was flying in a lightweight jacket, which was a bit more comfortable.

Later, we landed at Tok Junction. That night, we stayed at the *Golden Bear Hotel*, which only had one room available but luckily, it was a twin with two double beds so it worked just fine for us. After a good night's sleep, we had breakfast and made the required calls to the Canadian Immigration department as we were due to cross the border. We both also noticed that our backs felt incredibly itchy but we didn't give it too much thought. Over the coming days, the itching got worse and we realised that we'd been very badly bitten by bed bugs. Our shoulders and backs were covered in small bites that stayed with me for weeks before eventually clearing up.

Our destination for the day was Whitehorse, our first stop in Canada. Before we could depart, we needed to arrange fuel. The airport manager offered us *AVGAS* but we preferred to run unleaded petrol. There was a *Shell* filling station nearby and a small service road that ran adjacent to the road, so after some careful consideration, we decided to taxi the aircraft along the sidewalk to the filling station. We turned the engines off and pushed the gyros up to the pumps and started filling up. As you can imagine, this gained quite a lot of attention! It was a fun start to what looked to be another fairly easy day.

Highway One would take us all the way to our planned stop so we set off low-level in pretty good weather. We flew over some absolutely stunning lakes. One in particular was Kluane Lake and I managed to capture some amazing pictures where it looked like steam was rising off the lake. Not long after the lakes were behind us, we had around 30 minutes left before we would be arriving at Whitehorse. It was a particularly warm morning and the clouds had been building all day. We noticed some lightning in the distance but didn't think too much of it at first as it wasn't in the direction that we were heading. The cloud started to thicken up ahead of us and was getting darker so that we were now flying through light rain. "I'm not sure we can get through this," Norman said, as the rain was getting heavier. About 30 seconds later, a bolt of lightning struck a hill top only a few hundred metres away from me, off to my left side. It lit up the whole sky then, "BANG!" The crack of thunder was so loud that we heard it over the noise of our aircraft. "Turn around!" I said. If we were struck by lightning, the consequences would have been catastrophic. We realised that we couldn't fly all the way back to Tok Junction so it would just be a case of finding somewhere to land. We initially looked at a field as a possible landing site but there were fences and it may have been difficult to take off again.

I remembered that only a few minutes earlier, we had flown over a stretch of road that had a large pull-in area with a toilet, which would work as a potential landing site. We needed to get on the ground quickly and the cloud was coming in behind us as well. "Norman, fly back along the road – there's a layby that will work for us," I said. Thankfully, that stretch of highway was very quiet so cars would not be a problem, although every now and then we would see the occasional truck. As we turned around, another bolt of lightning jumped out of the clouds and struck the ground close by. I thought that the next one might hit us and my heart was racing with so much adrenaline pumping through me.

Norman was just in front of me and lined up for an approach on the road, as I warned him to watch out for wires. He landed smoothly on the road and I came in just behind him, before we taxied straight into the layby. Thankfully, the rain had eased off as we had flown out of it but now it was heading straight for us. We wrapped the gyros in their covers, I pulled out the camera and started filming. Just as I did, I managed to capture a massive lightning strike and quite possibly the loudest crack of thunder I have ever heard. The rain started coming down pretty heavily and the only place we could hide was in a toilet! Luckily, it was quite a big one so as we took shelter, we left the door open so we could see what was going on.

It was raining hard and the layby was starting to puddle up: we wouldn't be flying anywhere for a while. We had no signal on our phones so the only means of communication was via the *Garmin* tracker or the sat phone, which I used to call Eddie to update him on the situation. We were now in Canada but had not cleared Immigration so were technically in the country illegally at this point. Eddie informed Immigration and passed a message back with instructions to stay there. The Immigration officials from Whitehorse would drive out to us.

About an hour later, a family pulled up in an RV and, when they saw us standing in the doorway of a toilet sheltering from the rain, they came over and asked if we wanted a hot chocolate. "Oh yes please!" we both said. They were a lovely family and were on a road trip on their way back to Pennsylvania, quite literally thousands of miles away. We chatted and eventually they invited us into their RV for something to eat. Quite a bit of time had passed and we had expected the Immigration officials to have arrived by now.

The clouds were starting to clear and we discussed the idea of flying on, but we were mindful that the message had been relayed to stay where we were and not to move, so we didn't. Eventually it became a bit late to leave so we hitched a ride with the family into Whitehorse, where they dropped us off at a reasonable-looking hotel. Both Norman and I were quite anxious at the thought of leaving our aircraft in a layby by the side of the road. Of course, we had removed our equipment and they were completely covered up but it certainly wasn't ideal.

The next morning, we called Immigration and they came to the hotel to see us. They were pleasant enough and when we asked what had happened the night before and why no one had come out to us, they didn't really have an answer, which we weren't overly impressed with. The formalities were over quickly and we asked if they would give us a lift back out to the aircraft, which they couldn't, so it cost us $100 in a taxi instead!

All I wanted to do was get moving again and, to our immense relief, the gyros were still where we'd left them in the layby. However, the road was much busier and as we packed the aircraft, we had plenty of people pulling over to ask questions. When we said that we were going to take off soon, we got the reply "Oh man, I want to see this!" A truck driver very kindly stopped the traffic at one end of the road, then we waited until it was clear, lined up on the road and took off, one after the other, waving at the crowd that had gathered. Less than 24 hours after our arrival, the weather was now perfect. Although it had been risky landing on the road, it would have been far more dangerous to carry on and potentially get struck by lightning or crash into the ground due to poor visibility.

We were carrying enough fuel that we no longer needed to land at Whitehorse and we had cleared Customs, so decided to carry on to another smaller airfield at Carcross. We now had excellent phone signal, so much so that I could *FaceTime* Eddie whilst flying along. I started experimenting with *Facebook* Live, which worked perfectly and meant that I could share the flights via a live stream. We landed at Carcross and, similar to Tok Junction, we taxied onto a road and pulled into a petrol station.

We then landed at Dease Lake and managed to talk our way into a helicopter hangar for the night. The following morning at the hotel, there were motorcyclists everywhere on their large BMW adventure bikes. They looked like they were having a lot of fun, but so were we, on our flying motorbikes!

Over the next two days, we continued to enjoy some spectacular flying through the valleys and vast areas of outstanding beauty. Every time I saw a cyclist, I would buzz down low and give them a wave. I had many happy memories from cycling around the world, so seeing cyclists with their bikes loaded up brought back good memories. We eventually picked up Highway One again and crossed back into the US just south of Abbotsford. It was strange looking down as there was no visible border that we could see, apart from what looked like a small ditch. I'm sure there were checks in place but looking down from 800 feet, it looked like anyone was free to roam across.

20

West Coast Adventures

Eventually, I caught sight of the Seattle skyline. We noticed some military fighter jets flying low over the water and guessed that they were operating out of Whidbey Island Naval Air Station. We decided to fly low over the water at around 500 feet, which would put us below any other traffic that was flying in the local area. We landed at Jefferson International Airport; the "international" element makes it sound a lot bigger than it was but it was actually quite a small place which had Customs available on request. We had notified US Customs prior to leaving Canada, so an official came out to the airfield on our arrival. He was the most laid back US Customs official I've ever met in my life: he literally just wanted to see our passports and that was it. He didn't ask one question about what we were doing, where we were going, absolutely nothing!

A short while later, a young woman arrived to see me with her child. She was British and was living in Seattle; her mum lived in Basingstoke and had been following my journey, reading the fortnightly updates in the *Basingstoke Observer*. It is a very small world! Her little boy sat in the gyro whilst I pushed it into the Port Townsend Aero Museum, where we were permitted to store our aircraft overnight.

We were a little late leaving the following day due to low cloud and poor visibility but managed to get away in the early afternoon. Our destination for the day was Scappoose where we would meet up with Jim Vanek from *Sportcopter*, who manufactures gyros. Most of the flight was over trees and more beautiful lakes. The Columbia River was quite a sight, with huge, ocean-going cargo vessels and tankers slowly making their way upstream to Portland to load or offload their cargo on the river that separates the states of Washington and Oregon.

Scappoose air strip didn't appear to be particularly busy and was probably the perfect place for a gyroplane manufacturer. We were welcomed with open arms by Jim and his team. Norman had already visited on a previous trip so knew Jim fairly well. We packed the aircraft away and went straight out for dinner.

I hung out with Jim the next morning and he gave me an overview of some of the aircraft they were producing, which were incredibly impressive and extremely well-engineered. My front screen had picked up quite a few scratches along the way which I mentioned to Jim, who kindly had one of his colleagues polish them out. He did a great job and it was so clear when he finished that I could hardly tell that I was even looking through a screen. I was extremely impressed with Jim and everything he was doing; he is one of the most experienced gyro pilots and is well-known for performing loops in his *Sportcopter* machines. He was also very humble and I liked the fact that he was laid back, whilst also being extremely driven.

Norman had already set off for McMinnville early that morning, which marked a big day for him. More than four years earlier, he had flown back to Northern Ireland from McMinnville, having shipped his gyro from Japan. Now he was flying back there again and I felt that it was his moment to enjoy. If anyone deserved some recognition, it was him, although it wouldn't be quite the finish he had probably hoped for when he set off nine years earlier on his first attempt. Having overcome many problems and demonstrated incredible resilience, he had finally brought some closure to his endeavours. Over two separate journeys, flown more than four years apart, Norman *had* rounded the earth and crossed all lines of longitude, although the journeys would not be eligible for any official circumnavigation recognition by the *FAI* or *Guinness World Records.*

Later that afternoon, I flew to McMinnville to join Norman. I could see the large buildings of the Evergreen Aviation & Space Museum in the distance, with the *Boeing 747* on display at the front. I was due to land at the museum where Norman and his friend, who worked at the museum, were waiting for me. I flew a low pass and came in to land; there was plenty of space and no wind, which made it all very easy. We taxied both gyros to the back of the museum where they would be pushed through into the exhibition hall overnight.

The next two days would be some of the most spectacular flying I have ever experienced. We departed McMinnville and flew out to the coast, flying low-level along the beaches. The coastline was stunning, with miles of beautiful beaches, occasionally interspersed with rocky outcrops that we would either fly over or around. We often saw motocross bikes and 4x4 sand dune buggies racing along the beaches at almost 70 mph, which looked a lot of fun. There would often be people on the beaches and in the ocean enjoying the sunshine, so we flew over the water to avoid flying directly overhead.

Our first stop in California was Crescent City where we stayed overnight, then flew down to Half Moon Bay the following day. That was a flight that I will never forget! I was looking forward to seeing the Golden Gate Bridge and the San Francisco Bay area from the sky. I had cycled across the bridge on my round the world trip and had visited it a few times, the first being with my parents when I was around 10 years old, which I can still remember now. The bay area is notorious for fog and low cloud but someone was looking down on us that day, as there was hardly a cloud in the sky.

Just getting down to San Francisco was stunning: off to our right was the Pacific Ocean, sparkling as the sun's rays reflected off it, and to our left was the incredible Redwood National Park, home to some of the largest trees on earth. The air was fresh and occasionally (unless I was imagining it), I could smell the trees. As we rounded the headland, the Golden Gate Bridge came into view. "Wow," I thought to myself, "here I am." It was a magical sight.

As we got closer, the whole San Francisco city skyline opened up in front of us. We flew over the bridge on the south side and along the famous piers, descending to a lower level. Our turning point was the infamous Alcatraz and, as we rounded the island, I captured some fantastic footage with the Golden Gate Bridge in the foreground. The weather was perfect, just some light wind and crystal-clear visibility. As we flew back to the bridge, my mind was in a heightened state of readiness. I was aware of everything going on around me, checking my instruments and being extra vigilant for other traffic. However, it was surprisingly quiet and the only traffic I noticed was commercial airliners coming out of San Francisco International.

The bridge was getting bigger as we got closer. It really is an engineering marvel, considering it was built over 80 years ago. I knew that rotary aircraft flew under the bridge all the time and I had this gut feeling that it just felt right, being here doing what I was doing. My gyro was flying incredibly smoothly and I knew that I would never be here again in this very position with everything aligned so perfectly. As I got closer, I descended lower and positioned myself in the centre of the bridge so that I was level with the main deck. Trucks and lorries were whizzing by, totally unaware that this British adventurer, who had already flown half way around the world, was flying straight towards them.

My eyes were fixed on the bridge and I was scanning hard, looking for any ropes, wires or netting. Nothing. It was completely clear. I dropped some height and was below the main deck, with a clear view through. I was now absolutely committed; my heart rate was elevated and I could feel myself breathing heavier, with adrenaline coursing through my veins. I passed underneath and, within a few seconds, it was over and I was out the other side. "Woohoo, that's it, the Golden Gate Bridge!" I said to the camera. It felt incredible to know I had just flown my *Magni* gyro under what is arguably the world's most famous bridge!

We soon landed at Half Moon Bay, still buzzing from the flight. The excitement quickly wore off when Eddie told us the price of the local hotels! Luckily, we received an offer of hospitality from a local pilot who let us stay with him and his wife.

The next morning, I was up early. I had a lot of energy and was excited to be making good progress; I was also pleased as I had managed to capture some amazing footage the previous day. Although it was going to take a long time, I was eager to edit another video and get it out on *YouTube*. There were now literally thousands of people following the vlog and I wanted to upload more frequently but it was extremely time-consuming. When staying in someone's house, it's not polite to disappear to make videos when they are hosting you!

We set off from Half Moon Bay and soon found ourselves flying over Santa Cruz around Monterey Bay and out over the famous Pebble Beach golf course. We flew slightly slower so that we could enjoy the views and the moment. I wanted to take it all in and my senses were overloaded with different feelings. When you are 'in the zone' and really getting something done and making progress towards a worthy goal, it feels good – in fact, it feels very good and can become something that you crave. However, in order to get to these magical feelings, it's almost guaranteed that you will have to overcome frustration, difficulties and setbacks, which not everyone can get through. But when you make it to the other side, it really is worth it. Those few days flying down the Californian coastline were simply on another level.

Our destination for the day was Whiteman Airport, a fairly small airport to the north of Los Angeles. A fellow gyro pilot called Peter had been following our journey online and flew out to meet us; we eventually managed to make contact with him around the Ventura area. We followed him back into Whiteman where he had kindly arranged a hangar for us. We had a rest day planned, which we spent hanging out in LA. I could have easily stayed there for another few days. We found a pretty cool rooftop bar and I was able to catch up with a young lad and fellow Everest summiteer called William who I'd met whilst climbing in Nepal; he happened to be staying with a friend in the area.

Whilst in LA, I received an email from another *Magni* pilot, Mike, who had been following the journey and whose aircraft was based locally, not far from Whiteman. He asked if he could fly down to San Diego with me; I said that it would be an absolute pleasure to have another *Magni* fly with me.

The next day, Mike arrived at the airport in his almost brand new, yellow *Magni M16*, which looked pretty sweet! As soon as we were airborne, we were flying over one of the most densely populated areas on the planet. We flew out over the famous Hollywood sign, which I had to fly around twice in order to get the perfect selfie with it in the background! We then flew over to the coast with the high-rise skyscrapers of downtown LA towering above the rest of the city: it was one hell of a sight. We needed to cross LA International Airport, known as LAX. This was surprisingly easy as there was a VFR corridor for traffic to pass over that ran south easterly at 3,500 feet and north westerly at 4,500 feet. Looking down at all of the aircraft lined up was quite surreal; I noticed a *Boeing 747* taking off below us and, for all I knew, it could have been heading to London.

We had soon cleared LAX and were descending over Long Beach and along the famous Huntington Beach. The weather was perfect and it was great flying alongside Mike. He was very relaxed and was calling out all the sights, giving me a sightseeing tour from 500 feet. I loved it!

We were going into a fairly busy airport, Montgomery-Gibbs Executive. I had been in email contact with another pilot called Andy Keech, who had set many gyro records himself, as well as being an accomplished skydiver. I met Andy at the San Diego airfield and couldn't believe it when I saw him. At the age of 80, he had less body fat than most 20-year olds and was now an avid CrossFit athlete, who came third in the world in his age group. He was an extremely inspiring man and to think that he was an octogenarian was mind blowing! He was also a very knowledgeable person in the aviation world, kindly taking a real interest in what I was trying to achieve. Mike was staying with a friend and I was able to stay with Andy at his apartment. It was 4th July, Independence Day, so naturally there were celebrations, although we opted to watch the firework displays from Andy's balcony.

Eddie had put me in touch with another pilot called Robert DeLaurentis, who had already flown around the world and was now working on a project to fly pole to pole – an absolutely huge undertaking. Andy and I headed down to his hangar to meet up with him and check out his aircraft, which was very impressive indeed! We needed to get back to the airport to meet Mike who was flying back up to LA. Before he left, he made a personal contribution to my project, which was very kind and greatly appreciated.

Over the course of the next few days, Norman and I stayed with Robert in his penthouse apartment not far from downtown San Diego. I caught up with Eddie to discuss plans for the rest of the flights around the US, taking in all the lower states. I also used the time to get on top of any outstanding actions before things got busy again. San Diego is certainly a lovely place but I needed to get moving.

Norman was flying out towards Texas and I was flying into Arizona. We had flown almost halfway around the world and had shared some amazing adventures together but we were now going our separate ways. He was heading for the Oshkosh Airventure Air Show where his adventure came to an end. He had plenty of time to get there, whereas I was literally racing around the US in order to make the weather window for Greenland. "Good luck matey, go careful." That was the last time I heard Norman's distinctive accent over the radio. I also wished him well.

21

The Flying Cowboys

I was going to stay with a family in Tucson before heading to Phoenix and Las Vegas. I had stayed with them when I cycled around the world almost six years earlier so I was looking forward to seeing them again. I instantly recognised them when they came to collect me. I stayed in the same RV that they used to host guests as on the previous visit. I lay down that evening thinking about all the things that had happened since I was last in that very same bed. They dropped me back to the airfield early the following morning and it was already approaching 40 °C.

I was flying to Chandler Municipal Airport where I would be meeting another pilot and good friend, Bob, who I'd also met whilst cycling around the world. The flight up to Phoenix was only an hour so when I landed, I still had a full day with Bob. A hangar had been arranged with another gyro pilot who had a pretty good set-up with a beautiful, fixed-wing aircraft.

Bob took me to see his new cycle shop. He ran a not-for-profit scheme called *We Cycle USA* that helped young people have access to a bike who wouldn't ordinarily be able to afford one. In return for a bike, they had to donate their time at the shop and could become as involved as they wanted. Bob had built up a fantastic community over the years and had mentored many young individuals. The shop was bustling with activity and it was great to see so many kids working on bikes with smiles on their faces.

I arrived at the hangar the next day and my next stop was Las Vegas, Nevada. Once I had pulled the gyro out of the shaded hangar, I really wanted to just go as it was far too hot to stand around. In the gyro, I could at least climb up to an altitude where it was a bit cooler. Once I'd left Phoenix and was following the I10 Highway, there was no one around and nothing on the radio. The sheer size of the place is inspiring and the vast, arid landscape, which is also quite rocky, stretches for hundreds of miles. After the I10, I followed the Colorado River that would lead me all the way to Las Vegas. The river was quite busy with people water-skiing and generally having fun in boats. As I passed over Lake Havasu City, I was able to make out London Bridge below me. As I made my way upstream, I flew over Davis Dam which was an impressive sight holding back so much water, then over Lake Mohave. As I rounded the higher ground, I was very close – probably too close – to the controlled airspace of Las Vegas International Airport. I managed to reach the tower at Henderson Executive Airport and requested join instructions. It was quiet with very few aircraft movements so I landed and exited the runway.

Within a few minutes, my iPad stopped working and I got the overheating message. Boy, it was hot! I was also quite worried about the aircraft overheating as I was now on the ground with the engine still running and the heat was reflecting off the tarmac. It was unbearable, even though I only had a T-shirt on under my thin flying suit. To my amazement, the temperature gauge didn't move and the aircraft was unaffected by the scorching heat. By now, G-KTCH had flown through sub-zero temperatures and here it was almost 45 °C. The gyro just kept going, no matter what conditions were thrown at it.

I had never visited Las Vegas before and Eddie had worked his magic again. I was staying at the famous *Caesar's Palace*, which was a little more than I'd usually spend but it felt right! It was a great start and, although I was on my own, I was buzzing. I also had a day off planned, as well as an interview with a local newspaper back at the airport. The two days literally flew by. The place had a real buzz about it and I was given a room with amazing views overlooking the fountains. It was just as I'd imagined: non-stop, round the clock activity.

It was soon time to leave and there would be no prolonged stops for a while now. I wanted to get a move on as I literally had thousands of miles to fly through the US. On 12th July 2019, I set off from Las Vegas to Spanish Fork in Utah, just to the south of Salt Lake City, and followed Highway 15 the whole way there. The temperature was cooling off a little as the ground was starting to rise. I had been given the name of a guy called Mark Patey, who was based out of Spanish Fork with his twin brother, Mike, and they agreed to put me up for the night. Mark came down in his pick-up truck and opened up the hangar. This place was on another level: it was massive! There were planes, bikes, cars and even a private jet in their hangar. They were quite famous in the aviation world as they built an aircraft called Draco, which was a STOL aircraft (short take-off and landing) with a turboprop engine.

The following day, a group of Mark's friends came over in their cubs, a type of fixed-wing aircraft. They called themselves *The Flying Cowboys* and they made entertaining flying videos. They offered to fly in formation with me to give me a bit of a send-off, staying with me for about 20 minutes before heading back. Between flying and operating the camera, I managed to get some amazing footage of us together.

My route took me north to Preston, Idaho but not without flying over the Great Salt Lake. I was now starting to get into the higher ground and the elevation of the small airport was at 4,726 feet above sea level. To put it in perspective, the highest point in the UK is 4,400 feet! Flying from Idaho to Rock Springs in Wyoming would be the highest flight of the entire journey around the world. I flew slowly and maintained a gentle cruise climb up to 10,000 feet. I was blown away by the performance of the *Magni* – it just kept climbing and had massively surpassed my expectations.

I landed at Southwest Wyoming Regional Airport to refuel. It wasn't as hot as Las Vegas but I noticed that the temperature had certainly warmed up from my previous stop in Idaho. I didn't think a great deal of it as I taxied to the end of the runway; the airport was just under 7,000 feet above sea level so the runway was quite long to compensate for the density altitude. As I was taking off in hot conditions, fully loaded and already at altitude, I knew it would take a little longer to get off the ground. I built up speed and slowly climbed out, flying at the optimum climbing speed of around 65 mph, as I wanted to gain some height. I must have flown through some sinking air as the gyro started to lose height quickly, despite flying at full throttle! For a few seconds, my heart stopped as I watched the altimeter decreasing. I gently pushed the stick forward, gaining a little air speed, then brought the speed back to 65 mph. The natural instinct is to pull the stick back but if I'd done that in these hot and high conditions, it could have had devastating consequences by falling behind the power curve. Thankfully, my instructor had drilled into me the importance of staying calm and I was soon maintaining my height, but I can tell you, when you're expecting the aircraft to go up and it goes down, it certainly wakes you up!

The following day would see me fly through three more states, firstly stopping at a tiny, little place in Montana called Ekalaka. There was absolutely nobody around when I landed, which was frustrating as someone had to physically witness that I was there and sign my *FAI* paperwork. I spotted a young woman so I walked over to say hello and she was more than happy to sign my paperwork when I told her what I was doing. In a small place with a population of less than 400 people, I'm not sure she had encountered many British people but she was mesmerised by my good looks… I mean, accent!

The next stop was Bowman in North Dakota, where there were some young lads who were part of a weather-watching, storm chasing group at the airport; they were also happy to sign my paperwork. I was on the ground for about 30 minutes before I was off again to Sturgis in South Dakota. The terrain had changed a lot and it was now beautiful, rolling grasslands, no longer a parched, arid, rocky and dusty landscape. There was absolutely no one around so I flew low at around 20 feet off the ground. At this height, you have to be extremely cautious and always on the lookout for power lines, although they are easier to see than the smaller telegraph poles with thin wires. Flying this low gave me a real buzz, especially at 100 mph with the ground just whizzing past underneath me. If I saw any grazing animals, I'd usually give them a wide berth so as not to scare them. Occasionally, I'd see random pick-up trucks out in the middle of nowhere. If there were people outside, I'd give them a wave and would always end up getting an enthusiastic wave back.

After an overnight stop in Sturgis, I continued heading south, this time passing through two states: Scottsbuff in Nebraska and Yuma in Colorado. The terrain was now almost completely flat and all farmed on an absolutely gigantic scale, with fields that ran for miles and miles. I was having so much fun and the flying couldn't have been any easier. I was chatting with Eddie via *Facebook* as I still had a good signal, often *FaceTiming* him to show him what I was seeing in real time.

I had made up some time but I was fast running out of hours before the gyro needed another service. *Magni* had a dealer in Austin, where I was heading, so this looked like the best option. I phoned Dayton Dabbs who imports *Magni*; he couldn't have been more helpful and confirmed that he could service the gyro for me.

After leaving Yuma, I flew south into New Mexico, which was another dramatic change in terrain and scenery. It was now back to drier, dusty and rocky scenery, with large canyons that dropped away below me. The lush, green grass was now replaced with cacti and stony gravel, with few roads and buildings apart from the odd ranch. My first stop of the day was Clayton, which is located a few miles from the Texas border. I was meeting up with another *Magni* pilot, Doug Rhodes, who I'd been in contact with by email. I landed and was greeted by Doug, who was wearing a JK baseball cap that he'd ordered from my website! Doug had worked for *United Airlines* for most of his working life and was now retired, flying gyros for fun in his spare time. He passed me an ice-cold bottle of water which was just what I needed. We put the gyro in a hangar out of the sun and went out for some lunch. Spending a few hours with Doug was great: he was a kind, caring person and had given up his entire day to drive over five hours to Clayton to meet me. I felt humbled.

I was starting to feel quite tired and was debating whether to stay in Clayton or not but the weather was perfect and I knew it was just the food and heat that had made me feel a bit lethargic. Once I was up and moving, I'd be fine. I wanted to make some progress towards Austin so I opted for Plainview. I spent the few hours of flying mostly reflecting on how lucky I was to be meeting so many lovely people who wanted to support me. It wasn't just because I was flying my gyro

– each time I had cycled across the US, I had met so many wonderful people. They say you attract who and what you are, and in truth, I'm not sure how I come across as when I'm travelling, I'm usually busy working towards some kind of goal. However, I've always wondered why I end up meeting so many kind, friendly people who have helped me time and time again through various situations.

After landing at Plainview, I made my way to a hotel where I crashed out on the bed, waking up at around 11pm. I had been flying longer days and pushing myself harder and it was starting to take its toll. I was tired a lot of the time and felt drained so I wanted to get to Austin as soon as I could for a longer rest.

The following day, I made the flight to Taylor, a small airfield on the outskirts of Austin. I was pretty exhausted by now. I met Dayton and a friend of his, John Craparo, a fellow *Magni* pilot. Dayton had a few customer flights to do the next morning, so whilst he was flying, I cleaned G-KTCH in the hangar. Dayton had a sofa there which was useful as I suddenly felt very lethargic. It was probably a combination of the heat and tiredness but I lay on the sofa and fell asleep for about an hour. I still felt absolutely exhausted when I woke up but it was also very hot so I forced myself to drink as much water as I could and started to perk up. I had a visit from an old-school gyro pilot who asked me to sign his flying helmet for him, which was an honour. Later that afternoon, Dayton serviced the aircraft for me and took it for a quick test flight. He was extremely busy yet still made time to help me, for which I was grateful.

Dayton and John were heading off at 5am to fly to Oshkosh and they kindly said I could accompany them. They were flying together in a closed cockpit *M24* and another pilot called Russell arrived in his *American Ranger* gyro. We took off and headed to a small town called Winsbourgh, still in Texas, where we refuelled and met up with two other gyros flying to Oshkosh. We now had a five-ship formation flight so it was going to be fun. Everyone was very welcoming and friendly and we all had one thing in common: we loved flying gyroplanes.

Our first day saw us overnight in Gardner, Kansas with a stop in Tahlequah, Oklahoma to refuel. The following day, we passed through Centerville and Oelwein in Iowa, then through Caledonia in Minnesota. Our last flight of the day was to a small airport called Brennand, just north of Oshkosh. This last flight was by far the most spectacular. It was an evening flight and the air had cooled; the aircraft were flying smoothly, so we knew that we were going to be landing in the dark, something that I had not experienced. As the sun set, the lights of the towns and radio masts came to life and brightened up the horizon.

Just before the sun had set, Russell spoke to me on the radio and said he was messaging Kent, who was flying an *American Airlines* flight from San Francisco to New York. Kent had met me with his partner in Anchorage and it turned out that Russell was friends with him as well, and had actually sold him an old aircraft that he previously owned. What a small world! Russell had sent Kent a text with the frequency we were using and unbelievably, Kent came on the radio wishing us a good evening. I thought that was so cool! He was at least a hundred miles south of us but as he was cruising at 37,000 feet, he had no problem reaching us on the radio.

We were not far from Brennand when the runway lights became visible and we allowed a bit more spacing between aircraft for our final approach. I came in, careful not to fly too fast or too slow but before I could level off, the landing wheels slammed into the ground. Depth perception at night is often different than in the day. Luckily, no harm was done – it wasn't pretty but I had made my first night landing!

22

Pushing On

AirVenture Oshkosh is the largest annual air show in the US. *Magni* had a stand and I really wanted to support them by having my aircraft there. I wasn't going to be able to stay in Oshkosh the whole week but I was certainly able to enjoy a few days.

The *Magni* family arrived on their flight from Italy: it was great to see them all! The following morning, we were all up early as we had to fly our aircraft into Oshkosh. Once landed, we secured G-KTCH on the *Magni* stand. Over the next few days, I was able to walk around and check out the show. Its immense size really did blow my mind and I don't think there's another air show quite like it in the world. Just when I thought I'd seen everything, I found a little bit more. It didn't take long for the *Magni* stand to be buzzing with people, including many well-wishers who had been following my journey and who wanted to congratulate me on my efforts so far.

I had picked up some damage on my propeller, most likely from where I had landed on many gravel runways. It was a bit of a flying pit stop but the *Magni* team were impressed with how clean it still looked and they said you'd never have known that it had flown over halfway around the world!

Whilst I wanted to stay in Oshkosh a bit longer to catch up with new friends, I was finding it very hard to relax, knowing how much distance I still had left to fly. Every day not moving could cause me to miss precious weather windows once I made my way up into Canada and across to Greenland. After two full days, it was time to move on again and the next time I would see the *Magni* guys would be back at Popham.

Most of the remaining flights in the US weren't particularly long but had been meticulously planned to take in all the states that I needed to pass through. The first stop was Lansing in Illinois, and on to Sturgis in Michigan. I called Eddie and told him that I'd make one more flight for the day to Rochester in Indiana, where I would stay as I was now feeling really tired again. Rochester was a great stop, with an extremely friendly airport manager who arranged my fuel and gave me a hangar to use free of charge, as well as the use of a courtesy car.

The following day, I made a stop in Mentone, the home of the *PRA* (Popular Rotorcraft Association). Mentone was a small place with a great feel to it; I felt a bit bad that I couldn't stay overnight but I spent a lovely few hours there. I was treated to lunch and given a tour of their little museum of rotary aircraft.

I had a sponsorship commitment with *DHL* in Cincinnati which meant that I had to keep moving. I stopped in Harrison, Ohio first. I was excited at the prospect of flying into Cincinnati International: it's a large airport with four main runways, three that run parallel. In terms of passenger movements, it's not particularly busy, although there is a lot of cargo movement as it's *DHL*'s main US hub. I touched down just before the *DHL* apron and taxied under the instruction of the tower to my welcome party. I had also landed in the state of Kentucky.

I had activities lined up with *DHL* over the coming days, carrying out the various 'meet and greets' with *DHL* staff. I was overwhelmed with support and everyone I had met so far who was working for *DHL* was extremely positive and supportive of my mission. I was fortunate enough to be doing something that I was very passionate about and that makes all the difference.

I was psyched up to be on the move again. I made my way to Louisiana. I wasn't sure how far I'd get and agreed to take it one flight at a time before Eddie made any hotel reservations. I had been chatting with the airport staff who had never seen a gyroplane before. When I arrived back the next morning, the woman on reception said, "Ah Mr Ketchell, I've been Googling you last night." "None of it's true!" I joked. She carried on, bemused, "You never told us you had climbed Everest and spent God knows how many days rowing across the Atlantic Ocean." I just laughed and asked how her day was going so far. As I was packing the gyro in the hangar, one of the fuel guys passed me $50 and said, "I want you to have this, it's not much but I really want to contribute to your efforts and to say that what you're doing is amazing." He was an older guy, probably coming to the end of his working career, and it was another act of extreme kindness. I donated the money to the charities I was supporting.

My first flight that day was to Cape Girardeau in Missouri. For much of the next flight to Memphis, Tennessee, I was following the Mississippi River where the low-lying flood plains and swamps increased as I flew further south. I landed at a small airstrip on the outskirts of Memphis and literally on the edge of the Mississippi, before a short hop to Marianna, to land in the state of Arkansas.

I had already made the decision that I was going to push on for two more hours to Monroe in Louisiana. Eddie was concerned that I was pushing myself too hard but I felt good and conditions were optimal to continue. Initially, the terrain was mostly farmed land but it soon transitioned to dense swamp forest that would have been inhospitable in the event of an emergency, although it didn't faze me at all. It was now early evening; the temperature was starting to cool slightly, which made conditions a little more pleasant than the usual hot air blasting at me. I did, however, notice some large cumulonimbus clouds on the horizon with bolts of lightning striking out from below but thankfully, I was able to slide between them and landed safely at Monroe Regional Airport.

I was staying with Jeb Andrews and his wife. Their son, Mason Andrews, set a world record as the youngest person to fly around the world. I spoke with Mason on the phone briefly as he was away at the time I visited, and he wished me luck. He warned me that there is often a fair bit of rain and lightning around most afternoons as I got closer to Florida and also advised me to do as much flying as I could in the mornings.

I landed at Clark County, Mississippi later that day and I was now just flying in a T-shirt and jeans as it was too hot and humid to even wear my lightweight flying suit. My arms ended up getting quite badly burnt. The air flowing over them disguised the fact that they were baking in the sun without me realising – a mistake that I would only make once!

The next flight was to Enterprise, Alabama, where nothing really changed in terms of scenery or terrain, although I was greeted to a visit from a *Black Hawk* helicopter that came alongside me. I was not flying through any military or controlled air space at the time so I wasn't particularly concerned by its presence. I think they were probably more intrigued to take a closer look at this tiny, little rotor craft racing along!

I landed in Marianna for an overnight stop and parked up underneath a shaded hangar area. I was greeted by two young women dressed in hot pants and fairly tight T-shirts, who were exceptionally friendly. When I told them what I was doing, they were keen to find out more! I thought it would be a good idea to get a picture of us all standing next to G-KTCH. It would be useful to have if I was ever asked to prove I was there and I tried this at every stop if I remembered to. I paid for my fuel, picked up a courtesy car and drove to the hotel.

I was feeling absolutely exhausted and had a lot of work ahead of me that evening. I had fallen behind with editing the videos and other admin commitments. I spoke to Eddie who again expressed his concern that I was pushing myself too hard. He reminded me of how many people he knew who'd kept pushing because they needed to be somewhere, who kept going when the sensible thing would have been to fly another day, and who then made a fatal mistake. I was lucky to have Eddie supporting me and always prioritising my safety above all else. He had a lot of experience and his calm, logical demeanour leant itself well to working in aviation. I felt like I was flying within my limits and agreed with everything he said. I didn't get any work done that evening as I fell asleep as soon as I sat on the bed.

The following morning, I woke up and looked out of the window. With clear skies, I wanted to get going so headed back to the airport fast. Further south, there was a lot of rain and lightning around so I wasn't going to be able to make Pompano just outside Fort Lauderdale. We opted to fly south over the Apalachicola National Forest and to the Gulf of Mexico, where I flew low-level along the coast. Eventually I landed at Brooksville-Tampa Bay Regional Airport where I stopped for the night as there was too much lightning and heavy rain to the south.

The next day, I had a fairly short flight to Pompano Beach Airpark. Anything that was less than 200 nautical miles was something that I now classed as a 'short flight'! It's funny how things get easier just by repeating them: the thought of a 200-mile flight was hugely intimidating for me when I first passed my test. I remember my first flight from Popham to Land's End and back, which was a massive accomplishment for me at the time, and now I wouldn't even blink at it. It's amazing what becomes the new 'normal' when you have the discipline to push yourself every day.

I was aware of some rain and thunder coming in from the west and moving east, which meant that I couldn't fly south along the Gulf of Mexico. I would have run into bad weather so I routed south east passing Kissimmee to the south and made my way to the Atlantic coast, although not without encountering some very heavy rain. I could see it on the radar because I had my iPad tethered to my phone to receive data. I was receiving live weather updates via *Runway HD*, tracking weather systems in real time. I would fly around them or through them if they were small, and if I knew for certain that it was clear on the other side.

I could see on the radar that I was heading straight for the rain, which reduced visibility down to almost zero. I remained calm and flew off my artificial horizon; I could see the ground, I just couldn't see anything in front of me! The rain was collecting in the cockpit and gushing down the inside of the screen and soaking my instruments. I had a small hand towel under my legs which I used to try and soak up and dry the panels but my iPad was now rendered useless as it was too wet to use. I was particularly nervous at the amount of water that was collecting in the bottom of the gyro: it was sloshing around so I pitched the aircraft up and most of it poured out of the back. It's not wise to be flying in such conditions in an open cockpit gyro but as long as my instruments didn't short out, the aircraft would continue flying. Thankfully, the rain didn't last for long and I was soon out the other side, feeling very relieved. Within a few minutes I was back in the sunshine and drying out nicely.

I was now enjoying a fabulous flight with the Atlantic Ocean out to my left and the gator-infested swamplands to my right. I made contact with Pompano and they instructed me to hold for a few minutes over the coast before making my final approach. A golf ball was lying on the runway that needed to be cleared before I could land (the airpark backed on to a golf course, so someone must have hit a very poor shot)! I was chatting with the staff in reception when I got into a conversation with an Italian pilot called Lamberto. I told him how I had been on the road or in the air, as it were, for quite a while. I was very touched when he invited me to his house for a delicious home-cooked dinner with his wife and two children.

G-KTCH was safely tucked away in a hangar so I could forget about flying for a few days. I checked in to a hotel on the beach and spent the first day completely crashed out. I did force myself to get up and go for a walk along the beach but it was almost 100% humidity, so as soon as I left the comfort of the air-conditioned hotel, I was dripping with sweat. The plan was to have two rest days then move on again but I was still exhausted so I called Eddie and told him that I needed another day. He was pleased to hear that I was not pushing myself unnecessarily. If I had nothing to do except fly it wouldn't have been too difficult but I had a lot of other commitments and daily tasks to maintain, which added another challenging dimension to the project.

23

The Big Apple

I enjoyed my time in Florida, as I always do, but it was time to get moving again. I was now heading north and homeward bound! The weather was good and I soon landed in Fort Stewart, Georgia. It was just a quick pit stop for *FAI* paperwork and I was onwards to Summerville in South Carolina where I stayed with a lovely British family. It was strange to hear them speak in an accent I'm very familiar with but hadn't heard for some time.

Next, I flew to New Burn in North Carolina where I was greeted by another gyro pilot who had been following my journey. He lived nearby and had flown in to meet me, which was appreciated. My plan was to get to Kitty Hawk, where the Wright Brothers made the first powered flights in 1903 in their aircraft, the Wright Flyer. As I was trying to set an aviation record myself, it felt right to land there. However, the intense rain and lightning came between me and my destination that day. I had to divert to a tiny place called Hyde County, a small, unmanned airstrip with a little club house, that could be entered by punching in a code on the door that was the radio frequency! I waited around until the weather lifted and decided to carry on. It was clear but I wasn't able to get to Kitty Hawk which was still getting hit by the rain so I opted for Dare County Regional Airport just outside Manteo. The rain and thunder came back that evening with a vengeance but, as quickly and as violently as these storms came, they were gone again.

There wasn't a cloud in the sky the following morning and the previous day's weather had not really caused any delays. I left feeling motivated and eager to start another big day: four flights and three states. The first flight was literally a hop over the fence to Kitty Hawk's First Flight Airport. It was surprisingly small, with the famous monument paying tribute to the Wright Brothers. I managed to get my *FAI* paperwork stamped with a 'First Flight' airport logo! I then flew to Chesapeake in Virginia, where I had an unexpected surprise. A fellow gyro pilot who was based there was waiting for me and had kindly sponsored my fuel, as well as a dad and his kids who'd been tracking my journey and wanted to pop by to say hello.

I made the rest of the flights that day to Martinsburg in West Virginia and Fredrick in Maryland, where I was meeting up and staying with a gyro pilot called Frank. I could see someone waving a Union Jack flag, which I guessed was for me! We headed over to the airport restaurant, along with Victoria, another pilot and Frank's friend. Not only did I have the most amazing cheeseburger but the ride to the restaurant was certainly different…Frank had an electric three-seater sofa on wheels. One person had the controls via a little joystick, whilst the other two held on for dear life. It was great fun, as you can imagine!

We still had the whole evening ahead of us. I mentioned to Frank and Victoria that I would love to visit Washington DC, so they kindly agreed to show me round. We stopped off at a diner on the way home for chocolate milkshakes, which was a lovely way to finish a wonderful day. It was strange that I had not met Frank and Victoria before but I felt very comfortable with them, as if I'd known them for years.

The following day, I was heading to New York but had quite a few stops to make en route. Frank was going to fly his gyro with me initially so we departed for our first stop in Middleton, Delaware, to get my *FAI* paperwork signed. The next stop was a cool, little place called Spitfire Aerodrome in New Jersey; there was only one person around and he could barely speak English, so he phoned his wife who translated and got him to sign my paperwork for me. The next stop was West Chester in Pennsylvania and Frank's last flight with me before he headed home. We landed at Brandywine Airport, home to the American Helicopter Museum, where we were treated to a personal tour of the museum.

I wasn't able to fly a direct course to Poughkeepsie due to some temporary flight restrictions in place around the New York city area. It wasn't an issue as I was making very good progress, so a slightly longer flight didn't concern me at all. I also had a day off planned with Kristin and Kent, who I'd met in Anchorage. I landed at Hudson Valley Regional Airport and was met by Kristin and Kent, who both had big grins on their faces when they saw G-KTCH, sparkling in the sun outside their hangar.

I was very excited at the prospect of our flight the following day along the Hudson River and around New York City. Kent had checked the restricted airspace and it didn't affect our plans to fly around the Statue of Liberty. I was awake surprisingly early, considering I'd had another late night, replying to emails. Our plan was simple: to fly south from Poughkeepsie, pick up the Hudson River and follow it all the way to the famous lady. Kent and Kristin were in a small two-seater microlight – slightly smaller than the aircraft they fly for *American Airlines* – but just as much fun!

We flew a fairly tight formation on the west side of the river heading south; it didn't take long before the world-famous skyline came into view. The weather was near-perfect with a light wind and hardly a cloud in the sky. It was hard to take it all in. I just didn't know where to look first and my senses and emotions were overloaded. As we were flying south, with the skyline on our left, I was filming and taking pictures. For a brief moment, I thought of Captain 'Sully' Sullenberger, who landed his *US Airways* aircraft on the Hudson River and I wondered what went through his mind on that day, now famously dubbed *The Miracle on the Hudson.*

The Statue of Liberty was now clearly in sight and ahead of me. We circled around the statue four times and I descended to about 400 feet, slightly lower than I should have been. I could see people walking around the statue looking up at me and they would have certainly heard me! It was soon time to head back up the Hudson and I was now on the east side of the river. It felt like I could reach out and touch the buildings, they seemed so close. I was flying along looking up at the most iconic skyline on the planet, which was very surreal. Just two years earlier, I didn't even have a licence to fly and it had all seemed a totally unrealistic dream. But here I was, actually achieving my goal.

Although I was by no means finished, the feeling I had that day as I flew along the New York skyline is an experience I will never forget but something that I find hard to articulate. I posted a few pictures on Instagram later that day and, as one would expect, they received a lot of likes and comments. Kristin had taken some amazing air to air pictures but they didn't come close to reflecting all the effort and hard work that it had taken to get me there, which only my close friends and family fully understood.

As I said goodbye to Kent and Kristin, I thought to myself how funny it is how people come in and out of our lives. I believe our paths were meant to cross.

I had a fairly short flight to Danbury in Connecticut, then flew on to Newport Rhode Island, where I would be taking a few days off. Andy was arriving that evening from the UK to service G-KTCH one final time before I flew back across the north Atlantic. It was good to see him: seeing a familiar, friendly face when you are exhausted is different to meeting people for the first time and it was just what I needed.

I had pushed myself as hard as I could flying through America, not just with the flying, but with the work required when I wasn't flying: filming, editing, sponsorship commitments, engaging with schools online who were following the journey and general admin. I had many moments when I felt totally overwhelmed and wasn't sure if I could continue at the rate I was going but I just kept telling myself, "One more day and I'll take a rest." Then I'd say the same thing again and before I knew it, I got to the point where I realised, "This is all mental, it's all in my head." Of course I was tired but the truth is, I wasn't even close to my limit! I was doing it: I was stringing massive days together in the aircraft then working until sometimes 2am and still getting up the next day and doing it all over again, maintaining the pace that kept me going the whole way through the US. I was beginning to crave the feeling of pushing myself but knew I had to be careful. I planned to take some rest over the next couple of days but I still needed to arrange for somewhere to service the aircraft. Thankfully, I got chatting to Jeff, who owned *Newport Helicopter Tours*, a small, family-run business, which operated out of a hangar. He kindly let us use his hangar, which was a stroke of luck and an example of how sometimes you just have to trust that things will work out!

Over the next two days, Andy worked tirelessly. He is one of the best aircraft engineers around when it comes to working on *Magni* gyroplanes and his attention to detail is excellent. He was also very supportive of my journey, reminding me just how incredible it was to have even made it this far. I felt refreshed and eager to move on to my next stop, the island of Nantucket. The next time I would see Andy would be at Popham so I just needed to get myself safely back home. My confidence had grown considerably and, whilst I was nervous, I was now starting to realise that the gruelling schedule that I'd been pushing hard to achieve through the US was probably going to pay off as it looked like I would be able to fly up into Canada and Greenland before I lost the favourable weather that would be required to make the flights across to the UK.

I had one more engagement to fulfil on Nantucket, which I'd been looking forward to even before my trip had started. I had been introduced to an extremely enthusiastic lady called Betsey Sanpere who runs aviation camps for kids on the island. She had been following my journey since I'd left and I was excited to be meeting her and some of the kids. Betsey had various activities planned for me, which included a talk to some local children, who were eager to hear stories of fun and adventure.

Betsey introduced me to her friend Frank, the local Fire Chief, who had been living on the island for quite some time. He was a keen motorcyclist and one evening, we rode his motorbikes around the island. He had a beautiful *BMW* 1200cc adventure touring bike which I really liked; he also had a chopper-style bike but that wasn't really my thing, so I stuck with the *BMW*. Just like every other stop, the time went too quickly and I had to leave again, although not without a bit of a scare.

My aircraft was fuelled and checked, I had said all my goodbyes and was lined up behind the other aircraft waiting to take off. Eventually I was cleared for take-off and within minutes, the island was behind me and I was over the water. I noticed that my fuel gauge started to flutter and move up and down. I tried not to panic, wondering if I was losing fuel, but thought it was probably a faulty connection on the fuel gauge. However, I couldn't take any risks so I turned back and announced to the tower that I needed to land immediately. The airport was in sight and they gave me a direct heading, stopping all other traffic to allow me to land. The operator asked, "Do you want to declare an emergency and do you want fire trucks?" I declined but just wanted to get back on the ground. I checked everything over and as I thought, there were no leaks. I called Luca who advised me that it would most likely be a loose connection with a wire. He was right: I fiddled around and it appeared to be fine now.

I took off again and made the short flight across the water and landed at Marshfield just south of Boston, Massachusetts, where I would overnight. It was also the last point of land from which Charles Lindbergh made his famous flight to Paris on 20th May 1927. I was hoping to catch up with my good friend, Leo, who had rowed the Atlantic and attempted Mount Everest, all at well over 60 years old! He was a great guy with amazing stories from his time as a US marshal in New York, chasing down gun-toting gangsters and drug lords back in the eighties. Unfortunately, he was on holiday in Italy at the time so I checked into a hotel and prepped for the next day, which took me through Concord, New Hampshire and Fryeburg in Maine.

After a good night's sleep, I was now going to tick off my last state, Vermont, landing at Hartness State Airport on 18th August 2019 and completing all 49 mainland states. I had planned to leave America from Buffalo and cross into Canada via the Niagara Falls. I was going to stop in Guelph to see Joe, from *Exploring by the Seat of your Pants*, and his family. I had the range to make it to Buffalo, however, I was forced to divert and call it a day in Hamilton, New York, due to lightning and rain.

The following day, I was up early and had an easy flight to Buffalo, New York. I called Canadian Customs and informed them of my impending arrival, then asked the staff at the airport to sign my last *FAI* paperwork in America.

I was now bound for Canada. I wasn't able to fly directly over Niagara Falls so I crossed the border just to the south of the falls but could clearly see the spray from them. In my excitement before departure, I had seen Guelph on my *Runway HD* software and set that as my destination. As I made my approach, I was surprised at just how small it was, for an international airport. Apart from one lonely-looking fixed-wing aircraft, there was nothing. I checked my phone after landing and spotted a message from Eddie, which read, "What are you doing? You've landed at the wrong airport!" "Shit," I said to myself – I felt so stupid! I had indeed landed at the wrong airport, something that I thought would be almost impossible to do but it just proved how mistakes can easily be made. I was supposed to be landing at the Region of Waterloo International Airport which was very close but I had mixed the two up. I had Guelph on my mind and when I'd landed there, I quickly realised the mistake I'd made and felt pretty stupid. "I'm never going to hear the end of this," I joked with Eddie over the tracker. I landed at the correct airport just 15 minutes later and the authorities were none the wiser. My mistake was spotted by a few eagle-eyed people watching the tracker but I think it went relatively unnoticed at the time.

24

Colder Climes

O
ver the next couple of days, I made my way north east, following the St Lawrence River and passed through Brookville. I took a day off in the beautiful city of Quebec, due to extreme tiredness. I certainly liked the place and was looked after by the guys from *Gyro Adventure Canada*, a small gyroplane flying school.

The St Lawrence River starts to open out after Quebec. I was fortunate enough to have incredible weather and arrived in Sept Iles that afternoon after a stunning flight, flying low-level over the riverbanks.

I was excited about the prospect of going north but was getting concerned about finances. My bank account was literally running on fumes and I knew that things would be getting more expensive as they became more remote. Out of the blue, I received an email from John Craparo with whom I'd flown up to Oshkosh. He wanted to transfer some funds to me to help with my costs, which was so kind, and couldn't have come at a better time. I had flown 75% of the way around the world and felt ready to take on the unchartered landscape with no roads and limited airport options. There was a train line that ran all the way to Schefferville, which I planned to follow. This would be my only landing option if I had a problem. The flight was stunning: initially, there was some high ground but I stayed low and flew through the winding valleys until it flattened out a little. The railway line hugged the side of a river that meandered its way north and made for the most stunning pictures. Every so often, I would see trains pulling freight and more often than the trains, I would see gangs of workers on the lines who had specially fitted wheels on their trucks to drive along the rails. I always waved at them and most of the time, I received enthusiastic waves back. I landed at Schefferville, a small town that was established in the 1950's, whose main industry was the mining of iron ore deposits. I managed to get some support from *Air Inuit* who let me push G-KTCH into the back of their small hangar.

The following morning, I arranged my fuel with the airport manager. They didn't have any *AVGAS* readily available in the quantity that I needed, so I had to purchase a 200-litre drum of it. Someone ended up with the best part of 100 litres of free fuel, as I only needed around half of it. My destination for the day was Kuujjuaq, a small outpost at the mouth of the Koksoak River on Ungava Bay, south of the Hudson Strait. It was quite a windy day at around 20 knots gusting 30 knots at times, but thankfully it was a cross wind that didn't impact my speed across the ground. The terrain was slowly starting to change as my flight progressed north. There were still plenty of trees around but they were smaller and not so developed. As I looked out at the landscape, I could see many beautiful, blue lakes that sparkled in the sun.

Thankfully, *Air Inuit* had a fairly large base there so I taxied straight over to the hangar. I wasn't in any rush and got chatting with one of the mechanics, an old guy who was smoking like a chimney. It was quite apparent that there was very little for them to do when they were not working. I asked this old guy what he did for downtime and he said, with a totally straight face, "Ah, there's nothing to do here so I just watch porn and that's it."

The weather was excellent the following morning; the wind had now died off and there was not a cloud in the sky. It look me slightly longer than normal to get ready as I had to dig out my survival suit to fly over the Hudson Strait. I was very excited to be leaving the mainland and flying to Iqaluit on Baffin Island. I was kitted up, fuelled and had established comms with Eddie so was now ready to go. I took off into the smooth, cool air. It wasn't anywhere near freezing but the blistering heat of the lower 48 states was now long behind me. The aircraft flew well in the heat but it would always perform better in the colder, denser air. Apart from Eddie watching the tracker and being contactable via the *Garmin* messaging system, I was now on my own. There is no flight following up here unless you are flying at commercial flight levels but I was flying at my own levels, 50 feet above the ground!

The terrain was now just a vast, rocky, treeless tundra where the ground remains frozen for most of the year. There were a lot of huge boulders lying around and I wondered how they had managed to find their way into these random positions. The terrain was safe, to a degree. If the engine failed, I would have been able to land but probably not take off again as the landscape was too rocky. I was now heading into polar bear country and hoped I might see the odd one wandering around but sadly, never did. Flying low gave me an exhilarating feeling as the ground rushed past beneath me. I noticed the colour of stones and rocks, the crystal-clear water along the shore lines that formed rock pools and I could even see animal tracks. There were small, off-grid communities along the peninsula but as I flew right over Aupaluk, I didn't see a single person.

It wasn't long before I could see the blue horizon of the Hudson Strait and then it was around 80 nautical miles across to Baffin Island. As I coasted out and left the mainland behind me, I noticed something large sticking out the water in the distance. At the time, I presumed it was a boat, perhaps a research vessel, so I adjusted my course a few degrees and headed over to take a look. As I got closer, I realised that it was actually an iceberg, with just the top sticking out! It looked quite out of place floating on its own in the water with nothing around it. I scrambled through my pockets to get my phone and managed to get a great picture with the shadow of G-KTCH projecting down onto it as I flew over.

I could see the high ground of Baffin Island from almost 50 miles away. The flight across the water was less than an hour and I just had some hills to navigate before descending into Frobisher Bay for my arrival into Iqaluit. I got chatting to a couple of pilots who worked for a local company called *Air Nunavut*, who offered to let me bring the gyro into their workshop. I was pretty hyped up and had a fair bit of adrenaline running through me. I was able to get a ride to the local hotel.

My next planned stop was Greenland, however, there were no flyable weather windows for almost a week! That said, I had been watching the forecast for some time and it was very changeable, so I decided to stay put. I made sure that Norm, the workshop manager, was happy to keep my aircraft in his hangar, then went back to the *Frobisher Inn* for the night. However, at almost $200 a night, it certainly wasn't sustainable, so I had to find somewhere else to stay. As luck would have it, the following day I was chatting with the guys at the hangar who had a spare room in the house that the company rented for them. A lot of people living and working there were on shifts, working for a few months at a time until a fresh crew took over. They invited me to stay with them, which was a very kind gesture and just what I needed as my funds were running low. I spent the rest of the day at the hangar, catching up on emails, editing footage and spending a lot of time scrutinising the weather.

Over the next couple of days, I hung out with the guys from the house – Norm, Ryan and Thomas – who were all extremely supportive of what I was doing. For most of my time in Iqaluit, the weather was awful: heavy rain, low cloud and fog, with poor visibility.

My friend, Peter Wilson, who had vast experience flying in Greenland, was now in touch with Eddie and me on a daily basis, looking at weather windows to make the flight to Greenland and also examining the onward weather to safely transit through Greenland. My immediate goal and focus was to simply get to Nuuk and then I'd worry about the next flight. We eventually saw a viable day to make the crossing: after Iqaluit, it would be clear skies with tail winds the whole way across the Davis Strait to Nuuk. This was the break I needed and it came within a week of arriving. In the grand scheme of things, I wasn't stuck for long but my mind was playing tricks on me and I was becoming very anxious. If I didn't get away soon, I would be stuck in Iqaluit for the winter and would be forced to abandon my attempt until the following summer, which would have been a disaster in my eyes and not the same accomplishment any more.

It was 2nd September and I was up early. The flight to Nuuk was almost 500 nautical miles, which was only flyable with a tail wind, or at least no element of headwind. This was a serious flight to make which had been on my mind for some time. The aircraft had been fuelled free of charge the previous day by someone who purchased a drum of *AVGAS* and only needed half of it. Since I had done the same thing many times, it made me realise that what goes around comes around! I arrived at the airport feeling hyped up and lost count of how many times I looked at the *Windy* weather app to satisfy myself that it was good enough to depart. I received a call from Eddie to tell me that he hadn't heard back from the authorities in Greenland regarding my arrival and permissions. My heart sank. I had to leave as there was no other weather window and if I didn't leave now, I could be stuck there. My mind was racing at a thousand miles an hour but within a few seconds, a certain calmness came over me, enabling me to make a clear decision. I was going, no matter what.

I stepped into the aircraft in the light rain, strapped myself in, pushed the little red button and G-KTCH instantly came to life. I taxied to the threshold of Runway 34 and completed my power checks: both magnetos were working perfectly, all my temperatures and pressures were up and I was ready to go. I gently applied power and started to accelerate. The aircraft was off the ground surprisingly quickly, considering I was at maximum weight. As I climbed out, I made a 180 degree turn, heading for my first waypoint at the bottom of Frobisher Bay. If the weather had been clear, I would have departed to the north east over the high ground and flown a direct flight the whole way but due to low cloud, I had to route south east to get around the mountains.

I was quickly clear of Iqaluit and flying low at around 100 feet above the water in the bay below me. There were a few icebergs but the majority of the winter ice had now melted away. Although it was drizzling and the cloud base was very low, the horizontal visibility was clear, which gave me confidence. The grey sky and low clouds were behind me and I was soon flying into clear blue skies. The wind was also picking up and was pushing me forwards at 90 knots across the ground, which was fast.

I took a look over my left shoulder to see the vast Canadian mountains for one last time. There was now nothing but almost 400 nautical miles of open water to cross! I had packed food and drink into the small side pockets to keep me going. Strangely, I was not nervous: I was in fact very excited and I felt like I was truly alive.

I was soon flying at over 100 knots ground speed with a strong tail wind and was making excellent progress towards my goal. I climbed up to over 1,000 feet, thinking that I might perhaps catch some even stronger winds but it made very little difference. Another advantage of flying higher is that it gives you more time to put out an emergency call in the event of engine failure. I did have my life raft under my right leg which was slightly uncomfortable now as I'd flown with it all the way from Nantucket. I could see the water and ripples in great detail as they passed underneath me and it gave me a sense of speed that I didn't get if I flew higher up.

There was nobody to talk to on the radio, I just had Eddie and his watchful eye on the tracker. We had a protocol that, if my flight tracker stopped or showed anything unusual, he would wait until my predicted arrival time had passed and, if I had not arrived, he would initiate an emergency procedure. If I ended up in the water, as long as I could get clear of the aircraft and climb into the life raft without drowning, I knew that someone would be looking for me. I also carried my personal emergency beacon in my pocket. All of this made me feel much more comfortable.

I had downloaded some audio books and had my phone linked to my headset. It worked surprisingly well with the volume up, drowning out the noise of the engine to a degree and it took my mind to a place where I could still fly the aircraft and be aware of what was going on but at the same time, allowed my mind to drift into a different place as I listened. I had selected a book by David Goggins, an ex-Navy Seal. He'd had a difficult upbringing but had turned his life around. The book oozed testosterone and it was a very inspiring story. The most important part was that it made time pass more quickly. All through the flight, I was also communicating with Eddie and Peter, updating them on how the flight was going. It gave me something to do in addition to recording footage on my *GoPro*.

Due to my impressive ground speed, the flight wasn't going to take quite as long as I'd thought. This was particularly useful because for the first time on my journey, I was suffering with the cold quite badly. I often clenched up my toes to try and keep the blood flowing and I had every possible layer on, but I could feel my body temperature dropping and I was starting to shiver. As I crossed the half way point, I was now closer to Greenland than Canada, which gave me renewed energy. In a little over two hours, I would be in Nuuk! A technique that I'd used before when feeling very cold was to visualise myself in a nice hotel, relaxing in a warm shower. The intense cold was only temporary but at the time, it became almost unbearable. If I got too cold and lost dexterity in my fingers, despite having massive gloves on, I would find it hard to do crucial things such as changing the frequency on my radio and operating my iPad. Thankfully, I never reached that point.

At around 50 nautical miles out, I noticed something on the horizon resembling a land mass. As I got closer, the true beauty of Greenland slowly opened up as every mile passed. The wind had started to ease as I got closer to land. Nuuk eventually came into sight and I established communications with the tower. I landed and taxied onto the apron, feeling ecstatic that I had just completed a mammoth flight in just over five hours. Although I was geographically still on the north American continent, I was politically in Europe, which felt amazing. I noticed my phone vibrating, which was my dad calling via video messenger. I had full signal from a local mobile provider but I didn't think of the cost for roaming in Greenland, which soon maxed out my allowance!

I was now very cold and needed to warm up quickly. I headed to a hotel for a long-awaited shower and a hot meal. I couldn't resist having a surf and turf, and a beer – I felt like I'd earnt it! Later that evening,

I debriefed with Eddie and Peter: our plan had worked perfectly and no one at the airport had mentioned anything about permissions or what I was doing there. In fact, when I spoke to the controllers in the tower, they just wanted to buy me a beer for flying all that way in what they called a 'lawnmower'! With all the adrenaline that had been running through me, I crashed out that night.

After a much-needed rest day, it was time to move on again. Flying from Nuuk to Kulusuk in one flight up and over the ice cap would have been feasible; but I felt it was too risky due to the altitude I needed to fly at, as well as the changeable weather. Being caught in a white out, unable to differentiate between the ground and the sky, would have been very dangerous.

I taxied out and took off almost immediately, flying over the capital of Nuuk. It's a relatively small place with a population of around 20,000 people. As the city passed behind me, I was now flying over the mesmerising fjords with small icebergs all around. Most of Greenland's population is on the west coast where the land offers larger areas of flat rock to build on.

I received a message from Peter informing me that he had spoken to the controller at Narsarsuaq who advised me to stop at Paamiut. I would make the short flight down to Narsarsuaq the following morning, as fog and low cloud was rolling in and could make things difficult. I turned the aircraft around and headed back to Paamiut. I had soon landed and was in the crew room of the fire station which doubled up as the airport, chatting with the English-speaking crew.

The following day was going to be a big day so I tried to get some good rest. On arrival back at Paamiut Airport, I felt a real sense of urgency to move, but I couldn't take off before 9am due to their operating hours and I had the best part of eight hours' flying ahead of me. I was off the ground and into the air at 9.30am. One thing that I'd learnt on this journey was that everything takes twice as long as you think it will, no matter how organised you are. The weather was excellent and it felt good to be on my way again. After 2.5 hours, I was on my approach for Narsarsuaq. The airport was built by the Americans in World War Two as a stopover for aircraft that were coming off the production line in the US and needed to be flown to Europe. To this day, it's probably still the main stopover point for smaller aircraft between the US and Europe. I needed this to be a quick turnaround so I refuelled within minutes of landing, then raced into the terminal building and up to the tower to get my paperwork signed.

I took off and departed south of Narsarsuaq. I knew I had to get up to a minimum of 5,000 feet to clear the mountains before I could drop down to the east coast of Greenland. As I climbed, the views were simply breathtaking. It's hard to describe just how amazing the landscape is: it made me feel very small and insignificant, but it was also quite intimidating as the jagged mountains that I needed to pass over looked razor-sharp. I could also see the start of the icecap: a stunning, bright-white sheet of ice that is hundreds of millions of years old, which is sadly melting at an alarming rate due to climate change. I climbed up to 6,000 feet and could see the Atlantic Ocean in front of me. I was soon able to start my descent into a fjord that led out to the ocean and from where I would head north to Kulusuk.

As I made my way out through the fjords and turned north, the vast ocean opened up in front of me and to my left was the rugged east coast. I experimented with flying high over the ground but it felt more stable to be out over the water and flying at around 100 feet. Every now and then, a gust of wind coming down off the icecap would momentarily throw the aircraft around for a few seconds but then it was gone. As I progressed north, there were more and more icebergs floating around. The sheer beauty of Greenland was in a league of its own and I could see why it was such a popular tourist destination for outdoor enthusiasts.

As I got closer to Kulusuk, I began to relax a bit. I wasn't particularly cold but I was looking forward to landing as I was beginning to tire. As soon as I touched down in Kulusuk, I felt amazing. It had been one hell of a day: I had started on the west coast and finished on the east coast! The aircraft had performed outstandingly well, as it always did. As I unpacked my kit and got out of the survival suit, I was handed a cup of coffee, which was just what I needed. I had no idea what to expect in terms of the hotel but when I arrived, it was absolutely outstanding for such a small place. The restaurant would have not looked out of place in a high street in Britain; I couldn't believe my luck when I noticed steak and jacket potatoes on the menu!

I knew I needed to get going again the next day, otherwise I would be stuck with no workable weather window at all in the current forecast. It was one of the challenges of flying across this part of the world in September: good weather days would now be few and far between.

25

Island Hopping

I felt surprisingly refreshed the next morning and suited up ready for the 'big one' – the flight I had been visualising ever since this dream of flying around the world came to fruition.

As I had already spent many hours flying over the water, I wasn't particularly worried about the flight to Iceland – in fact, it would be an easier day than the previous day's flight to Kulusuk. This was just one flight in a straight line for the best part of five hours. The weather was forecast to be good enough with a slight chance of some light rain, but nothing that should have caused any problems.

I took off and as soon as I had cleared the runway, I was out over the water. It was a situation I had been in quite a few times before but this time I was above the water and not on it! One of the first things that went through my mind was that this journey would take me 10 days if I was rowing across. It's crazy to think that I would now cover the same distance in just five hours!

I had already established comms with Peter and Eddie on the ground but was now firing off messages to let them know that all was well.

There was some grey cloud around but in general, visibility was very good. The first two hours passed quickly, probably because I was hyped up and running on adrenaline. As much as I tried to balance drinking the right amount of fluids to stay hydrated without needing to use the toilet mid-flight, I had misjudged this flight and had developed a bit of a headache; it was bearable but enough to notice it.

I could see in the distance that I was flying towards a wall of grey cloud which turned to rain as I got closer. I kept a hand towel under my left leg to dry the screen and wipe down the instruments when they got wet. I also had another small towel that I placed over my iPad to stop it getting wet and rendering the screen useless. The rain was manageable but the visibility had really started to deteriorate. The cloud was very low and I was flying at just over 100 feet above the water. For the first time, I really felt out of my comfort zone and the headache wasn't helping! I told myself to stay calm but I was now flying using the artificial horizon on the *Garmin* as I couldn't see in front of me, just the ocean passing by below me.

For about an hour, the conditions would fluctuate, getting worse and then improving. This is when time really does slow up… I thought a lot about my nephew, Max. My brother, Jeremy, had sent me a picture of Max looking very grown up in his new school uniform on his first day of school, the very school that my brother and I had attended. I spent the majority of that hour looking at the picture of Max. I truly believed that it was not my time to go. I was really looking forward to seeing Max and of course spoiling him, which is what all good uncles do.

I knew that all I had to do was keep going and eventually I would reach Iceland. I just hoped that the weather would improve as this was the only time that the conditions I was experiencing did not reflect the forecast. The first glimpse of land was the mountains to the north of the island. Although the weather had now improved, my headache had deteriorated into a serious migraine. I could see myself getting closer on the GPS and I eventually spotted the coast. There was a lot of cloud lingering over the island, especially in the direction that I was heading. As I got closer, I could see that the only gap in the cloud was in the general direction of my destination, Reykjavik Airport. "What are the chances of that!" I thought to myself.

That's when I knew that this flight was meant to be: had I not had so much experience by now, the outcome of that flight could have been quite different. The entire way I had been listening to Elon Musk's audio book, which was excellent. I thought that I pushed myself, but this guy was on another level! As I was given a direct approach for Runway 19, I was coming to the end of the book and really wanted to finish it before landing, but it was not to be. I touched down so smoothly that I didn't even feel the wheels make contact with the ground. I had never been so pleased to be back on the ground. I checked my phone and it was pinging like crazy, as messages of congratulations started coming through. There must have been lots of people watching the tracker that day!

It was all a bit surreal. Only four days ago, I was in Canada and now I was on the other side of the Atlantic Ocean in Iceland. It looked like I would be in Iceland for a few days according to the weather forecast so I decided to enjoy some enforced rest days. That evening, I took a stroll into the city and had a glass of wine in a steakhouse, along with a steak, of course! As I sat there people watching and generally pondering over the past week, it was crazy to think what I had achieved. Although I still had some big flights across hundreds of miles of water to get back to the UK, something had changed mentally. I felt overwhelmingly happy and was now 100% confident that I was going to complete this flight around the world. I spoke with Peter on the phone at the airport and the first thing he said was, "Very well done, you are going to do this, you are almost home."

Looking back, the decision to leave Iqaluit when I had the weather window, despite there being some uncertainty around permission logistics, was without doubt the defining moment in making it back across the Atlantic. At the time, I was feeling stressed and anxious but it's at those times that you need to push through as there will always be something worth having on the other side. I lay awake for hours that night, thinking about all the memories that I'd made so far and the experiences that I'd been fortunate enough to have. I looked through all the messages that I had received, including many recorded video messages from various *Magni* pilots, sending their congratulations from Italy, which was lovely.

I slept in the following morning, having eventually fallen asleep in the early hours. I was meeting a guy called John, who had been following my journey. He had offered to take me for a tour around Reykjavik; sadly, the weather wasn't particularly good but it didn't dampen our spirits and we had a great time. That evening, John and his wife kindly took me to a wonderful restaurant. The following day was a general rest day and catch up. *Newgate Communications* were now working on the PR plan for my arrival back home, although it was difficult to pin down an exact date. As I enjoyed some rest in Reykjavik, the east coast of the United States was getting battered by Hurricane Dorian and it was heading across the Atlantic. Although I was well in front of it for the time being, I knew it was coming. We were unsure if it would cause a delay or not but continued to focus on one flight at a time. I managed to process some video footage and eventually responded to all the messages; if someone took the time to send me a message, I would always try to reply. I also had an interview at the hangar with a local news outlet, which I was told aired that evening.

The weather looked to be good to fly direct from Reykjavik to Vagar in the Faroe Islands, another long flight. Of all the flights across long open water, I was most concerned about this one: not because I was over the water, but the fact that there would be no alternative options other than to land at Vagar.

Situated between Iceland and Norway in the North Atlantic Ocean, the volcanic Faroe Islands offer some of the most stunning natural landscapes with their steep, coastal cliffs that harbour a vast array of seabirds. However, the islands are known for their furious storms and wild weather which passes through on a regular basis. The islands also receive a large amount of rainfall per year and are often shrouded in cloud, which can make landing an aircraft extremely difficult. I needed to be 100% sure that the weather was going to be good enough to land safely. Once I was there, I was totally committed and would be landing no matter what. This was all in the back of my mind before setting off and I just had to trust my intuition.

As always, I was very thorough with my pre-flight checks, for my own peace of mind. At times, I had been doing a lot of comfort eating in hotels, especially in America, and now my survival suit was 'snug' once I'd squeezed myself into it! I took off to the south and immediately noticed the beauty of Iceland from the air. Before heading out over the Atlantic, I had an hour of the most stunning beach and coastal scenery, flying low to take in the amazing views and environment. Once I coasted out and left the relative safety of the smooth beaches and flat coastal road beneath me, I decided to listen to the Elon Musk audio book which I had almost finished on the flight from Greenland. The time passed quickly and it wasn't long before over half of the flight was completed. The last flight into Reykjavik had been a tough one, with less than ideal weather and a headache from hell, but this time around, the weather was good and I took some paracetamol before I departed as a precaution. I felt energised, alert and motivated, which was probably due to the fact that I'd had a couple of rest days and I was almost back in the UK.

Seeing the Faroe Islands come into view was a stunning sight, with their steep cliff edges rising up out of the water. They wouldn't have looked out of place on a *Jurassic Park* film set, we just needed some dinosaurs running around to complete the look! As I had suspected, there was a lot of lingering, broken cloud cover but I was confident that I could pick my way through it to Vagar. There is a back door entrance into the airport when there is low cloud and turbulence that is only really available for light aircraft. To the south of the airport, there is a beautiful lake that funnels out to a waterfall and into the Atlantic Ocean. When there is low cloud, light aircraft usually fly alongside the cliff and when they get to the waterfall, they come in to land over the lake and follow it round until the airport opens up in front.

As I flew closer, I called the tower who advised using the waterfall approach. I had the large cliffs off to my left, the Atlantic Ocean to my right as far as the eye could see and in front of me, I could see the spray from the waterfall just coming into sight. There were patches of sunlight streaking through the broken clouds. When the sun's rays hit the rock face and lit up the water beneath me, it looked like something out of a film, as if I was discovering lost, uninhabited lands. The view would have no doubt been the same for thousands, if not millions, of years before my arrival.

The beautiful waterfall appeared beneath me; I made a turn to the left and flew straight over the glistening lake. I still couldn't quite see the airport runway but I knew it was there as I started my slow descent. I had been filming with the *GoPro* as I made my approach over the waterfall but now I needed to put the camera down and have both hands on the controls as I landed. At the time, I didn't realise that the airport website had a webcam but Eddie had shared the link on social media prior to my arrival, so when I checked my phone, I had loads of messages showing a screen shot of me on the webcam. It was pretty crazy to think that so many people were now tracking my flights!

On arrival, I was told I could taxi to the *Atlantic Airways* hangar. I wasn't sure how long I was going to be there, which is one of the first questions I was often asked. I was aware that Hurricane Dorian was making her way across the Atlantic and would soon be passing through, meaning that no aircraft would be flying for some time. However, I was also aware of a possible weather window to fly to Scotland the following day but I was reluctant to fly in less than ideal weather. There was no rain forecast but it was the fact that I would have had to punch into a strong headwind of almost 30 knots to make it back to Scotland, making it an extremely slow flight. I had the fuel capacity to do it but something just told me to rest and wait. I only had one flight back to the UK but I didn't want to jeopardise the entire journey around the world.

I got chatting to one of the senior aircraft technicians, Elfinn, who was on shift. When I told him that I hadn't booked anywhere to stay, he kindly arranged accommodation for the evening at his mum's B&B guesthouse and he also drove me there later that afternoon. I arrived at the lovely guesthouse in Sandavágur, a village to the south of the airport. I informed Elfinn the following morning that it looked like I'd be around for the best part of a week. Thankfully, his mum's B&B was available so I was able to stay there. I did, however, need some way of getting around because I couldn't ask for lifts or keep getting taxis for the whole week. As luck would have it, Elfinn's work colleague had a side line business renting cars to tourists during the holiday season, which was now long finished. I was able to pick up a little *Peugeot* for my independence on the islands.

For the first few days, I caught up on some sleep but to be honest, that made me feel even more tired and lethargic. I quickly snapped out of that and got straight into editing some footage that I had recently shot and caught up with admin chores. I had been in touch with Guy and Louise from *Newgate* and, until now, we had not selected a date for arriving back to Popham. However, they would not be able to send the press release out and inform the media of my arrival until we had a fixed date in the diary for my return. We selected Sunday 22nd September, which was still almost two weeks away, giving me a few days' contingency.

I was very aware that, although I was only one flight from the UK, I was still a fair way from home and it was far from over. Guy and Louise got to work managing the press and I also informed Popham Airfield of my arrival date. There was a surprisingly long 'To Do' list but it was nothing I couldn't organise from the Faroe Islands.

The remnants of Hurricane Dorian were now pummelling the islands with no let up. One evening, I honestly thought that the B&Bs windows were going to be blown in as the wind was so strong. It was relentless for a good few days until the wind and rain eventually eased, although it would be a while before the conditions were good enough for me to fly again.

I ended up spending most evenings back at the *Atlantic Airways* hangar with Elfinn and his colleagues, just hanging out and chatting. He was a motivated guy and we had a lot of similar interests. He arranged for me to go along in the *Atlantic Airways* helicopter, an *Augusta Westland 139*, for a local pickup of some residents on one of the smaller islands (the pilots also doubled up as the Search & Rescue crew using the same machine). It was only a quick flight but it was really good of them to take me out for a quick spin. As we skirted under the clouds, it was still blowing fairly hard but it was no problem for the heavy *Augusta*.

After a week on the main island, I had pretty much seen everything. It was a lovely place but by now, I had been away for half a year and I was ready to get home. The weather was starting to improve and a solid window of opportunity to make the flight to Scotland had now presented itself. Favourable winds, very little cloud and no rain would make for perfect conditions.

26

Making History

Having spent eight days on the Faroe Islands, I set off for Wick on 17th September. As I departed Vagar, I flew low over the hangar, waving at Elfinn who had come in on his day off to see me depart. I weaved my way between the beautiful valleys and out into the North Atlantic. As flights go, it wasn't particularly long at just over 200 nautical miles. I wanted to enjoy the flight as I knew it would be the last time for the foreseeable future that I would make a long flight like that over water.

I was about to enter UK airspace and I hadn't yet considered the route I was going to take from Scotland back to Popham. I just knew that I needed to be back at Popham in five days' time, without fail.

Waiting it out on the Faroe Islands had been the right decision, as I was now enjoying an easy flight and perfect weather conditions. As I entered UK airspace and saw the slight hint of land on the horizon, I experienced a similar euphoric feeling to the first time I saw land after rowing for 110 days across the Atlantic. It was as if time had slowed down whilst I was thinking about all the people

I had met and the different places that I'd experienced, almost not wanting it to end.

I called Wick on the radio and was cleared for a direct approach. Within a few minutes, I had touched down in the UK. My phone was lighting up with messages left, right and centre, and my brain was running at 100 miles an hour, taking in all the different feelings and emotions. I hopped out of G-KTCH and was taken straight to the flight office, which was a converted World War Two building. It had a real frontier feel to it, with pictures on the walls of pilots who were either about to start their crossings to North America or had just arrived, like myself.

I was chatting with my flying instructor, Steve, who mentioned that Perth would be a good stop-off point. There was also a gyroplane school there run by a guy called Kevin; it was part of the *Gyrocopter Experience*, which Steve was part of. I left Wick and flew straight out over the North Sea as I wanted to take a direct route to Perth. Eventually, the controller at Wick passed me over to Lossiemouth. Half an hour later, I was back over land and passed over to Aberdeen air traffic control to continue my journey over the rolling highlands to Perth, where I landed a short while later.

I was hosted that night by a fellow gyro pilot and one of Kevin's friends who kindly took us out for a lovely meal. The following morning, I needed to move on from Perth to continue making my way south. It made logical sense to stop at York to see Phil, who set up and runs the *Gyrocopter Experience*. Once I reached England and the Northumberland coastline, I slowed down to take it all in, as I didn't need to fly flat out any more, which I'd done most of the way through the US and back to the UK.

As I made my way south along the coast, I flew very close by Newcastle controlled airspace so I picked up a basic flight following service from their air traffic control. There were a few other aircraft on the frequency but it was relatively quiet. I was minding my own business when I heard another aircraft ask the controller if they could pass a message to me. I then heard, "Golf-Charlie-Hotel, I just wanted to congratulate you on your flight around the world, very well done!" I quickly replied, thanking him, but couldn't believe that someone else who was flying at the same time and who happened to be on the same frequency as me had obviously been aware of my flight and wanted to congratulate me. I thought that was really cool.

I continued my way south and adjusted my heading to fly over the North Yorkshire Moors and into Rufforth airfield. I had not flown in there before and was aware that they shared the airfield with gliders, although I couldn't see any when I arrived. I was, however, greeted with a gyroplane guard of honour as I taxied up to Phil's hangar. All of Phil's students and other gyro pilots from the local area had flown in to meet me, which I wasn't expecting but was incredibly humbled by. Phil and his wife, Katie, kindly hosted me for the evening and we went out for pizza with the rest of Phil's students who were staying for a week of flying instruction.

It was now 19th September and, in terms of flight times, I was only a few hours from Popham. I couldn't arrive early as everything had been planned for Sunday 22nd September. I knew I needed to get a little closer to home, leaving myself a very short flight on the Sunday. *Sky News* had already confirmed that they would cover the arrival, which was great, especially as they'd been offered a spot in the helicopter with Peter to capture my last flight. I was also starting to get press enquiries coming direct to me, requesting interviews. I was under strict instructions from *Newgate Communications* not to engage with any media before Sunday as it could potentially undo everything that they had lined up. With this in mind, I needed to go somewhere quiet where I could guarantee that media crews wouldn't just turn up to take photos and publish the story prematurely.

We also had the dilemma of the weather which was fast becoming a talking point within the team as it was deteriorating on the Sunday but looked gorgeous for the Saturday. I decided the best thing to do was to get down to a holding location near Popham, as Peter was flying the *Sky News* crew alongside me to capture the arrival. It made sense to fly to White Waltham, leaving only a 20-minute flight for my arrival into Popham.

I departed York that afternoon and I couldn't have asked for better conditions. There was not a cloud in the sky and it was surprisingly warm for late September. As I left York, I flew south east to avoid some controlled airspace until I crossed the Humber River. I then had a straight course the whole way back to White Waltham. As I started to get closer, I needed to be a bit careful with my height and position as they are located on the western edge of Heathrow's controlled airspace and regularly have problems with airspace infringements from visiting pilots. I wanted to avoid this at all costs.

After I landed, I taxied to the *Helicopter Services* hangar. It was great to see Peter again; it was weird to think that when I first met him, I had only just passed my test and was worried I had bitten off far more than I could chew! I was able to stay with Peter and his family because I didn't feel that I should go home to my parents' house until I had finished once and for all. No sooner had I landed and made it back to Peter's house, things started getting busy.

The weather was now causing a problem and Sunday was looking like rain for most of the day. I had a call with Guy and Louise to discuss our options: if we moved the arrival from Sunday to Saturday, we would likely lose the media outlets who had committed to coming along and covering the story. There was no viable option other than to stick with the Sunday. It wasn't just me I needed to think about, I also had two wonderful charities that I was raising money for and many sponsors who had kindly supported me. To arrive a day early, just to drink champagne in the sun and potentially lose the media support, would have been very foolish. Onlookers may have wondered why I was deliberately choosing to fly in the rain on a less than ideal day, but I owed it to my sponsors and charities to try and secure maximum media coverage. Without these people, there simply would have been no flight around the world. I could not overlook that in my quest for a fairy-tale ending in the sun. An arrival on Sunday would also put the project into a good position for the Monday papers to run the story. The *Magni* family had already booked their flights from Italy and planned to arrive on the Sunday. The Mayor of Basingstoke had also confirmed her attendance, along with several sponsors.

The morning of 22nd September came round. *Sky News* had a reporter and cameraman arriving at the hangar fairly early so we made sure we arrived ahead of them. It was absolutely pouring down with rain when we arrived but we knew it was due to improve. As time passed, I was in touch with Mike, who was managing proceedings at Popham. The good news was that it was clear there and people were starting to arrive.

Steve Boxall had kindly agreed to take a cameraman up in his gyro to get some air to air pictures of the arrival. We had agreed to meet in the air over Overton, a small village to the north of Popham. I was getting quite a few phone calls from people asking me what time I was going to arrive. It was now midday and I'd still not left yet. There were a lot of people waiting, including David, the CEO of Barratt Homes, as well as other sponsors and friends.

We waited for another 20 minutes and could see the cloud clearing and brightening up. "This is the gap we have been waiting for so I think we need to go now," I said to Peter. I was already in my flying suit and pushed G-KTCH outside onto the grass. I was ready and had already completed my pre-flight checks. This was it – my last flight back to Popham. At times on the journey, I had wondered what this day was going to be like. Despite the conditions, I was very excited but that voice in the back of my mind kept saying, "You have not completed this until you safely touch down." It was as though someone was there reminding me to stay focused and calm. I had flown hundreds of hours by now and this would ordinarily have been a very simple flight, but my mind was racing hard and I had to keep a level head.

Once we left White Waltham, I flew just ahead of Peter as he manoeuvred G-DIGA, a *Robinson 66* helicopter, close enough to capture the footage that *Sky News* needed. At only 17 nautical miles, it was certainly a short flight, but that was the plan. Within a few minutes, I could see the town of Reading below me, just off to my right. Peter changed sides a number of times to get some variations with the camera angle. As fast as we were up in the air and dancing around each other to get the perfect shots, it was over and Peter went ahead to land at Popham before my arrival.

It was now starting to rain a bit harder and the other gyros that had flown out to meet me headed back to Popham. All I needed to do was just land but I needed to give the guys time to get down before me. I managed to find some clear air a few miles to the north where there was no rain lashing down, so I made a few orbits to pass the time. "OK James, we are ready for you," Steve said over the radio.

As I had Popham in my sights – or at least, I was looking in the direction of Popham – all I could see was a wall of dark cloud. "I'm going to get pretty wet here," I thought to myself. Mike had planned to put the radio at his end to a microphone that was linked up to a PA system so I could thank the crowd as I flew by. I thought it was a great idea and was initially thinking of going with, "Today is one small flight but one giant leap for gyroplanes" but I felt that was a little cheesy! So I decided to keep it simple and thanked the crowd for waiting in the rain and apologised for being an hour late.

As I made my approach, I could see everyone patiently waiting for me: it was an amazing sight. I flew low and slow past everyone waving and I'm not sure if it was my imagination or not, but I was sure I could hear the cheers and claps over the sound of the engine. I turned downwind and lined myself up for a short final approach. I touched down on Runway 21 as light as a feather, which was a good job as there were a lot of eyes and cameras on me. I let the rotors spin down and taxied slowly over towards the crowd. Mike marshalled me into position and I shut the aircraft down for the last time. I had done it, I had achieved another dream…which is the best feeling in the world! Why not give it a go yourself?

Epilogue

After much deliberation, I decided the best way to finish this book was to write an epilogue. As I sit here typing, it's coming to the end of 2020. It would be an understatement to say it has been an interesting year, not just for me but for every person on this planet.

If you had told me when I arrived home on 22nd September 2019, having completed my record-breaking journey, that a year later we would be in the middle of a global pandemic and everyday life as we know it would no longer exist, I would have said, "Not a chance." However, what sounds like a Hollywood script would in fact become reality. I am often reminded how lucky I was to have completed my flight when I did. If I'd set off a year later, I wouldn't have got very far. In fact, I wouldn't have even made it to France! I guess when something is meant to be, it's meant to be.

After landing back at Popham, my feet hardly touched the ground. Within 24 hours of arriving home, I was in London fulfilling media requests, and within five days, I was on stage in front of 500 people at a black-tie charity dinner in Cardiff.

A month later, I was touring theatres all over the UK, from Cornwall to Inverness. It was a speaking tour that had been planned long before I set off on my flight around the world. The tour was called *Chasing Extremes*, which I thought was quite fitting. I had been an established speaker in the corporate world for many years, but this was my first public tour. I wondered how it would be received and if anybody would pay money to come and hear my story, but thankfully it went very well, with venues close to being sold out.

2020 got off to a good start. G-KTCH was packed up into a cargo plane and flown out to Abu Dhabi where it was on display at a *DHL* event. The records that I set on my gyro flight around the world were all ratified. The *FAI* "speed around the world" as it stands is the first and only *FAI* ratified circumnavigation in a gyroplane. Additionally, *Guinness World Records* recognised my flight as the first circumnavigation in an autogyro. And my journey earned the highest accolade to be presented by the *Royal Aero Club*, The Britannia Trophy.

Just before this book was published, I also learnt that I had been awarded one of the most prestigious awards of my adventure career, the Segrave Trophy. This is awarded by the *Royal Automobile Club* to the British national who demonstrates "Outstanding Skill, Courage and Initiative on Land, Water and in the Air with the spirit of Adventure". To be listed among such names as Sterling Moss, Lewis Hamilton, Donald Campbell, Amy Johnson, Richard Branson and Ken Wallis is certainly a huge honour.

These records are as much attributable to my sponsors and flight team as they are to me, as I simply wouldn't have them if it wasn't for the support I received and the significant team effort.

As great as world records are, it's the journey itself and going through the processes to complete it that are the most rewarding parts for me. Crushing lows to stratospheric highs, I experienced them all. Learning through adversity is not for the faint-hearted but it can certainly reap the greatest rewards. I have laid out my exact route around the world with full ICAO codes (on the following pages), which will hopefully be useful for any budding RTW pilot.

When I started the trip, my mission was to reach over one million young people with the aim of inspiring them to pursue their own goals and dreams. It's hard to measure the actual number of young people reached: obviously I didn't see a million people in person, but taking into account the media reach, via press and social media, that figure would have been exceeded by a long way.

During the six months that I was flying around the world, I found it difficult to stay in shape. I would often eat hotel meals and when the flying days got longer in the US, I was fighting a losing battle with my evening runs that I had started in Europe. The end result wasn't pretty but I quickly got back in shape on my return to the UK. I had always wanted to take part in an *Ironman* competition and subsequently booked myself on to the *Ironman* event in Florida, for November 2020. Due to Covid-19 restrictions, I was not able to travel to the US, so will now (hopefully) be competing in the Florida *Ironman* event in 2021 instead and have a Greenland expedition lined up in 2022.

I managed to catch up recently with Ash, who is doing exceptionally well, in both his career and home life, having not suffered an epileptic seizure in over two years. For me personally, the Indian Ocean is something that I would like to pick up again at some point in the future, as I feel it is unfinished business.

On a final note, I would encourage anyone with a desire to travel, have an adventure or to set up a business, to just go for it! The only thing worse than failing is the feeling of regret, wishing you had taken the opportunity when it presented itself and always wondering, "What if?" The experiences I have gained, the people I have met and the lessons I have learnt are things that will stay with me forever.

I now live by the mantra "It's all mental." For me, this is living my life to my full potential as opposed to the limits my mind often tries to impart on me. Most people know what they want or need to be doing on a daily basis, but something is just holding them back.

Almost everything we do in life is governed by our minds. I have been fortunate enough to have met some high-achieving individuals and they all have one thing in common: they are in control of their mental state with their minds working for them, not against them. You'll be interested to know that 90% of all the things I worried about never happened on the flight around the world.

As I type this, I am closer to forty than thirty and, having circumnavigated the globe twice and been in some extremely precarious situations over the last ten years, I feel I'm well-qualified to tell you this… the world is full of opportunity and it's all waiting for you, if you want it badly enough. If someone else is doing it, it means you can be doing it too! If you have the right mindset, a positive and determined attitude, your life can be close to limitless.

In terms of my goals moving forward, I have another big project in the pipeline that is going to push me beyond anything that I've ever worked on before. So, watch this space and follow me on Instagram (@ketchelljames) or on my website: www.jamesketchell.net.

Thank you for all the continued support. Until the next book…out for now!

Gyroplane World Route

ICAO (International Civil Aviation Organisation) codes	City/Town/Airfield	Country
EGHP	Popham	England
EGHR	Goodwood	England
LFAT	LeTouquet	France
LFQF	Alencon	France
LFQB	Troyes	France
LFGA	Colmar	France
EDNY	Fridrichschafen	Germany
EDDP	Leipzeg	Germany
EPMR	Mirosalwice	Poland
EPNT	Nowy Targ	Poland
EPBC	Warsaw Babice	Poland
EYKA	Kaunas	Lithuania
EETU	Tartu	Estonia
ULOO	Pskov	Russia
ULOR	Seredka	Russia
UUBM	Moscow	Russia
UWKS	Choboksary	Russia
UWUO	Pervushino	Russia
USSS	Yekaterinburg	Russia
USTR	Tyumen	Russia
UNOL	Omsk	Russia
UNNT	Novosibirsk	Russia
UNKK	Krasnoyarsk	Russia
UIBM	Bratsk	Russia
UITK	Kazachinskoe	Russia
UIKG	Taksimo	Russia
UEMO	Olyokminsk	Russia

ICAO (International Civil Aviation Organisation) codes	City/Town/Airfield	Country
UEMM	Yakutsk	Russia
UEMJ	Tomtor	Russia
UHMM	Magadan	Russia
UHMW	Evensk	Russia
UHMO	Markovo	Russia
UHMA	Anadyr	Russia
UHMD	Provideniya Bay	Russia
PAOM	Nome	USA
PAMC	McGrath	USA
PAUO	Willow	USA
PAMR	Merril Field/Anchorage	USA
PFTO	Tok Junction	USA
Takhin Valley	Emergency landing on road	Canada
CYDL	Dease Lake	Canada
CYYD	Smithers	Canada
CZML	108 Mile	Canada
KO59	Jefferson	USA
KSPB	Scappoose	USA
KMMV	McMinnville	USA
KCEC	Crecsent City	USA
KHAF	Halfmoon Bay (San Fran)	USA
KWHP	Whiteman (LA)	USA
KMYF	San Diego	USA
KRYN	Tucson	USA
KCHD	Phoenix	USA
KHND	Las Vegas	USA
KSPK	Spanish Fork	USA
U10	Preston	USA

ICAO (International Civil Aviation Organisation) codes	City/Town/Airfield	Country
KRKS	Rocksprings	USA
KCPR	Casper	USA
97M	Ekalaka	USA
KBWW	Bowman	USA
49B	Sturgis	USA
KBFF	Scottsbuff	USA
2V6	Yuma	USA
KCAO	Clayton	USA
KPVW	Plainview	USA
T74	Taylor	USA
F51	Winsbourgh	USA
KTQH	Tahlequah	USA
K34	Gardner	USA
KTUK	Centerville	USA
KOLZ	Oelwein	USA
KCHU	Caledonia	USA
79C	Brennand	USA
KIGO	Lansing	USA
KIRS	Sturgis	USA
KRCR	Rochester	USA
C92	Mentone	USA
I67	Harrison	USA
KCVG	Cincinatti	USA
KCGI	Gape Girardeue	USA
MO1	Memphis	USA
6M7	Marianna	USA
KMLU	Monroe	USA
23M	Clark County	USA

ICAO (International Civil Aviation Organisation) codes	City/Town/Airfield	Country
KEDN	Enterprise	USA
KMAI	Marianna	USA
KBKV	Brooksville	USA
KPMP	Pompano	USA
KLHW	Ft Stewart	USA
KDYB	Summerville	USA
KEWN	New Burn	USA
7W6	Hyde County	USA
KMQI	Manteo	USA
KFFA	Kitty Hawk	USA
KCDK	Chesapeake	USA
KMRB	Martinsburg	USA
KFDK	Fredrick	USA
KEVY	Middleton	USA
7N7	Spitfire	USA
KOQN	West Chester	USA
KPOU	Poughkeepsie	USA
No Code	Old Rhineback Airfield	USA
KDXR	Danbury	USA
KUUU	Newport	USA
KACK	Nantucket	USA
KGHG	Marshfield (Boston)	USA
KCON	Concord	USA
KIZG	Fryeburg	USA
KUSF	Springfield	USA
KVGC	Hamilton	USA
KIAG	Niagara Falls	USA
CYKF	Kitchener	Canada

ICAO (International Civil Aviation Organisation) codes	**City/Town/Airfield**	**Country**
CNL3	Brookville	Canada
CNV9	Newville	Canada
CYZV	Sept Iles	Canada
CYKL	Schefferville	Canada
CYVP	Kuujjuaq	Canada
CYFB	Iqualuit	Canada
BGGH	Nuuk	Greenland
BGPT	Paamiut	Greenland
BGBW	Narrsaruaq	Greenland
BGKK	Kulusuk	Greenland
BIRK	Reykjavik	Iceland
EKVG	Vagar	Faroe Islands
EGPC	Wick	Scotland
EGPT	Perth	Scotland
No Code	York/Rufforth	England
EGLM	White Waltham	England
EGHP	Popham	Engand